BOOKS BY TRUMAN CAPOTE

Music for
Chameleons

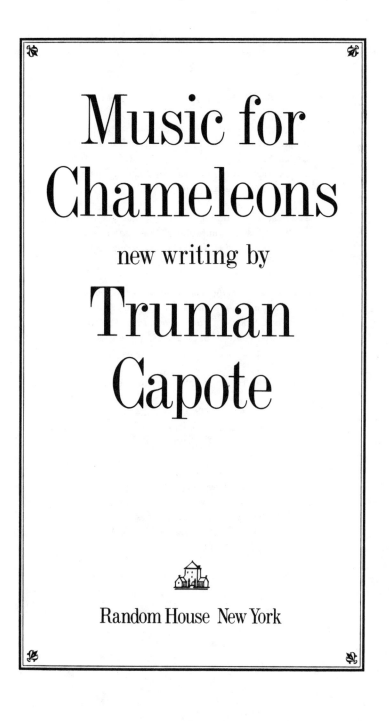

Music for Chameleons

new writing by

Truman Capote

Random House New York

Library of Congress Cataloging in Publication Data
Capote, Truman, 1924–
Music for chameleons.
I. Title.
PS3505.A59M8   813′54   79–5532
ISBN 0–394–50826–2
0–394–51464–5 (limited edition)

Manufactured in the United States of America
Typography and binding design by J. K. Lambert
2 4 6 8 9 7 5 3

A limited first edition of this book has been printed.

FOR
Tennessee Williams

Contents

Preface

My life—as an artist, at least—can be charted as precisely as a fever: the highs and lows, the very definite cycles.

I started writing when I was eight—out of the blue, uninspired by any example. I'd never known anyone who wrote; indeed, I knew few people who read. But the fact was, the only four things that interested me were: reading books, going to the movies, tap dancing, and drawing pictures. Then one day I started writing, not knowing that I had chained myself for life to a noble but merciless master. When God hands you a gift, he also hands you a whip; and the whip is intended solely for self-flagellation.

But of course I didn't know that. I wrote adventure stories, murder mysteries, comedy skits, tales that had been told me by former slaves and Civil War veterans. It was a lot of fun—at first. It stopped being fun when I discovered the difference between good writing and bad, and then made an even more alarming discovery: the difference between very good writing and true art; it is subtle, but savage. And after that, the whip came down!

As certain young people practice the piano or the violin four and five hours a day, so I played with my papers and pens. Yet I never discussed my writing with anyone; if someone asked what I was up to all those hours, I told them I was doing my school homework. Actually, I never did any homework. My literary tasks kept me fully occupied: my apprenticeship at the altar of technique, craft; the devilish intricacies of paragraphing, punctuation, dialogue placement. Not to mention the grand overall design, the great demanding arc of middle-beginning-end. One had to learn so much, and from so many sources: not only from books, but from music, from painting, and just plain everyday observation.

In fact, the most interesting writing I did during those days was the plain everyday observations that I recorded in my journal. Descriptions of a neighbor. Long verbatim accounts of overheard conversations. Local gossip. A kind of reporting, a style of "seeing" and "hearing" that would later seriously influence me, though I was unaware of it then, for all my "formal" writing, the stuff that I polished and carefully typed, was more or less fictional.

By the time I was seventeen, I was an accomplished writer. Had I been a pianist, it would have been the moment for my first public concert. As it was, I decided I was ready to publish. I sent off stories to the principal literary quarterlies, as well as to the national magazines, which in those days published the best so-called "quality" fiction—*Story, The New Yorker, Harper's Bazaar, Mademoiselle, Harper's, Atlantic Monthly*—and stories by me duly appeared in those publications.

Then, in 1948, I published a novel: *Other Voices, Other Rooms*. It was well received critically, and was a best seller. It was also, due to an exotic photograph of the author on the dust jacket, the start of a certain notoriety that has kept close step with me these many years. Indeed, many people attributed the commercial success of the novel to the photograph. Others dismissed the book as though it were a freakish accident: "Amazing that anyone so young can write that well." Amazing? I'd only been writing day in and day out for fourteen years! Still, the novel was a satisfying conclusion to the first cycle in my development.

A short novel, *Breakfast at Tiffany's*, ended the second cycle in 1958. During the intervening ten years I experimented with almost every aspect of writing, attempting to conquer a variety of techniques, to achieve a technical virtuosity as strong and flexible as a fisherman's net. Of course, I failed in several of the areas I invaded, but it is true that one learns more from a failure than one does from a success. I know I did, and later I was able to apply what I had learned to great advantage. Anyway, during that decade of exploration I wrote short-story collections (*A Tree of Night, A Christmas Memory*), essays and portraits (*Local Color, Observations*, the work contained in *The Dogs Bark*), plays (*The Grass Harp, House of Flowers*), film scripts (*Beat the Devil, The Innocents*), and a great deal of factual reportage, most of it for *The New Yorker*.

In fact, from the point of view of my creative destiny, the most interesting writing I did during the whole of this second phase first appeared in *The New Yorker* as a series of articles and subsequently as a book entitled *The Muses Are Heard*. It concerned the first cultural exchange between the U.S.S.R. and the U.S.A.: a tour, undertaken in 1955, of Russia by a company of black Americans in *Porgy and Bess*. I conceived of the whole adventure as a short comic "nonfiction novel," the first.

Some years earlier, Lillian Ross had published *Picture*, her account of the making of a movie, *The Red Badge of Courage*; with its fast cuts, its flash forward and back, it was itself like a movie, and as I read it I wondered what would happen if the author let go of her hard linear straight-reporting discipline and handled her material as if it were fictional—would the book gain or lose? I decided, if the right subject came along, I'd like to give it a try: *Porgy and Bess* and Russia in the depths of winter seemed the right subject.

The Muses Are Heard received excellent reviews; even sources usually unfriendly to me were moved to praise it. Still, it did not attract any special notice, and the sales were moderate. Nevertheless, that book was an important event for me: while writing it, I realized I just might have found a solution to what had always been my greatest creative quandary.

For several years I had been increasingly drawn toward journalism as an art form in itself. I had two reasons. First, it didn't seem to me that anything truly innovative had oc-curred in prose writing, or in writing generally, since the 1920s; second, journalism as art was almost virgin terrain, for the simple reason that very few literary artists ever wrote narrative journalism, and when they did, it took the form of travel essays or autobiography. *The Muses Are Heard* had set me to thinking on different lines altogether: I wanted to pro-duce a journalistic novel, something on a large scale that would have the credibility of fact, the immediacy of film, the depth and freedom of prose, and the precision of poetry.

It was not until 1959 that some mysterious instinct di-rected me toward the subject—an obscure murder case in an isolated part of Kansas—and it was not until 1966 that I was able to publish the result, *In Cold Blood.*

In a story by Henry James, I think *The Middle Years*, his character, a writer in the shadows of maturity, laments: "We live in the dark, we do what we can, the rest is the madness of art." Or words to that effect. Anyway, Mr. James is laying it on the line there; he's telling us the truth. And the darkest part of the dark, the maddest part of the madness, is the relentless gambling involved. Writers, at least those who take genuine risks, who are willing to bite the bullet and walk the plank, have a lot in common with another breed of lonely men—the guys who make a living shooting pool and dealing cards. Many people thought I was crazy to spend six years wandering around the plains of Kansas; others rejected my whole concept of the "nonfiction novel" and pronounced it unworthy of a "serious" writer; Norman Mailer described it as a "failure of imagination"—meaning, I assume, that a novelist should be writing about something imaginary rather than about something real.

Yes, it was like playing high-stakes poker; for six nerve-shattering years I didn't know whether I had a book or not. Those were long summers and freezing winters, but I just kept on dealing the cards, playing my hand as best I could. Then it turned out I *did* have a book. Several critics complained that "nonfiction novel" was a catch phrase, a hoax, and that there was nothing really original or new about what I had done. But there were those who felt differently, other writers who realized the value of my experiment and moved swiftly to put it to their own use—none more swiftly than Norman Mailer, who has made a lot of money and won a lot of prizes writing nonfiction novels (*The Armies of the Night, Of a Fire on the Moon, The Executioner's Song*), although he has always been careful never to describe them as "nonfiction novels." No matter; he is a good writer and a fine fellow and I'm grateful to have been of some small service to him.

The zigzag line charting my reputation as a writer had reached a healthy height, and I let it rest there before moving into my fourth, and what I expect will be my final, cycle. For four years, roughly from 1968 through 1972, I spent most of my time reading and selecting, rewriting and indexing my own letters, other people's letters, my diaries and journals (which contain detailed accounts of hundreds of scenes and conversations) for the years 1943 through 1965. I intended to use much of this material in a book I had long been planning: a variation on the nonfiction novel. I called the book *Answered Prayers*, which is a quote from Saint Thérèse, who said: "More tears are shed over answered prayers than unanswered ones." In 1972 I began work on this book by writing the last chapter first (it's always good to know where one's going). Then I wrote the first chapter, "Unspoiled Monsters." Then the fifth, "A Severe Insult to the Brain." Then the seventh, "La Côte Basque." I went on in this manner, writing different chapters out of sequence. I was able to do this only because the plot—or rather plots—was true, and all the characters were real: it wasn't difficult to keep it all in mind, for I hadn't invented anything. And yet *Answered Prayers* is not intended as any ordinary roman à clef, a form where facts are disguised as fiction. My intentions are the reverse: to remove disguises, not manufacture them.

In 1975 and 1976 I published four chapters of the book in *Esquire* magazine. This aroused anger in certain circles, where it was felt I was betraying confidences, mistreating friends and/or foes. I don't intend to discuss this; the issue involves social politics, not artistic merit. I will say only that all a writer has to work with is the material he has gathered as the result of his own endeavor and observations, and he cannot be denied the right to use it. Condemn, but not deny.

However, I did stop working on *Answered Prayers* in September 1977, a fact that had nothing to do with any public reaction to those parts of the book already published. The halt happened because I was in a helluva lot of trouble: I was suffering a creative crisis and a personal one at the same time. As the latter was unrelated, or very little related, to the former, it is only necessary to remark on the creative chaos.

Now, torment though it was, I'm glad it happened; after all, it altered my entire comprehension of writing, my attitude toward art and life and the balance between the two, and my understanding of the difference between what is true and what is *really* true.

To begin with, I think most writers, even the best, overwrite. I prefer to underwrite. Simple, clear as a country creek. But I felt my writing was becoming too dense, that I was taking three pages to arrive at effects I ought to be able to achieve in a single paragraph. Again and again I read all that I had written of *Answered Prayers*, and I began to have doubts—not about the material or my approach, but about the texture of the writing itself. I reread *In Cold Blood* and had the same reaction: there were too many areas where I was not writing as well as I could, where I was not delivering the total potential. Slowly, but with accelerating alarm, I read every word I'd ever published, and decided that never, not once in my writing life, had I completely exploded all the energy and esthetic excitements that material contained. Even when it was good, I could see that I was never working with more than half, sometimes only a third, of the powers at my command. Why?

The answer, revealed to me after months of meditation, was simple but not very satisfying. Certainly it did nothing to lessen my depression; indeed, it thickened it. For the answer created an apparently unsolvable problem, and if I couldn't solve it, I might as well quit writing. The problem was: how can a writer successfully combine within a single form—say the short story—all he knows about every other form of writing? For this was why my work was often insufficiently illuminated; the voltage was there, but by restricting myself to the techniques of whatever form I was working in, I was not using everything I knew about writing—all I'd learned from film scripts, plays, reportage, poetry, the short story, novellas, the novel. A writer ought to have all his colors, all his abilities available on the same palette for mingling (and, in suitable instances, simultaneous application). But how?

I returned to *Answered Prayers*. I removed one chapter and rewrote two others. An improvement, definitely an improvement. But the truth was, I had to go back to kindergarten. Here I was—off again on one of those grim gambles! But I was excited; I felt an invisible sun shining on me. Still, my first experiments were awkward. I truly felt like a child with a box of crayons.

From a technical point, the greatest difficulty I'd had in writing *In Cold Blood* was leaving myself completely out of it. Ordinarily, the reporter has to use himself as a character, an eyewitness observer, in order to retain credibility. But I felt that it was essential to the seemingly detached tone of that book that the author should be absent. Actually, in all my reportage, I had tried to keep myself as invisible as possible.

Now, however, I set myself center stage, and reconstructed, in a severe, minimal manner, commonplace conversations with everyday people: the superintendent of my building, a masseur at the gym, an old school friend, my dentist. After writing hundreds of pages of this simple-minded sort of thing, I eventually developed a style. I had found a framework into which I could assimilate everything I knew about writing.

Later, using a modified version of this technique, I wrote a nonfiction short novel (*Handcarved Coffins*) and a number of short stories. The result is the present volume: *Music for Chameleons*.

And how has all this affected my other work-in-progress, *Answered Prayers*? Very considerably. Meanwhile, I'm here alone in my dark madness, all by myself with my deck of cards—and, of course, the whip God gave me.

I
Music for Chameleons

One

✤

Music for Chameleons

She is tall and slender, perhaps seventy, silver-haired, soigné, neither black nor white, a pale golden rum color. She is a Martinique aristocrat who lives in Fort de France but also has an apartment in Paris. We are sitting on the terrace of her house, an airy, elegant house that looks as if it was made of wooden lace: it reminds me of certain old New Orleans houses. We are drinking iced mint tea slightly flavored with absinthe.

Three green chameleons race one another across the terrace; one pauses at Madame's feet, flicking its forked tongue, and she comments: "Chameleons. Such exceptional creatures. The way they change color. Red. Yellow. Lime. Pink. Lavender. And did you know they are very fond of music?" She regards me with her fine black eyes. "You don't believe me?"

During the course of the afternoon she had told me many

curious things. How at night her garden was filled with mammoth night-flying moths. That her chauffeur, a dignified figure who had driven me to her house in a dark green Mercedes, was a wife-poisoner who had escaped from Devil's Island. And she had described a village high in the northern mountains that is entirely inhabited by albinos: "Little pink-eyed people white as chalk. Occasionally one sees a few on the streets of Fort de France."

"Yes, of course I believe you."

She tilts her silver head. "No, you don't. But I shall prove it."

So saying, she drifts into her cool Caribbean salon, a shadowy room with gradually turning ceiling fans, and poses herself at a well-tuned piano. I am still sitting on the terrace, but I can observe her, this chic, elderly woman, the product of varied bloods. She begins to perform a Mozart sonata.

Eventually the chameleons accumulated: a dozen, a dozen more, most of them green, some scarlet, lavender. They skittered across the terrace and scampered into the salon, a sensitive, absorbed audience for the music played. And then not played, for suddenly my hostess stood and stamped her foot, and the chameleons scattered like sparks from an exploding star.

Now she regards me. "*Et maintenant? C'est vrai?*"

"Indeed. But it seems so strange."

She smiles. "*Alors.* The whole island floats in strangeness. This very house is haunted. Many ghosts dwell here. And not in darkness. Some appear in the bright light of noon, saucy as you please. Impertinent."

"That's common in Haiti, too. The ghosts there often stroll about in daylight. I once saw a horde of ghosts working in a field near Petionville. They were picking bugs off coffee plants."

She accepts this as fact, and continues: *"Oui. Oui.* The Haitians work their dead. They are well known for that. Ours we leave to their sorrows. And their frolics. So coarse, the Haitians. So Creole. And one can't bathe there, the sharks are so intimidating. And their mosquitoes: the size, the audacity! Here in Martinique we have no mosquitoes. None."

"I've noticed that; I wondered about it."

"So do we. Martinique is the only island in the Caribbean not cursed with mosquitoes, and no one can explain it."

"Perhaps the night-flying moths devour them all."

She laughs. "Or the ghosts."

"No. I think ghosts would prefer moths."

"Yes, moths are perhaps more ghostly fodder. If I was a hungry ghost, I'd rather eat anything than mosquitoes. Will you have more ice in your glass? Absinthe?"

"Absinthe. That's something we can't get at home. Not even in New Orleans."

"My paternal grandmother was from New Orleans."

"Mine, too."

As she pours absinthe from a dazzling emerald decanter: "Then perhaps we are related. Her maiden name was Dufont. Alouette Dufont."

"Alouette? Really? Very pretty. I'm aware of two Dufont families in New Orleans, but I'm not related to either of them."

"Pity. It would have been amusing to call you cousin. *Alors.* Claudine Paulot tells me this is your first visit to Martinique."

"Claudine Paulot?"

"Claudine and Jacques Paulot. You met them at the Governor's dinner the other night."

I remember: he was a tall, handsome man, the First President of the Court of Appeals for Martinique and French

Guiana, which includes Devil's Island. "The Paulots. Yes. They have eight children. He very much favors capital punishment."

"Since you seem to be a traveler, why have you not visited here sooner?"

"Martinique? Well, I felt a certain reluctance. A good friend was murdered here."

Madame's lovely eyes are a fraction less friendly than before. She makes a slow pronouncement: "Murder is a rare occurrence here. We are not a violent people. Serious, but not violent."

"Serious. Yes. The people in restaurants, on the streets, even on the beaches have such severe expressions. They seem so preoccupied. Like Russians."

"One must keep in mind that slavery did not end here until 1848."

I fail to make the connection, but do not inquire, for already she is saying: "Moreover, Martinique is *très cher*. A bar of soap bought in Paris for five francs costs twice that here. The price of everything is double what it should be because everything has to be imported. If these troublemakers got their way, and Martinique became independent of France, then that would be the close of it. Martinique could not exist without subsidy from France. We would simply perish. *Alors*, some of us have serious expressions. Generally speaking, though, do you find the population attractive?"

"The women. I've seen some amazingly beautiful women. Supple, suave, such beautifully haughty postures; bone structure as fine as cats. Also, they have a certain alluring aggressiveness."

"That's the Senegalese blood. We have much Senegalese here. But the men—you do not find them so appealing?"

"No."

"I agree. The men are not appealing. Compared to our women, they seem irrelevant, without character: *vin ordinaire*. Martinique, you understand, is a matriarchal society. When that is the case, as it is in India, for example, then the men never amount to much. I see you are looking at my black mirror."

I am. My eyes distractedly consult it—are drawn to it against my will, as they sometimes are by the senseless flickerings of an unregulated television set. It has that kind of frivolous power. Therefore, I shall overly describe it—in the manner of those "avant-garde" French novelists who, having chosen to discard narrative, character, and structure, restrict themselves to page-length paragraphs detailing the contours of a single object, the mechanics of an isolated movement: a wall, a white wall with a fly meandering across it. So: the object in Madame's drawing room is a black mirror. It is seven inches tall and six inches wide. It is framed within a worn black leather case that is shaped like a book. Indeed, the case is lying open on a table, just as though it were a deluxe edition meant to be picked up and browsed through; but there is nothing there to be read or seen—except the mystery of one's own image projected by the black mirror's surface before it recedes into its endless depths, its corridors of darkness.

"It belonged," she is explaining, "to Gauguin. You know, of course, that he lived and painted here before he settled among the Polynesians. That was his black mirror. They were a quite common artifact among artists of the last century. Van Gogh used one. As did Renoir."

"I don't quite understand. What did they use them for?"

"To refresh their vision. Renew their reaction to color, the tonal variations. After a spell of work, their eyes fatigued, they rested themselves by gazing into these dark mirrors. Just as gourmets at a banquet, between elaborate courses, re-awaken their palates with a *sorbet de citron.*" She lifts the small volume containing the mirror off the table and passes it to me. "I often use it when my eyes have been stricken by too much sun. It's soothing."

Soothing, and also disquieting. The blackness, the longer one gazes into it, ceases to be black, but becomes a queer silver-blue, the threshold to secret visions; like Alice, I feel on the edge of a voyage through a looking-glass, one I'm hesitant to take.

From a distance I hear her voice—smoky, serene, culti-vated: "And so you had a friend who was murdered here?"

"Yes."

"An American?"

"Yes. He was a very gifted man. A musician. A com-poser."

"Oh, I remember—the man who wrote operas! Jewish. He had a mustache."

"His name was Marc Blitzstein."

"But that was long ago. At least fifteen years. Or more. I understand you are staying at the new hotel. La Bataille. How do you find it?"

"Very pleasant. In a bit of a turmoil because they are in the process of opening a casino. The man in charge of the casino is called Shelley Keats. I thought it was a joke at first, but that really happens to be his name."

"Marcel Proust works at Le Foulard, that fine little sea-food restaurant in Schoelcher, the fishing village. Marcel is a waiter. Have you been disappointed in our restaurants?"

"Yes and no. They're better than anywhere else in the Caribbean, but too expensive."

"*Alors.* As I remarked, everything is imported. We don't even grow our own vegetables. The natives are too lackadaisical." A hummingbird penetrates the terrace and casually balances on the air. "But our sea-fare is exceptional."

"Yes and no. I've never seen such enormous lobsters. Absolute whales; prehistoric creatures. I ordered one, but it was tasteless as chalk, and so tough to chew that I lost a filling. Like California fruit: splendid to look at, but without flavor."

She smiles, not happily: "Well, I apologize"—and I regret my criticism, and realize I'm not being very gracious.

"I had lunch at your hotel last week. On the terrace overlooking the pool. I was shocked."

"How so?"

"By the bathers. The foreign ladies gathered around the pool wearing nothing above and very little below. Do they permit that in your country? Virtually naked women parading themselves?"

"Not in so public a place as a hotel pool."

"Exactly. And I don't think it should be condoned here. But of course we can't afford to annoy the tourists. Have you bothered with any of our tourist attractions?"

"We went yesterday to see the house where Empress Josephine was born."

"I never advise anyone to visit there. That old man, the curator, what a chatterbox! And I can't say which is worse— his French or his English or his German. Such a bore. As though the journey getting there weren't tiring enough."

Our hummingbird departs. Far off we hear steel-drum bands, tambourines, drunken choirs (*"Ce soir, ce soir nous danserons sans chemise, sans pantalons"*: Tonight, tonight we dance without shirts, without pants), sounds reminding us that it is Carnival week in Martinique.

"Usually," she announces, "I leave the island during Carnival. It's impossible. The racket, the stench."

When planning for this Martinique experience, which included traveling with three companions, I had not known our visit would coincide with Carnival; as a New Orleans native, I've had my fill of such affairs. However, the Martinique variation proved surprisingly vital, spontaneous and vivid as a bomb explosion in a fireworks factory. "We're enjoying it, my friends and I. Last night there was one marvelous marching group: fifty men carrying black umbrellas and wearing silk tophats and with their torsos painted with phosphorescent skeleton bones. I love the old ladies with gold-tinsel wigs and sequins pasted all over their faces. And all those men wearing their wives' white wedding gowns! And the millions of children holding candles, glowing like fireflies. Actually, we did have one near-disaster. We borrowed a car from the hotel, and just as we arrived in Fort de France, and were creeping through the midst of the crowds, one of our tires blew out, and immediately we were surrounded by red devils with pitchforks—"

Madame is amused: "*Oui. Oui.* The little boys who dress as red devils. That goes back centuries."

"Yes, but they were dancing all over the car. Doing terrific damage. The roof was a positive samba floor. But we couldn't abandon it, for fear they'd wreck it altogether. So the calmest of my friends, Bob MacBride, volunteered to change the tire then and there. The problem was that he had on a new white linen suit and didn't want to ruin it."

"Therefore, he disrobed. Very sensible."

"At least it was funny. To watch MacBride, who's quite a solemn sort of fellow, stripped to his briefs and trying to change a tire with Mardi Gras madness swirling around him and red devils jabbing at him with pitchforks. Paper pitchforks, luckily."

"But Mr. MacBride succeeded."

"If he hadn't, I doubt that I'd be here abusing your hospitality."

"Nothing would have happened. We are not a violent people."

"Please. I'm not suggesting we were in any danger. It was just—well, part of the fun."

"Absinthe? *Un peu?*"

"A mite. Thank you."

The hummingbird returns.

"Your friend, the composer?"

"Marc Blitzstein."

"I've been thinking. He came here once to dinner. Madame Derain brought him. And Lord Snowdon was here that evening. With his uncle, the Englishman who built all those houses on Mustique—"

"Oliver Messel."

"*Oui. Oui.* It was while my husband was still alive. My husband had a fine ear for music. He asked your friend to play the piano. He played some German songs." She is standing now, moving to and fro, and I am aware of how exquisite her figure is, how ethereal it seems silhouetted inside a frail green lace Parisian dress. "I remember that, yet I can't recall how he died. Who killed him?"

All the while the black mirror has been lying in my lap, and once more my eyes seek its depths. Strange where our passions carry us, floggingly pursue us, forcing upon us unwanted dreams, unwelcome destinies.

"Two sailors."

"From here? Martinique?"

"No. Two Portuguese sailors off a ship that was in harbor. He met them in a bar. He was here working on an opera, and he'd rented a house. He took them home with him—"

"I *do* remember. They robbed him and beat him to death. It was dreadful. An appalling tragedy."

"A tragic accident." The black mirror mocks me: Why did you say that? It wasn't an accident.

"But our police caught those sailors. They were tried and sentenced and sent to prison in Guiana. I wonder if they are still there. I might ask Paulot. He would know. After all, he is the First President of the Court of Appeals."

"It really doesn't matter."

"Not matter! Those wretches ought to have been guillotined."

"No. But I wouldn't mind seeing them at work in the fields in Haiti, picking bugs off coffee plants."

Raising my eyes from the mirror's demonic shine, I notice my hostess has momentarily retreated from the terrace into her shadowy salon. A piano chord echoes, and another. Madame is toying with the same tune. Soon the music lovers assemble, chameleons scarlet, green, lavender, an audience that, lined out on the floor of the terra-cotta terrace, resembles a written arrangement of musical notes. A Mozartean mosaic.

Two

✿

Mr. Jones

During the winter of 1945 I lived for several months in a rooming house in Brooklyn. It was not a shabby place, but a pleasantly furnished, elderly brownstone kept hospital-neat by its owners, two maiden sisters.

Mr. Jones lived in the room next to mine. My room was the smallest in the house, his the largest, a nice big sunshiny room, which was just as well, for Mr. Jones never left it: all his needs, meals, shopping, laundry, were attended to by the middle-aged landladies. Also, he was not without visitors; on the average, a half-dozen various persons, men and women, young, old, in-between, visited his room each day, from early morning until late in the evening. He was not a drug dealer or a fortuneteller; no, they came just to talk to him and apparently they made him small gifts of money for his conversation and advice. If not, he had no obvious means of support.

I never had a conversation with Mr. Jones myself, a circumstance I've often since regretted. He was a handsome man, about forty. Slender, black-haired, and with a distinctive face; a pale, lean face, high cheekbones, and with a birthmark on his left cheek, a small scarlet defect shaped like a star. He wore gold-rimmed glasses with pitch-black lenses: he was blind, and crippled, too—according to the sisters, the use of his legs had been denied him by a childhood accident, and he could not move without crutches. He was always dressed in a crisply pressed dark grey or blue three-piece suit and a subdued tie—as though about to set off for a Wall Street office.

However, as I've said, he never left the premises. Simply sat in his cheerful room in a comfortable chair and received visitors. I had no notion of why they came to see him, these rather ordinary-looking folk, or what they talked about, and I was far too concerned with my own affairs to much wonder over it. When I did, I imagined that his friends had found in him an intelligent, kindly man, a good listener in whom to confide and consult with over their troubles: a cross between a priest and a therapist.

Mr. Jones had a telephone. He was the only tenant with a private line. It rang constantly, often after midnight and as early as six in the morning.

I moved to Manhattan. Several months later I returned to the house to collect a box of books I had stored there. While the landladies offered me tea and cakes in their lace-curtained "parlor," I inquired of Mr. Jones.

The women lowered their eyes. Clearing her throat, one said: "It's in the hands of the police."

The other offered: "We've reported him as a missing person."

The first added: "Last month, twenty-six days ago, my sister carried up Mr. Jones's breakfast, as usual. He wasn't there. All his belongings were there. But he was gone."

"It's odd—"

"—how a man totally blind, a helpless cripple—"

Ten years pass.

Now it is a zero-cold December afternoon, and I am in Moscow. I am riding in a subway car. There are only a few other passengers. One of them is a man sitting opposite me, a man wearing boots, a thick long coat and a Russian-style fur cap. He has bright eyes, blue as a peacock's.

After a doubtful instant, I simply stared, for even without the black glasses, there was no mistaking that lean distinctive face, those high cheekbones with the single scarlet star-shaped birthmark.

I was just about to cross the aisle and speak to him when the train pulled into a station, and Mr. Jones, on a pair of fine sturdy legs, stood up and strode out of the car. Swiftly, the train door closed behind him.

Three

❧

A Lamp in a Window

Once I was invited to a wedding; the bride suggested I drive up from New York with a pair of other guests, a Mr. and Mrs. Roberts, whom I had never met before. It was a cold April day, and on the ride to Connecticut the Robertses, a couple in their early forties, seemed agreeable enough—no one you would want to spend a long weekend with, but not bad.

However, at the wedding reception a great deal of liquor was consumed, I should say a third of it by my chauffeurs. They were the last to leave the party—at approximately 11 P.M.—and I was most wary of accompanying them; I knew they were drunk, but I didn't realize *how* drunk. We had driven about twenty miles, the car weaving considerably, and Mr. and Mrs. Roberts insulting each other in the most extraordinary language (really, it was a moment out of *Who's Afraid of Virginia Woolf?*), when Mr. Roberts, very understandably, made a wrong turn and got lost on a dark country road. I kept asking them, finally begging them, to stop the car and let me out, but they were so involved in their invectives that they ignored me. Eventually the car stopped of its own accord (temporarily) when it swiped against the side of a tree. I used the opportunity to jump out the car's back door and run into the woods. Presently the cursed vehicle drove off, leaving me alone in the icy dark. I'm sure my hosts never missed me; Lord knows I didn't miss them.

But it wasn't a joy to be stranded out there on a windy cold night. I started walking, hoping I'd reach a highway. I walked for half an hour without sighting a habitation. Then, just off the road, I saw a small frame cottage with a porch and a window lighted by a lamp. I tiptoed onto the porch and looked in the window; an elderly woman with soft white hair and a round pleasant face was sitting by a fireside reading a book. There was a cat curled in her lap, and several others slumbering at her feet.

I knocked at the door, and when she opened it I said, with chattering teeth: "I'm sorry to disturb you, but I've had a sort of accident; I wonder if I could use your phone to call a taxi."

"Oh, dear," she said, smiling. "I'm afraid I don't have a phone. Too poor. But please, come in." And as I stepped through the door into the cozy room, she said: "My goodness, boy. You're freezing. Can I make coffee? A cup of tea? I have a little whiskey my husband left—he died six years ago."

I said a little whiskey would be very welcome.

While she fetched it I warmed my hands at the fire and glanced around the room. It was a cheerful place occupied by six or seven cats of varying alley-cat colors. I looked at the title of the book Mrs. Kelly—for that was her name, as I later learned—had been reading: it was *Emma* by Jane Austen, a favorite writer of mine.

When Mrs. Kelly returned with a glass of ice and a dusty quarter-bottle of bourbon, she said: "Sit down, sit down. It's not often I have company. Of course, I have my cats. Anyway, you'll spend the night? I have a nice little guest room that's been waiting such a long time for a guest. In the morning you can walk to the highway and catch a ride into town, where you'll find a garage to fix your car. It's about five miles away."

I wondered aloud how she could live so isolatedly, without transportation or a telephone; she told me her good friend, the mailman, took care of all her shopping needs. "Albert. He's really so dear and faithful. But he's due to retire next year. After that I don't know what I'll do. But something will turn up. Perhaps a kindly new mailman. Tell me, just what sort of accident did you have?"

When I explained the truth of the matter, she responded indignantly: "You did exactly the right thing. I wouldn't set foot in a car with a man who had sniffed a glass of sherry. That's how I lost my husband. Married forty years, forty happy years, and I lost him because a drunken driver ran him down. If it wasn't for my cats . . ." She stroked an orange tabby purring in her lap.

We talked by the fire until my eyes grew heavy. We talked about Jane Austen ("Ah, Jane. My tragedy is that I've read all her books so often I have them memorized"), and other admired authors: Thoreau, Willa Cather, Dickens, Lewis Carroll, Agatha Christie, Raymond Chandler, Hawthorne, Chekhov, De Maupassant—she was a woman with a good and varied mind; intelligence illuminated her hazel eyes like the small lamp shining on the table beside her. We talked about the hard Connecticut winters, politicians, far places ("I've never been abroad, but if ever I'd had the chance, the place I would have gone is Africa. Sometimes I've dreamed of it, the green hills, the heat, the beautiful giraffes, the elephants walking about"), religion ("Of course, I was raised a Catholic, but now, I'm almost sorry to say, I have an open mind. Too much reading, perhaps"), gardening ("I grow and can all my own vegetables; a necessity"). At last: "Forgive my babbling on. You have no idea how much pleasure it gives me. But it's way past your bedtime. I know it is mine."

She escorted me upstairs, and after I was comfortably arranged in a double bed under a blissful load of pretty scrap-quilts, she returned to wish me goodnight, sweet dreams. I lay awake thinking about it. What an exceptional experience —to be an old woman living alone here in the wilderness and have a stranger knock on your door in the middle of the night and not only open it but warmly welcome him inside and offer him shelter. If our situations had been reversed, I doubt that I would have had the courage, to say nothing of the generosity.

The next morning she gave me breakfast in her kitchen. Coffee and hot oatmeal with sugar and tinned cream, but I was hungry and it tasted great. The kitchen was shabbier than the rest of the house; the stove, a rattling refrigerator, everything seemed on the edge of expiring. All except one large, somewhat modern object, a deep-freeze that fitted into a corner of the room.

She was chatting on: "I love birds. I feel so guilty about not tossing them crumbs during the winter. But I can't have them gathering around the house. Because of the cats. Do you care for cats?"

"Yes, I once had a Siamese named Toma. She lived to be twelve, and we traveled everywhere together. All over the world. And when she died I never had the heart to get another."

"Then maybe you will understand this," she said, leading me over to the deep-freeze, and opening it. Inside was nothing but cats: stacks of frozen, perfectly preserved cats—dozens of them. It gave me an odd sensation. "All my old friends. Gone to rest. It's just that I couldn't bear to lose them. *Completely.*" She laughed, and said: "I guess you think I'm a bit dotty."

A bit dotty. Yes, a bit dotty, I thought as I walked under grey skies in the direction of the highway she had pointed out to me. But radiant: a lamp in a window.

Four

✤

Mojave

At 5 P.M. that winter afternoon she had an appointment with Dr. Bentsen, formerly her psychoanalyst and currently her lover. When their relationship had changed from the analytical to the emotional, he insisted, on ethical grounds, that she cease to be his patient. Not that it mattered. He had not been of much help as an analyst, and as a lover—well, once she had watched him running to catch a bus, two hundred and twenty pounds of shortish, fiftyish, frizzly-haired, hip-heavy, myopic Manhattan Intellectual, and she had laughed: how was it possible that she could love a man so ill-humored, so ill-favored as Ezra Bentsen? The answer was she didn't; in fact, she disliked him. But at least she didn't associate him with resignation and despair. She feared her husband; she was not afraid of Dr. Bentsen. Still, it was her husband she loved.

She was rich; at any rate, had a substantial allowance from her husband, who was rich, and so could afford the studio-apartment hideaway where she met her lover perhaps once a week, sometimes twice, never more. She could also afford gifts he seemed to expect on these occasions. Not that he appreciated their quality: Verdura cuff links, classic Paul Flato cigarette cases, the obligatory Cartier watch, and (more to the point) occasional specific amounts of cash he asked to "borrow."

He had never given *her* a single present. Well, one: a mother-of-pearl Spanish dress comb that he claimed was an heirloom, a mother-treasure. Of course, it was nothing she could wear, for she wore her own hair, fluffy and tobacco-colored, like a childish aureole around her deceptively naïve and youthful face. Thanks to dieting, private exercises with Joseph Pilatos, and the dermatological attentions of Dr. Orentreich, she looked in her early twenties; she was thirty-six.

The Spanish comb. Her hair. That reminded her of Jaime Sanchez and something that had happened yesterday. Jaime Sanchez was her hairdresser, and though they had known each other scarcely a year, they were, in their own way, good friends. She confided in him somewhat; he confided in her considerably more. Until recently she had judged Jaime to be a happy, almost overly blessed young man. He shared an apartment with an attractive lover, a young dentist named Carlos. Jaime and Carlos had been schoolmates in San Juan; they had left Puerto Rico together, settling first in New Orleans, then New York, and it was Jaime, working as a beautician, a talented one, who had put Carlos through dental school. Now Carlos had his own office and a clientele of prosperous Puerto Ricans and blacks.

However, during her last several visits she had noticed

that Jaime Sanchez's usually unclouded eyes were somber, yellowed, as though he had a hangover, and his expertly articulate hands, ordinarily so calm and capable, trembled a little.

Yesterday, while scissor-trimming her hair, he had stopped and stood gasping, gasping—not as though fighting for air, but as if struggling against a scream.

She had said: "What is it? Are you all right?"

"No."

He had stepped to a washbasin and splashed his face with cold water. While drying himself, he said: "I'm going to kill Carlos." He waited, as if expecting her to ask him why; when she merely stared, he continued: "There's no use talking any more. He understands nothing. My words mean nothing. The only way I can communicate with him is to kill him. Then he will understand."

"I'm not sure that I do, Jaime."

"Have I ever mentioned to you Angelita? My cousin Angelita? She came here six months ago. She has always been in love with Carlos. Since she was, oh, twelve years old. And now Carlos is in love with her. He wants to marry her and have a household of children."

She felt so awkward that all she could think to ask was: "Is she a nice girl?"

"Too nice." He had seized the scissors and resumed clipping. "No, I mean that. She is an excellent girl, very petite, like a pretty parrot, and much too nice; her kindness becomes cruel. Though she doesn't understand that she is being cruel. For example . . ." She glanced at Jaime's face moving in the mirror above the washbasin; it was not the merry face that had often beguiled her, but pain and perplexity exactly reflected. "Angelita and Carlos want me to live with them after they are married, all of us together in one apartment. It was her idea, but Carlos says yes! yes! we must all stay together and from now on he and I will live like brothers. That is the reason I have to kill him. He could never have loved me, not if he could ignore my enduring such hell. He says, 'Yes, I love you, Jaime; but Angelita—this is different.' There is no difference. You love or you do not. You destroy or you do not. But Carlos will never understand that. Nothing reaches him, nothing can—only a bullet or a razor."

She wanted to laugh; at the same time she couldn't because she realized he was serious and also because she well knew how true it was that certain persons could only be made to recognize the truth, be made to *understand*, by subjecting them to extreme punishment.

Nevertheless, she did laugh, but in a manner that Jaime would not interpret as genuine laughter. It was something comparable to a sympathetic shrug. "You could never kill anyone, Jaime."

He began to comb her hair; the tugs were not gentle, but she knew the anger implied was against himself, not her. "Shit!" Then: "No. And that's the reason for most suicides. Someone is torturing you. You want to kill them, but you can't. All that pain is because you love them, and you can't kill them because you love them. So you kill yourself instead."

Leaving, she considered kissing him on the cheek, but settled for shaking his hand. "I know how trite this is, Jaime. And for the moment certainly no help at all. But remember—there's always somebody else. Just don't look for the same person, that's all."

The rendezvous apartment was on East Sixty-fifth Street; today she walked to it from her home, a small town house on Beekman Place. It was windy, there was leftover snow on the sidewalk and a promise of more in the air, but she was snug enough in the coat her husband had given her for Christmas —a sable-colored suede coat that was lined with sable.

A cousin had rented the apartment for her in his own name. The cousin, who was married to a harridan and lived in Greenwich, sometimes visited the apartment with his secretary, a fat Japanese woman who drenched herself in noseboggling amounts of Mitsouko. This afternoon the apartment reeked of the lady's perfume, from which she deduced that her cousin had lately been dallying here. That meant she would have to change the sheets.

She did so, then prepared herself. On a table beside the bed she placed a small box wrapped in shiny cerulean paper; it contained a gold toothpick she had bought at Tiffany, a gift for Dr. Bentsen, for one of his unpleasing habits was constantly picking his teeth, and, moreover, picking them with an endless series of paper matches. She had thought the gold pick might make the whole process a little less disagreeable. She put a stack of Lee Wiley and Fred Astaire records on a phonograph, poured herself a glass of cold white wine, undressed entirely, lubricated herself, and stretched out on the bed, humming, singing along with the divine Fred and listening for the scratch of her lover's key at the door.

To judge from appearances, orgasms were agonizing events in the life of Ezra Bentsen: he grimaced, he ground his dentures, he whimpered like a frightened mutt. Of course, she was always relieved when she heard the whimper; it meant that soon his lathered carcass would roll off her, for he was not one to linger, whispering tender compliments: he just rolled right off. And today, having done so, he greedily reached for the blue box, knowing it was a present for him. After opening it, he grunted.

She explained: "It's a gold toothpick."

He chuckled, an unusual sound coming from him, for his sense of humor was meager. "That's kind of cute," he said, and began picking his teeth. "You know what happened last night? I slapped Thelma. But good. And I punched her in the stomach, too."

Thelma was his wife; she was a child psychiatrist, and by reputation a fine one.

"The trouble with Thelma is you can't talk to her. She doesn't understand. Sometimes that's the only way you can get the message across. Give her a fat lip."

She thought of Jaime Sanchez.

"Do you know a Mrs. Roger Rhinelander?" Dr. Bentsen said.

"Mary Rhinelander? Her father was my father's best friend. They owned a racing stable together. One of her horses won the Kentucky Derby. Poor Mary, though. She married a real bastard."

"So she tells me."

"Oh? Is Mrs. Rhinelander a new patient?"

"Brand-new. Funny thing. She came to me for more or less the particular reason that brought you; her situation is almost identical."

The particular reason? Actually, she had a number of problems that had contributed to her eventual seduction on Dr. Bentsen's couch, the principal one being that she had not been capable of having a sexual relationship with her husband since the birth of their second child. She had married when she was twenty-four; her husband was fifteen years her senior. Though they had fought a lot, and were jealous of each other, the first five years of their marriage remained in her memory as an unblemished vista. The difficulty started when he asked her to have a child; if she hadn't been so much in love with him, she would never have consented—she had been afraid of children when she herself was a child, and the company of a child still made her uneasy. But she had given him a son, and the experience of pregnancy had traumatized her: when she wasn't actually suffering, she imagined she was, and after the birth she descended into a depression that continued more than a year. Every day she slept fourteen hours of Seconal sleep; as for the other ten, she kept awake by fueling herself with amphetamines. The second child, another boy, had been a drunken accident—though she suspected that really her husband had tricked her. The instant she knew she was pregnant again she had insisted on having an abortion; he had told her that if she went ahead with it, he would divorce her. Well, he had lived to regret that. The child had been born two months prematurely, had nearly died, and because of massive internal hemorrhaging, so had she; they had both hovered above an abyss through months of intensive care. Since then, she had never shared a bed with her husband; she wanted to, but she couldn't, for the naked presence of him, the thought of his body inside hers, summoned intolerable terrors.

Dr. Bentsen wore thick black socks with garters, which he never removed while "making love"; now, as he was sliding his gartered legs into a pair of shiny-seated blue serge trousers, he said: "Let's see. Tomorrow is Tuesday. Wednesday is our anniversary . . ."

"Our anniversary?"

"Thelma's! Our twentieth. I want to take her to . . . Tell me the best restaurant around now?"

"What does it matter? It's very small and very smart and the owner would never give you a table."

His lack of humor asserted itself: "That's a damn strange thing to say. What do you mean, he wouldn't give me a table?"

"Just what I said. One look at you and he'd know you had hairy heels. There are *some* people who won't serve people with hairy heels. He's one of them."

Dr. Bentsen was familiar with her habit of introducing unfamiliar lingo, and he had learned to pretend he knew what it signified; he was as ignorant of her ambience as she was of his, but the shifting instability of his character would not allow him to admit it.

"Well, then," he said, "is Friday all right? Around five?"

She said: "No, thank you." He was tying his tie and stopped; she was still lying on the bed, uncovered, naked; Fred was singing "By Myself." "No, thank you, darling Dr. B. I don't think we'll be meeting here any more."

She could see he was startled. Of course he would miss her—she was beautiful, she was considerate, it never bothered her when he asked her for money. He knelt beside the bed and fondled her breast. She noticed an icy mustache of sweat on his upper lip. "What is this? Drugs? Drink?"

She laughed and said: "All I drink is white wine, and not much of that. No, my friend. It's simply that you have hairy heels."

Like many analysts, Dr. Bentsen was quite literal-minded; just for a second she thought he was going to strip off his socks and examine his feet. Churlishly, like a child, he said: "I *don't* have hairy heels."

"Oh, yes you do. Just like a horse. All ordinary horses have hairy heels. Thoroughbreds don't. The heels of a well-bred horse are flat and glistening. Give my love to Thelma."

"Smart-ass. Friday?"

The Astaire record ended. She swallowed the last of the wine.

"Maybe. I'll call you," she said.

As it happened, she never called, and she never saw him

again—except once, a year later, when she sat on a banquette next to him at La Grenouille; he was lunching with Mary Rhinelander, and she was amused to see that Mrs. Rhinelander signed the check.

The promised snow had arrived by the time she returned, again on foot, to the house on Beekman Place. The front door was painted pale yellow and had a brass knocker shaped like a lion's claw. Anna, one of four Irishwomen who staffed the house, answered the door and reported that the children, exhausted from an afternoon of ice-skating at Rockefeller Center, had already had their supper and been put to bed.

Thank God. Now she wouldn't have to undergo the half-hour of playtime and tale-telling and kiss-goodnight that customarily concluded her children's day; she may not have been an affectionate mother, but she was a dutiful one—just as her own mother had been. It was seven o'clock, and her husband had phoned to say he would be home at seven-thirty; at eight they were supposed to go to a dinner party with the Sylvester Hales, friends from San Francisco. She bathed, scented herself to remove memories of Dr. Bentsen, remodeled her makeup, of which she wore the most modest quantity, and changed into a grey silk caftan and grey silk slippers with pearl buckles.

She was posing by the fireplace in the library on the second floor when she heard her husband's footsteps on the stairs. It was a graceful pose, inviting as the room itself, an unusual octagonal room with cinnamon lacquered walls, a yellow lacquered floor, brass bookshelves (a notion borrowed from Billy Baldwin), two huge bushes of brown orchids ensconced in yellow Chinese vases, a Marino Marini horse standing in a corner, a South Seas Gauguin over the mantel, and a delicate fire fluttering in the fireplace. French windows offered a view of a darkened garden, drifting snow, and lighted tugboats floating like lanterns on the East River. A voluptuous couch, upholstered in mocha velvet, faced the fireplace, and in front of it, on a table lacquered the yellow of the floor, rested an ice-filled silver bucket; embedded in the bucket was a carafe brimming with pepper-flavored red Russian vodka.

Her husband hesitated in the doorway, and nodded at her approvingly: he was one of those men who truly noticed a woman's appearance, gathered at a glance the total atmosphere. He was worth dressing for, and it was one of her lesser reasons for loving him. A more important reason was that he resembled her father, a man who had been, and forever would be, the man in her life; her father had shot himself, though no one ever knew why, for he was a gentleman of almost abnormal discretion. Before this happened, she had terminated three engagements, but two months after her father's death she met George, and married him because in both looks and manners he approximated her great lost love.

She moved across the room to meet her husband halfway. She kissed his cheek, and the flesh against her lips felt as cold as the snowflakes at the window. He was a large man, Irish, black-haired and green-eyed, handsome even though he had lately accumulated considerable poundage and had gotten a bit jowly, too. He projected a superficial vitality; both men and women were drawn to him by that alone. Closely observed, however, one sensed a secret fatigue, a lack of any real optimism. His wife was severely aware of it, and why not? She was its principal cause.

She said: "It's such a rotten night out, and you look so tired. Let's stay home and have supper by the fire."

"Really, darling—you wouldn't mind? It seems a mean thing to do to the Haleses. Even if she is a cunt."

"*George!* Don't use that word. You know I hate it."

"Sorry," he said; he was, too. He was always careful not to offend her, just as she took the same care with him: a consequence of the quiet that simultaneously kept them together and apart.

"I'll call and say you're coming down with a cold."

"Well, it won't be a lie. I think I am."

While she called the Haleses, and arranged with Anna for a soup and soufflé supper to be served in an hour's time, he chugalugged a dazzling dose of the scarlet vodka and felt it light a fire in his stomach; before his wife returned, he poured himself a respectable shot and stretched full length on the couch. She knelt on the floor and removed his shoes and began to massage his feet: God knows, *he* didn't have hairy heels.

He groaned. "Hmm. That feels good."

"I love you, George."

"I love you, too."

She thought of putting on a record, but no, the sound of the fire was all the room needed.

"George?"

"Yes, darling."

"What are you thinking about?"

"A woman named Ivory Hunter."

"You really know somebody named Ivory Hunter?"

"Well. That was her stage name. She'd been a burlesque dancer."

She laughed. "What is this, some part of your college adventures?"

"I never knew her. I only heard about her once. It was the summer after I left Yale."

He closed his eyes and drained his vodka. "The summer I hitchhiked out to New Mexico and California. Remember? That's how I got my nose broke. In a bar fight in Needles, California." She liked his broken nose, it offset the extreme gentleness of his face; he had once spoken of having it re-broken and reset, but she had talked him out of it. "It was early September, and that's always the hottest time of the year in Southern California; over a hundred almost every day. I ought to have treated myself to a bus ride, at least across the desert. But there I was like a fool, deep in the Mojave, hauling a fifty-pound knapsack and sweating until there was no sweat in me. I swear it was a hundred and fifty in the shade. Except there wasn't any shade. Nothing but sand and mesquite and this boiling blue sky. Once a big truck drove by, but it wouldn't stop for me. All it did was kill a rattlesnake that was crawling across the road.

"I kept thinking something was bound to turn up some-where. A garage. Now and then cars passed, but I might as well have been invisible. I began to feel sorry for myself, to understand what it means to be helpless, and to understand why it's a good thing that Buddhists send out their young monks to beg. It's chastening. It rips off that last layer of baby fat.

"And then I met Mr. Schmidt. I thought maybe it was a mirage. An old white-haired man about a quarter mile up the highway. He was standing by the road with heat waves rip-pling around him. As I got closer I saw that he carried a cane and wore pitch-black glasses, and he was dressed as if headed for church—white suit, white shirt, black tie, black shoes.

"Without looking at me, and while some distance away, he called out: 'My name is George Schmidt.'

"I said: 'Yes. Good afternoon, sir.'

"He said: '*Is* it afternoon?'

" 'After three.'

" 'Then I must have been standing here two hours or more. Would you mind telling me where I am?'

" 'In the Mojave Desert. About eighteen miles west of Needles.'

" 'Imagine that,' he said. 'Leaving a seventy-year-old blind man stranded alone in the desert. Ten dollars in my pocket, and not another rag to my name. Women are like flies: they settle on sugar or shit. I'm not saying I'm sugar, but she's sure settled for shit now. My name is George Schmidt.'

"I said: 'Yes, sir, you told me. I'm George Whitelaw.' He wanted to know where I was going, what I was up to, and when I said I was hitchhiking, heading for New York, he asked if I would take his hand and help him along a bit, maybe until we could catch a ride. I forgot to mention that he had a German accent and was extremely stout, almost fat; he looked as if he'd been lying in a hammock all his life. But when I held his hand I felt the roughness, the immense strength of it. You wouldn't have wanted a pair of hands like that around your throat. He said: 'Yes, I have strong hands. I've worked as a masseur for fifty years, the last twelve in Palm Springs. You got any water?' I gave him my canteen, which was still half full. And he said: 'She left me here without even a drop of water. The whole thing took me by surprise. Though I can't say it should have, knowing Ivory good as I did. That's my wife. Ivory Hunter, she was. A stripper; she played the Chicago World's Fair, 1932, and she would have been a star if it hadn't been for that Sally Rand. Ivory invented this fan-dance thing and that Rand woman stole it off her. So Ivory said. Probably just more of her bullshit. Uh-oh, watch out for that rattler, he's over there someplace, I can hear him really singing. There's two things I'm scared of. Snakes and women. They have a lot in common. One thing they have in common is: the last thing that dies is their tail.'

"A couple of cars passed and I stuck out my thumb and the old man tried to flag them down with his stick, but we must have looked too peculiar—a dirty kid in dungarees and a blind fat man dressed in his city best. I guess we'd still be out there if it hadn't been for this truckdriver. A Mexican. He was parked by the road fixing a flat. He could speak about five words of Tex-Mex, all of them four-letter, but I still remembered a lot of Spanish from the summer with Uncle Alvin in Cuba. So the Mexican told me he was on his way to El Paso, and if that was our direction, we were welcome aboard.

"But Mr. Schmidt wasn't too keen. I had practically to drag him into the caboose. 'I hate Mexicans. Never met a Mexican I liked. If it wasn't for a Mexican . . . Him only nineteen and her I'd say from the touch of her skin, I'd say Ivory was a woman way past sixty. When I married her a couple of years ago, she said she was fifty-two. See, I was living in this trailer camp out on Route 111. One of those trailer camps halfway between Palm Springs and Cathedral City. Cathedral City! Some name for a dump that's nothing but honky-tonks and pool halls and fag bars. The only thing you can say about it is Bing Crosby lives there. If that's saying something. Anyway, living next to me in this other trailer is my friend Hulga. Ever since my wife died—she died the same day Hitler died—Hulga had been driving me to work; she works as a waitress at this Jew club where I'm the masseur. All the waiters and waitresses at the club are big blond Germans. The Jews like that; they really keep them stepping. So one day Hulga tells me she has a cousin coming to visit. Ivory Hunter. I forget her legal name, it was on the marriage certificate, but I forget. She had about three husbands before; she probably didn't remember the name she was born with. Anyway, Hulga tells me that this cousin of hers, Ivory, used to be a famous dancer, but now she's just come out of the hospital and she's lost her last husband on account of she's spent a year in the hospital with TB. That's why Hulga asked her out to Palm Springs. Because of the air. Also, she didn't have any place else to go. The first night she was there, Hulga invited me over, and I liked her cousin right away; we didn't talk much, we listened to the radio mostly, but I liked Ivory. She had a real nice voice, real slow and gentle, she sounded like nurses ought to sound; she said she didn't smoke or drink and she was a member of the Church of God, same as me. After that, I was over at Hulga's almost every night.'"

George lit a cigarette, and his wife tilted out a jigger more of the pepper vodka for him. To her surprise, she poured one for herself. A number of things about her husband's narrative had accelerated her ever-present but usually Librium-subdued anxiety; she couldn't imagine where his memoir was leading, but she knew there was some destination, for George seldom rambled. He had graduated third in his class at Yale Law School, never practiced law but had gone on to top his class at Harvard Business School; within the past decade he had been offered a presidential Cabinet post, and an ambassadorship to England or France or wherever he wanted. However, what had made her feel the need for red vodka, a ruby bauble burning in the firelight, was the disquieting manner in which George Whitelaw had become Mr. Schmidt;

her husband was an exceptional mimic. He could imitate certain of their friends with infuriating accuracy. But this was not casual mimicry; he seemed entranced, a man fixed in another man's mind.

"'I had an old Chevy nobody had driven since my wife died. But Ivory got it tuned up, and pretty soon it wasn't Hulga driving me to work and bringing me home, but Ivory. Looking back, I can see it was all a plot between Hulga and Ivory, but I didn't put it together then. Everybody around the trailer park, and everybody that met her, all they said was what a lovely woman she was, big blue eyes and pretty legs. I figured it was just good-heartedness, the Church of God—I figured that was why she was spending her evenings cooking dinner and keeping house for an old blind man. One night we were listening to the *Hit Parade* on the radio, and she kissed me and rubbed her hand along my leg. Pretty soon we were doing it twice a day—once before breakfast and once after dinner, and me a man of sixty-nine. But it seemed like she was as crazy about my cock as I was about her cunt—'"

She tossed her vodka into the fireplace, a splash that made the flames hiss and flourish; but it was an idle protest: Mr. Schmidt would not be reproached.

"'Yes, sir, Ivory was all cunt. Whatever way you want to use the word. It was exactly one month from the day I met her to the day I married her. She didn't change much, she fed me good, she was always interested to hear about the Jews at the club, and it was me that cut down on the sex—*way* down, what with my blood pressure and all. But she never complained. We read the Bible together, and night after night she would read aloud from magazines, good magazines like *Reader's Digest* and *The Saturday Evening Post*, until I fell asleep. She was always saying she hoped she died before I did because she would be heartbroken and destitute. It was true I didn't have much to leave. No insurance, just some bank-savings that I turned into a joint account, and I had the trailer put in her name. No, I can't say there was a harsh word between us until she had the big fight with Hulga.

"'For a long time I didn't know what the fight was about. All I knew was that they didn't speak to each other any more, and when I asked Ivory what was going on, she said: "Nothing." As far as she was concerned, she hadn't had any falling-out with Hulga: "But you know how much she drinks." That was true. Well, like I told you, Hulga was a waitress at the club, and one day she comes barging into the massage room. I had a customer on the table, had him there spread out buck-naked, but a lot she cared—she smelled like a Four Roses factory. She could hardly stand up. She told me she had just got fired, and suddenly she started swearing and pissing. She was hollering at me and pissing all over the floor. She said everybody at the trailer park was laughing at me. She said Ivory was an old whore who had latched onto me because she was down and out and couldn't do any better. And she said what kind of a chowderhead was I? Didn't I know my wife was fucking the balls off Freddy Feo since God knows when?

"'Now, see, Freddy Feo was an itinerant Tex-Mex kid—he was just out of jail somewhere, and the manager of the trailer park had picked him up in one of those fag bars in Cat City and put him to work as a handyman. I don't guess he could have been one-hundred-percent fag because he was giving plenty of the old girls around there a tickle for their money. One of them was Hulga. She was loop-de-do over him. On hot nights him and Hulga used to sit outside her trailer on her swing-seat drinking straight tequila, forget the lime, and he'd play the guitar and sing spic songs. Ivory described it to me as a green guitar with his name spelled out in rhinestone letters. I'll say this, the spic could sing. But Ivory always claimed she couldn't stand him; she said he was a cheap little greaser out to take Hulga for every nickel she had. Myself, I don't remember exchanging ten words with him, but I didn't like him because of the way he smelled. I have a nose like a bloodhound and I could smell him a hundred yards off, he wore so much brilliantine in his hair, and something else that Ivory said was called Evening in Paris.

"'Ivory swore up and down it wasn't so. Her? *Her* let a Tex-Mex monkey like Freddy Feo put a finger on her? She said it was because Hulga had been dumped by this kid that she was crazy and jealous and thought he was humping everything from Cat City to Indio. She said she was insulted that I'd listen to such lies, even though Hulga was more to be pitied than reviled. And she took off the wedding ring I'd given her—it had belonged to my first wife, but she said that didn't make any difference because she knew I'd loved Hedda and that made it all the better—and she handed it to me and she said if I didn't believe her, then here was the ring and she'd take the next bus going anywhere. So I put it back on her finger and we knelt on the floor and prayed together.

"'I did believe her; at least I thought I did; but in some way it was like a seesaw in my head—yes, no, yes, no. And Ivory had lost her looseness; before she had an easiness in her body that was like the easiness in her voice. But now it was all wire—tense, like those Jews at the club that keep whining and scolding because you can't rub away all their worries. Hulga got a job at the Miramar, but out at the trailer park I always turned away when I smelled her coming. Once she sort of whispered up beside me: "Did you know that sweet wife of yours gave the greaser a pair of gold earrings! But his

boyfriend won't let him wear them." I don't know. Ivory
prayed every night with me that the Lord would keep us
together, healthy in spirit and body. But I noticed . . . Well,
on those warm summer nights when Freddy Feo would be
out there somewhere in the dark, singing and playing his
guitar, she'd turn off the radio right in the middle of Bob
Hope or Edgar Bergen or whatever, and go sit outside and
listen. She said she was looking at the stars: "I bet there's no
place in the world you can see the stars like here." But suddenly it turned out she hated Cat City and the Springs. The
whole desert, the sandstorms, summers with temperatures up
to a hundred thirty degrees, and nothing to do if you wasn't
rich and belonged to the Racquet Club. She just announced
this one morning. She said we should pick up the trailer and
plant it down anywhere where the air was cool. Wisconsin.
Michigan. I felt good about the idea; it set my mind to rest as
to what might be going on between her and Freddy Feo.

    "'Well, I had a client there at the club, a fellow from
Detroit, and he said he might be able to get me on as a
masseur at the Detroit Athletic Club; nothing definite, only
one of them maybe deals. But that was enough for Ivory.
Twenty-three skidoo, and she's got the trailer uprooted, fifteen years of planting strewn all over the ground, the Chevy
ready to roll, and all our savings turned into traveler's checks.
Last night she scrubbed me top to bottom and shampooed
my hair, and this morning we set off a little after daylight.

    "'I realized something was wrong, and I'd have known
what it was if I hadn't dozed off soon as we hit the highway.
She must have dumped sleeping pills in my coffee.

    "'But when I woke up I smelled him. The brilliantine
and the dime-store perfume. He was hiding in the trailer.
Coiled back there somewhere like a snake. What I thought
was: Ivory and the kid are going to kill me and leave me for

the buzzards. She said, "You're awake, George." The way she said it, the slight fear, I could tell she knew what was going on in my head. That I'd guessed it all. I told her, *Stop the car*. She wanted to know what for? Because I had to take a leak. She stopped the car, and I could hear she was crying. As I got out, she said: "You been good to me, George, but I didn't know nothing else to do. And you got a profession. There'll always be a place for you somewhere."

" 'I got out of the car, and I really did take a leak, and while I was standing there the motor started up and she drove away. I didn't know where I was until you came along, Mr. . . .?'

" 'George Whitelaw.' And I told him: 'Jesus, that's just like murder. Leaving a blind man helpless in the middle of nowhere. When we get to El Paso we'll go to the police station.'

"He said: 'Hell, no. She's got enough trouble without the cops. She settled on shit—leave her to it. Ivory's the one out in nowhere. Besides, I love her. A woman can do you like that, and still you love her.' "

George refilled his vodka; she placed a small log on the fire, and the new rush of flame was only a little brighter than the furious red suddenly flushing her cheeks.

"That *women* do," she said, her tone aggressive, challenging. "Only a crazy person . . . Do you think I could do something like that?"

The expression in his eyes, a certain visual silence, shocked her and made her avert her eyes, withdrawing the question. "Well, what happened to him?"

"Mr. Schmidt?"

"Mr. Schmidt."

He shrugged. "The last I saw of him he was drinking a glass of milk in a diner, a truck stop outside El Paso. I was lucky; I got a ride with a trucker all the way to Newark. I sort of forgot about it. But for the last few months I find myself wondering about Ivory Hunter and George Schmidt. It must be age; I'm beginning to feel old myself."

She knelt beside him again; she held his hand, interweaving her fingers with his. "Fifty-two? And you feel *old*?"

He had retreated; when he spoke, it was the wondering murmur of a man addressing himself. "I always had such confidence. Just walking the street, I felt such a *swing*. I could feel people looking at me—on the street, in a restaurant, at a party—envying me, wondering who is that guy. Whenever I walked into a party, I knew I could have half the women in the room if I wanted them. But that's all over. Seems as though old George Whitelaw has become the invisible man. Not a head turns. I called Mimi Stewart twice last week, and she never returned the calls. I didn't tell you, but I stopped at Buddy Wilson's yesterday, he was having a little cocktail thing. There must have been twenty fairly attractive girls, and they all looked right through me; to them I was a tired old guy who smiled too much."

She said: "But I thought you were still seeing Christine."

"I'll tell you a secret. Christine is engaged to that Rutherford boy from Philadelphia. I haven't seen her since November. He's okay for her; she's happy and I'm happy for her."

"Christine! Which Rutherford boy? Kenyon or Paul?"

"The older one."

"That's Kenyon. You knew that and didn't tell me?"

"There's so much I haven't told you, my dear."

Yet that was not entirely true. For when they had stopped sleeping together, they had begun discussing together—indeed, collaborating on—each of his affairs. Alice

Kent: five months; ended because she'd demanded he divorce
and marry her. Sister Jones: terminated after one year when
her husband found out about it. Pat Simpson: a *Vogue* model
who'd gone to Hollywood, promised to return and never had.
Adele O'Hara: beautiful, an alcoholic, a rambunctious scene-
maker; he'd broken that one off himself. Mary Campbell,
Mary Chester, Jane Vere-Jones. Others. And now Christine.

A few he had discovered himself; the majority were "ro-
mances" she herself had stage-managed, friends she'd introduced him to, confidantes she had trusted to provide him
with an outlet but not to exceed the mark.

"Well," she sighed. "I suppose we can't blame Christine.
Kenyon Rutherford's rather a catch." Still, her mind was running, searching like the flames shivering through the logs: a
name to fill the void. Alice Combs: available, but too dull.
Charlotte Finch: too rich, and George felt emasculated by
women—or men, for that matter—richer than himself. Perhaps the Ellison woman? The soigné Mrs. Harold Ellison
who was in Haiti getting a swift divorce . . .

He said: "Stop frowning."

"I'm not frowning."

"It just means more silicone, more bills from Orentreich.
I'd rather see the human wrinkles. It doesn't matter whose
fault it is. We all, sometimes, leave each other out there
under the skies, and we never understand why."

An echo, caverns resounding: Jaime Sanchez and Carlos and
Angelita; Hulga and Freddy Feo and Ivory Hunter and Mr.
Schmidt; Dr. Bentsen and George, George and herself, Dr.
Bentsen and Mary Rhinelander . . .

He gave a slight pressure to their interwoven fingers, and
with his other hand, raised her chin and insisted on their eyes

meeting. He moved her hand up to his lips and kissed its palm.

"I love you, Sarah."

"I love you, too."

But the touch of his lips, the insinuated threat, tautened her. Below stairs, she heard the rattle of silver on trays: Anna and Margaret were ascending with the fireside supper.

"I love you, too," she repeated with pretended sleepiness, and with a feigned languor moved to draw the window draperies. Drawn, the heavy silk concealed the night river and the lighted riverboats, so snow-misted that they were as muted as the design in a Japanese scroll of winter night.

"George?" An urgent plea before the supper-laden Irishwomen arrived, expertly balancing their offerings: "*Please*, darling. We'll think of somebody."

Five

❧

Hospitality

Once upon a time, in the rural South, there were farmhouses and farm wives who set tables where almost any passing stranger, a traveling preacher, a knife-grinder, an itinerant worker, was welcome to sit down to a hearty midday meal. Probably many such farm wives still exist. Certainly my aunt does, Mrs. Jennings Carter. Mary Ida Carter.

As a child I lived for long periods of time on the Carters' farm, small then, but today a considerable property. The house was lighted by oil lamps in those days; water was pumped from a well and carried, and the only warmth was provided by fireplaces and stoves, and the only entertainment was what we ourselves manufactured. In the evenings, after supper, likely as not my uncle Jennings, a handsome, virile man, would play the piano accompanied by his pretty wife, my mother's younger sister.

They were hard-working people, the Carters. Jennings, with the help of a few sharecropping field hands, cultivated his land with a horse-drawn plow. As for his wife, her chores were unlimited. I helped her with many of them: feeding the pigs, milking the cows, churning milk into butter, husking corn, shelling peas and pecans—it was fun, except for one assignment I sought to avoid, and when forced to perform, did so with my eyes shut: I just plain hated wringing the necks of chickens, though I certainly didn't object to eating them afterward.

This was during the Depression, but there was plenty to eat on Mary Ida's table for the principal meal of the day, which was served at noon and to which her sweating husband and his helpers were summoned by clanging a big bell. I loved to ring the bell; it made me feel powerful and beneficent.

It was to these midday meals, where the table was covered with hot biscuits and cornbread and honey-in-the-comb and chicken and catfish or fried squirrel and butter beans and black-eyed peas, that guests sometimes appeared, sometimes expected, sometimes not. "Well," Mary Ida would sigh, seeing a footsore Bible salesman approaching along the road, "we don't need another Bible. But I guess we'd better set another place."

Of all those we fed, there were three who will never slip my memory. First, the Presbyterian missionary, who was traveling around the countryside soliciting funds for his Christian duties in unholy lands. Mary Ida said she couldn't afford a cash contribution, but she would be pleased to have him take dinner with us. Poor man, he definitely looked as though he needed one. Arrayed in a rusty, dusty, shiny black suit, creaky black undertaker shoes, and a black-greenish hat, he was thin as a stalk of sugar cane. He had a long red wrinkled neck with a bobbing Adam's apple the size of a goiter. I never saw a greedier fellow; he sucked up a quart of buttermilk in three swallows, devoured a whole platter of chicken single-handed (or rather, double-handedly, for he was eating with both hands), and so many biscuits, dripping with butter and molasses, that I lost count. However, for all his gobbling, he managed to give us hair-raising accounts of his exploits in perilous territories. "I'll tell you somethin'. I've seen cannibals roast black men and white men on a spit—just like you'd roast a pig—and eat every morsel, toes, brains, ears, and all. One of them cannibals told me the best eatin' is a roasted newborn baby; said it tasted just like lamb. I spec the reason they didn't eat me is 'cause I didn't have enough meat on my bones. I've seen men hung by their heels till blood gushed out their ears. Once I got bit by a green mamba, the deadliest snake in the world. I was kinda nauseated there for a spell, but I didn't die, so the black men figured I was a god and they gave me a coat made of leopard skins."

After the gluttonous preacher had departed, Mary Ida felt dizzy; she was sure she would have bad dreams for a month. But her husband, comforting her, said: "Oh, honey, you didn't believe any of that malarkey? That man's no more a missionary than I am. He's just a heathen liar."

Then there was the time we entertained a convict who had escaped from a chain gang at the Alabama State Prison in Atmore. Obviously, we didn't *know* he was a dangerous character serving a life sentence for umpteen armed robberies. He simply appeared at our door and told Mary Ida he was hungry and could she give him something to eat. "Well, sir," she said, "you've come to the right place. I'm just putting dinner on the table now."

Somehow, probably by raiding a washline, he had exchanged his convict stripes for overalls and a worn blue work shirt. I thought he was nice, we all did; he had a flower tattooed on his wrist, his eyes were gentle, he was gently spoken. He said his name was Bancroft (which, as it turned out, *was* his true name). My uncle Jennings asked him: "What's your line of work, Mr. Bancroft?"

"Well," he drawled, "I'm just lookin' for some. Like most everybody else. I'm pretty handy. Can do most anythin'. You wouldn't have somethin' for me?"

Jennings said: "I sure could use a man. But I can't afford him."

"I'd work for most nothin'."

"Yeah," said Jennings. "But nothing is what I've got."

Unpredictably, for it was a subject seldom alluded to in that household, crime came into the conversation. Mary Ida complained: "Pretty Boy Floyd. And that Dillinger man. Running around the country shooting people. Robbing banks."

"Oh, I don't know," said Mr. Bancroft. "I got no sympathy with them banks. And Dillinger, he's real smart, you got to hand him that. It kinda makes me laugh the way he knocks off them banks and gets clean away with it." Then he actually laughed, displaying tobacco-tinted teeth.

"Well," Mary Ida countered, "I'm slightly surprised to hear you say that, Mr. Bancroft."

Two days later Jennings drove his wagon into town and returned with a keg of nails, a sack of flour, and a copy of the *Mobile Register*. On the front page was a picture of Mr. Bancroft—"Two-Barrels" Bancroft, as he was colloquially known to the authorities. He had been captured in Evergreen, thirty miles away. When Mary Ida saw his photo, she rapidly fanned her face with a paper fan, as though to prevent a fainting fit. "Heaven help me," she cried. "He could have killed us all."

Jennings said sourly: "There was a reward. And we missed out on it. *That's* what gets my goat."

Next, there was a girl called Zilla Ryland. Mary Ida discovered her bathing a two-year-old baby, a red-haired boy, in a creek that ran through the woods back of the house. As Mary Ida described it: "I saw her before she saw me. She was standing naked in the water bathing this beautiful little boy. On the bank there was a calico dress and the child's clothes and an old suitcase tied together with a piece of rope. The boy was laughing, and so was she. Then she saw me, and she was startled. Scared. I said: 'Nice day. But hot. The water must feel good.' But she snatched up the baby and scampered out of the creek, and I said: 'You don't have to be frightened of me. I'm only Mrs. Carter that lives just over yonder. Come on up and rest a spell.' Then she commenced to cry; she was only a little thing, no more than a child herself. I asked what's the matter, honey? But she wouldn't answer. By now she had pulled on her dress and dressed the boy. I said maybe I could help you if you'd tell me what's wrong. But she shook her head, and said there was nothing wrong, and I said well, we don't cry over nothing, do we? Now you just follow me up to the house and we'll talk about it. And she did."

Indeed she did.

I was swinging in the porch swing reading an old *Saturday Evening Post* when I noticed them coming up the path, Mary Ida toting a broken-down suitcase and this barefooted girl carrying a child in her arms.

Mary Ida introduced me: "This is my nephew, Buddy. And—I'm sorry, honey, I didn't catch your name."

"Zilla," the girl whispered, eyes lowered.

"I'm sorry, honey. I can't hear you."

"Zilla," she again whispered.

"Well," said Mary Ida cheerfully, "that sure is an unusual name."

Zilla shrugged. "My mama give it to me. Was her name, too."

Two weeks later Zilla was still with us; she proved to be as unusual as her name. Her parents were dead, her husband had "run off with another woman. She was real fat, and he liked fat women, he said I was too skinny, so he run off with her and got a divorce and married her up in Athens, Georgia." Her only living kin was a brother: Jim James. "That's why I come down here to Alabama. The last I heard, he was located somewhere around here."

Uncle Jennings did everything in his power to trace Jim James. He had good reason, for, although he liked Zilla's little boy, Jed, he'd come to feel quite hostile toward Zilla—her thin voice aggravated him, and her habit of humming mysterious tuneless melodies.

Jennings to Mary Ida: "Just the hell how much longer is our boarder going to hang around?" Mary Ida: "Oh, Jennings. Shhh! Zilla might hear you. Poor soul. She's got nowhere to go." So Jennings intensified his labors. He brought the sheriff into the case; he even *paid* to place an ad in the local paper—and that was really going far. But nobody hereabouts had ever heard of Jim James.

At last Mary Ida, clever woman, had an idea. The idea was to invite a neighbor, Eldridge Smith, to evening supper, usually a light meal served at six. I don't know why she hadn't thought of it before. Mr. Smith was not much to look at, but he was a recently widowed farmer of about forty with two school-aged children.

After that first supper Mr. Smith got to stopping by almost every twilight. After dark we all left Zilla and Mr. Smith alone, where they swung together on the creaking porch swing and laughed and talked and whispered. It was driving Jennings out of his mind because he didn't like Mr. Smith any better than he liked Zilla; his wife's repeated requests to "Hush, honey. Wait and see" did little to soothe him.

We waited a month. Until finally one night Jennings took Mr. Smith aside and said: "Now look here, Eldridge. Man to man, what are your intentions toward this fine young lady?" The way Jennings said it, it was more like a threat than anything else.

Mary Ida made the wedding dress on her foot-pedaled Singer sewing machine. It was white cotton with puffed sleeves, and Zilla wore a white silk ribbon bow in her hair, especially curled for the occasion. She looked surprisingly pretty. The ceremony was held under the shade of a mulberry tree on a cool September afternoon, the Reverend Mr. L. B. Persons presiding. Afterward everybody was served cupcakes and fruit punch spiked with scuppernong wine. As the newlyweds rode away in Mr. Smith's mule-drawn wagon, Mary Ida lifted the hem of her skirt to dab at her eyes, but Jennings, eyes dry as a snake's skin, declared: "Thank you, dear Lord. And while You're doing favors, my crops could use some rain."

Six

❧

Dazzle

She fascinated me.

She fascinated everyone, but most people were ashamed of their fascination, especially the proud ladies who presided over some of the grander households of New Orleans' Garden District, the neighborhood where the big plantation owners lived, the shipowners and oil operators, the richest professional men. The only persons not secretive about their fascination with Mrs. Ferguson were the servants of these Garden District families. And, of course, some of the children, who were too young or guileless to conceal their interest.

I was one of those children, an eight-year-old boy temporarily living with Garden District relatives. However, as it happened, I did keep my fascination to myself, for I felt a certain guilt: I had a secret, something that was bothering me, something that was really worrying me very much, something I was afraid to tell anybody, *any*body—I couldn't imagine what their reaction would be, it was such an odd thing that was worrying me, that had been worrying me for almost two years. I had never heard of anyone with a problem like the one that was troubling me. On the one hand it seemed maybe silly; on the other . . .

I wanted to tell my secret to Mrs. Ferguson. Not *want* to, but felt I had to. Because Mrs. Ferguson was said to have magical powers. It was said, and believed by many serious-minded people, that she could tame errant husbands, force proposals from reluctant suitors, restore lost hair, recoup squandered fortunes. In short, she was a witch who could make wishes come true. I had a wish.

Mrs. Ferguson did not seem clever enough to be capable of magic. Not even card tricks. She was a plain woman who might have been forty but was perhaps thirty; it was hard to tell, for her round Irish face, with its round full-moon eyes, had few lines and little expression. She was a laundress, probably the only white laundress in New Orleans, and an artist at her trade: the great ladies of the town sent for her when their finest laces and linens and silks required attention. They sent for her for other reasons as well: to obtain desires —a new lover, a certain marriage for a daughter, the death of a husband's mistress, a codicil to a mother's will, an invitation to be Queen of Comus, grandest of the Mardi Gras galas. It was not merely as a laundress that Mrs. Ferguson was courted. The source of her success, and principal income, was her alleged abilities to sift the sands of daydreams until she produced the solid stuff, golden realities.

Now, about this wish of my own, the worry that was with me from first thing in the morning until last thing at night: it wasn't anything I could just straight out ask her. It required the right time, a carefully prepared moment. She seldom came to our house, but when she did I stayed close by, pretending to watch the delicate movements of her thick ugly fingers as they handled lace-trimmed napkins, but really attempting to catch her eye. We never talked; I was too nervous and she was too stupid. Yes, stupid. It was just something I sensed; powerful witch or not, Mrs. Ferguson was a stupid woman. But now and again our eyes did lock, and dumb as she was, the intensity, the *fascination* she saw in my gaze told her that I desired to be a client. She probably thought I wanted a bike, or a new air rifle; anyway, she wasn't about to concern herself with a kid like me. What could I give her? So she would turn her tiny lips down and roll her full-moon eyes elsewhere.

About this time, early December in 1932, my paternal grandmother arrived for a brief visit. New Orleans has cold winters; the chilly humid winds from the river drift deep into your bones. So my grandmother, who was living in Florida, where she taught school, had wisely brought with her a fur coat, one she had borrowed from a friend. It was made of black Persian lamb, the belonging of a rich woman, which my grandmother was not. Widowed young, and left with three sons to raise, she had not had an easy life, but she never complained. She was an admirable woman; she had a lively mind, and a sound, sane one as well. Due to family circumstances, we rarely met, but she wrote often and sent me small gifts. She loved me and I wanted to love her, but until she died, and she lived beyond ninety, I kept my distance, behaved indifferently. She felt it, but she never knew what caused my apparent coldness, nor did anyone else, for the reason was part of an intricate guilt, faceted as the dazzling yellow stone dangling from a slender gold-chain necklace that she often wore. Pearls would have suited her better, but she attached great value to this somewhat theatrical gewgaw, which I understood her own grandfather had won in a card game in Colorado.

Of course the necklace wasn't valuable; as my grandmother always scrupulously explained to anyone who inquired, the stone, which was the size of a cat's paw, was not a "gem" stone, not a canary diamond, nor even a topaz, but a chunk of rock-crystal deftly faceted and tinted dark yellow. Mrs. Ferguson, however, was unaware of the trinket's true worth, and when one afternoon, during the course of my grandmother's stay, the plump youngish witch arrived to stiffen some linen, she seemed spellbound by the brilliant bit of glass swinging from the thin chain around my grandmother's neck. Her ignorant moon eyes glowed, and that's a fact: they truly glowed. I now had no difficulty attracting her attention; she studied me with an interest absent heretofore.

As she departed, I followed her into the garden, where there was a century-old wisteria arbor, a mysterious place even in winter when the foliage had shriveled, stripping this leaf-tunnel of its concealing shadows. She walked under it and beckoned to me.

Softly, she said: "You got something on your mind?"

"Yes."

"Something you want done? A favor?"

I nodded; she nodded, but her eyes shifted nervously: she didn't want to be seen talking to me.

She said: "My boy will come. He will tell you."

"*When?*"

But she said hush, and hurried out of the garden. I watched her waddle off into the dusk. It dried my mouth to think of having all my hopes pinned on this stupid woman. I couldn't eat supper that night; I didn't sleep until dawn.

Aside from the thing that was worrying me, now I had a whole lot of new worries. If Mrs. Ferguson did what I wanted her to do, then what about my clothes, what about my name, where would I go, who would I be? Holy smoke, it was enough to drive you crazy! Or was I already crazy? That was part of the problem: I must be crazy to want Mrs. Ferguson to do this thing I wanted her to do. That was one reason why I couldn't tell anybody: they would think I was crazy. Or something worse. I didn't know what that something worse could be, but instinctively I felt that people saying I was crazy, my family and their friends and the other kids, might be the least of it.

Because of fear and superstition combined with greed, the servants of the Garden District, some of the snobbiest mammies and haughtiest housemen who ever tread a parquet floor, spoke of Mrs. Ferguson with respect. They also spoke of her in quiet tones, and not only because of her peculiar gifts, but because of her equally peculiar private life, various details of which I had gradually collected by eavesdropping on the tattletale of these elegant blacks and mulattoes and Creoles, who considered themselves the real royalty of New Orleans, and certainly superior to any of their employers. As for Mrs. Ferguson—she was not a madame, merely a mamselle: an unmarried woman with a raft of children, at least six, who came from East Texas, one of those redneck hamlets across the border from Shreveport. At the age of fifteen she had been tied to a hitching post in front of the town post office and publicly flogged with a horsewhip by her own father. The reason for this terrible punishment was a child she had borne, a boy with green eyes but unmistakably the product of a black father. With the baby, who was called Skeeter and was now fourteen and said to be a devil himself, she came to New Orleans and found work as a housekeeper for an Irish Catholic priest, whom she seduced, had a second baby by, abandoned for another man, and went on from there, living with a succession of handsome lovers, men she could only have succeeded in acquiring through potions poured into their wine, for after all, without her particular powers, who was she? White trash from East Texas who carried on with black men, the mother of six bastards, a laundress, a servant herself. And yet they respected her; even Mme. Jouet, the head mammy of the Vaccaro family, who owned the United Fruit Company, always addressed her civilly.

Two days after my conversation with Mrs. Ferguson, a Sunday, I accompanied my grandmother to church, and as we were walking home, a matter of a few blocks, I noticed that someone was following us: a well-built boy with tobacco-colored skin and green eyes. I knew at once that it was the infamous Skeeter, the boy whose birth had caused his mother to be flogged, and I knew that he was bringing me a message. I felt nauseated, but also elated, almost tipsy, enough so to make me laugh.

Merrily, my grandmother asked: "Ah, you know a joke?"

I thought: No, but I know a secret. However, I only said: "It was just something the minister said."

"Really? I'm glad you found some humor. It struck me as a very dry sermon. But the choir was good."

I refrained from making the following comment: "Well, if they're just going to talk about sinners and hell, when they don't know what hell is, they ought to ask me to preach the sermon. I could tell them a thing or two."

"Are you happy here?" my grandmother asked, as if it were a question she had been considering ever since her arrival. "I know it's been difficult. The divorce. Living here, living there. I want to help; I don't know how."

"I'm fine. Everything's hunky-dory."

But I wished she'd shut up. She did, with a frown. So at least I'd got one wish. One down and one to go.

When we reached home my grandmother, saying she felt the start of a migraine and might try to ward it off with a pill and a nap, kissed me and went inside the house. I raced through the garden toward the old wisteria arbor and hid myself inside it, like a bandit in a bandit's cave waiting for a confederate.

Soon Mrs. Ferguson's son arrived. He was tall for his age, just shy of six feet, and muscular as a dockworker. He resembled his mother in no respect. It wasn't only his dark coloring; his features were nicely defined, the bone structure quite precise—his father must have been a handsome man. And unlike Mrs. Ferguson, his emerald eyes were not dumb comic-strip dots, but narrow and mean, weapons, bullets threateningly aimed and primed to explode. I wasn't surprised when, not many years later, I heard he'd committed a double murder in Houston and died in the electric chair at Texas State Prison.

He was natty, dressed like the adult sharp-guy hoodlums who lounged around the waterfront hangouts: Panama hat, two-toned shoes, a tight stained white linen suit that some much slighter man must have given him. An impressive cigar jutted from his handkerchief pocket: a Havana Castle Morro, the connoisseur's cigar Garden District gentlemen served along with their after-dinner absinthe and framboise. Skeeter Ferguson lit his cigar with movie-gangster showmanship, constructed an impeccable smoke ring, blew it straight into my face, and said: "I've come to get you."

"*Now?*"

"Just as soon as you bring me the old lady's necklace."

It was useless to stall, but I tried: "What necklace?"

"Save your breath. Go get it and then we'll head somewhere. Or else we won't. And you'll never have another
chance."

"But she's wearing it!"

Another smoke ring, professionally manufactured, effort-
lessly projected. "How you get it ain't none of my beeswax.
I'll just be right here. Waiting."

"But it may take a long time. And suppose I can't do
it?"

"You will. I'll wait till you do."

The house sounded empty when I entered through the
kitchen door, and except for my grandmother, it was; everyone else had driven off to visit a newly married cousin who
lived across the river. After calling my grandmother's name,
and hearing silence, I tiptoed upstairs and listened at her
bedroom door. She must be asleep. Accepting the risk, I
inched the door open.

The curtains were drawn and the room dark except for
the hot shine of coal burning inside a porcelain stove. My
grandmother was lying in bed with covers drawn up to her
chin; she must have taken the headache pill, for her breathing was deep and even. Still, I drew back the quilt covering
her with the meticulous stealth of a robber tumbling the dials
of a bank safe. Her throat was naked; she was wearing only
an undergarment, a pink slip. I found the necklace on a
bureau; it was lying in front of a photograph of her three
sons, one of them my father. I hadn't seen him for so long
that I'd forgotten what he looked like—and after today, I'd
probably never see him again. Or if I did, he wouldn't know
who I was. But I had no time to think about that. Skeeter
Ferguson was waiting for me, standing inside the wisteria
arbor tapping his foot and sucking on his millionaire's cigar.
Nevertheless, I hesitated.

I had never stolen anything before; well, some Hershey bars from the candy counter at the movies, and a few books I'd not returned to the public library. But this was so important. My grandmother would forgive me if she knew why I had to steal the necklace. No, she wouldn't forgive me; nobody would forgive me if they knew *exactly* why. But I had no choice. It was like Skeeter said: if I didn't do it now, his mother would never give me another chance. And the thing that was worrying me would go on and on, maybe forever and forever. So I took it. I stuffed it in my pocket and fled the room without even closing the door. When I rejoined Skeeter, I didn't show him the necklace, I just told him I had it, and his green eyes grew greener, turned nastier, as he issued one of his big-shot smoke rings and said: "Sure you do. You're just a born rascal. Like me."

First we walked, then we took a trolley car down Canal Street, usually so crowded and cheerful but spooky now with the stores closed and a Sabbath stillness hovering over it like a funeral cloud. At Canal and Royal we changed trolleys and rode all the way across the French Quarter, a familiar neighborhood where many of the longer-established families lived, some with purer lineage than any names the Garden District could offer. Eventually we started walking again; we walked miles. The stiff churchgoing shoes I was still wearing hurt, and now I didn't know where we were, but wherever it was I didn't like it. It was no use questioning Skeeter Ferguson, for if you did, he smiled and whistled, or spit and smiled and whistled. I wonder if he whistled on his way to the electric chair.

I really had no idea where we were; it was a section of the city I'd not seen before. And yet there was nothing unusual about it, except that there were fewer white faces around than one was accustomed to, and the farther we walked the scarcer they became: an occasional white resident surrounded by blacks and Creoles. Otherwise it was an ordinary collection of humble wooden structures, rooming houses with peeling paint, modest family homes, mostly poorly kept but with some exceptions. Mrs. Ferguson's house, when at last we reached it, was one of the exceptions.

It was an old house but a *real* house, with seven or eight rooms; it didn't look as though the first strong breeze from the Gulf would blow it away. It was painted an ugly brown, but at least the paint was not sun-blistered and flaking. And it stood inside a well-tended yard that contained a big shade tree—a chinaberry tree with old rubber tires, several of them, suspended on ropes from its branches: swings for children. And there were other playthings scattered around the yard: a tricycle, buckets, and little shovels for making mud pies— evidence of Mrs. Ferguson's fatherless brood. A mongrel puppy held captive by a chain attached to a stake began bouncing about and yapping the second he glimpsed Skeeter.

Skeeter said: "Here we are. Just open the door and walk in."

"Alone?"

"She's expectin' you. Do what I tell you. Walk right in. And if you catch her in the middle of a hump, keep your eyes open: that's how I got to be a champion humper."

The last remark, meaningless to me, ended with a chuckle, but I followed his instructions, and as I started toward the front door, glanced back at him. It didn't seem possible, but he was already gone, and I never saw him again —or if I did, I don't remember it.

The door opened directly into Mrs. Ferguson's parlor. At least it was furnished as a parlor (a couch, easy chairs, two wicker rocking chairs, maplewood side tables), though the floor was covered with a brown kitchen linoleum that perhaps was meant to match the color of the house. When I came into the room Mrs. Ferguson was tilting to and fro in one of the rocking chairs, while a good-looking young man, a Creole not many years older than Skeeter, rocked away in the other. A bottle of rum rested on a table between them, and they were both drinking from glasses filled with the stuff. The young man, who was not introduced to me, was wearing only an undershirt and somewhat unbuttoned bell-bottom sailor's trousers. Without a word he stopped rocking, stood up, and swaggered down a hall, taking the rum bottle with him. Mrs. Ferguson listened until she heard a door close.

Then all she said was: "Where is it?"

I was sweating. My heart was acting funny. I felt as though I had run a hundred miles and lived a thousand years in just the last few hours.

Mrs. Ferguson stilled her chair, and repeated herself: "Where is it?"

"Here. In my pocket."

She held out a thick red hand, palm up, and I dropped the necklace into it. Rum had already done something to alter the usual dullness of her eyes; the dazzling yellow stone did more. She turned it this way and that, staring at it; I tried not to, I tried to think of other things, and found myself wondering if she had scars on her back, lash marks.

"Am I expected to guess?" she asked, never removing her gaze from the bijou dangling from its fragile gold chain. "Well? Am I supposed to tell you why you are here? What it is you want?"

She didn't know, she couldn't, and suddenly I didn't want her to. I said: "I like to tap-dance."

For an instant her attention was diverted from the sparkling new toy.

"I want to be a tap dancer. I want to run away. I want

to go to Hollywood and be in the movies." There was some truth in this; running away to Hollywood was high on my list of escape-fantasies. But that wasn't what I'd decided not to tell her, after all.

"Well," she drawled. "You sure are pretty enough to be in picture shows. Prettier than any boy ought to be."

So she *did* know. I heard myself shouting: "Yes! Yes! That's it!"

"That's what? And stop hollering. I'm not deaf."

"I don't want to be a boy. I want to be a girl."

It began as a peculiar noise, a strangled gurgling far back in her throat that bubbled into laughter. Her tiny lips stretched and widened; drunken laughter spilled out of her mouth like vomit, and it seemed to be spurting all over me— laughter that sounded like vomit smells.

"Please, please. Mrs. Ferguson, you don't understand. I'm very worried. I'm worried all the time. There's something wrong. Please. You've got to understand."

She went on rocking with laughter and her rocking chair rocked with her.

Then I said: "You *are* stupid. Dumb and stupid." And I tried to grab the necklace away from her.

The laughter stopped as though she had been struck by lightning; a storm overtook her face, total fury. Yet when she spoke her voice was soft and hissing and serpentine: "You don't know what you want, boy. I'll show you what you want. Look at me, boy. Look here. I'll show you what you want."

"Please. I don't want anything."

"Open your eyes, boy."

Somewhere in the house a baby was crying.

"Look at me, boy. Look here."

What she wanted me to look at was the yellow stone. She was holding it above her head, and slightly swinging it. It seemed to have gathered up all the light in the room, accumulated a devastating brilliance that plunged everything else into blackness. Swing, spin, dazzle, dazzle.

"I hear a baby crying."

"That's you you hear."

"Stupid woman. Stupid. Stupid."

"Look here, boy."

Spindazzlespinspindazzledazzledazzle.

It was still daylight, and it was still Sunday, and here I was back in the Garden District, standing in front of my house. I don't know how I got there. Someone must have brought me, but I don't know who; my last memory was the noise of Mrs. Ferguson's laughter returning.

Of course, a huge commotion was made over the missing necklace. The police were not called, but the whole household was upside down for days; not an inch was left unsearched. My grandmother was very upset. But even if the necklace had been of high value, a jewel that could have been sold and assured her of comfort the rest of her life, I still would not have accused Mrs. Ferguson. For if I did, she might reveal what I'd told her, the thing I never told anyone again, not ever. Finally it was decided that a thief had stolen into the house and taken the necklace while my grandmother slept. Well, that was the truth. Everyone was relieved when my grandmother concluded her visit and returned to Florida. It was hoped that the whole sad affair of the missing jewel would soon be forgotten.

But it was not forgotten. Forty-four years evaporated, and it was not forgotten. I became a middle-aged man, riddled with quirks and quaint notions. My grandmother died, still sane and sound of mind despite her great age.

A cousin called to inform me of her death, and to ask when I would be arriving for the funeral; I said I'd let her know. I was ill with grief, inconsolable; and it was absurd, out of all proportion. My grandmother was not someone I had loved. Yet how I grieved! But I did not travel to the funeral, nor even send flowers. I stayed home and drank a quart of vodka. I was very drunk, but I can remember answering the telephone and hearing my father identify himself. His old man's voice trembled with more than the weight of years; he vented the pent-up wrath of a lifetime, and when I remained silent, he said: "You sonofabitch. She died with your picture in her hand." I said "I'm sorry," and hung up. What was there to say? How could I explain that all through the years any mention of my grandmother, any letter from her or thought of her, evoked Mrs. Ferguson? Her laughter, her fury, the swinging, spinning yellow stone: spindazzle-dazzle.

II

Handcarved
Coffins

✤

Handcarved Coffins
A Nonfiction Account of an American Crime

March, 1975.

A town in a small Western state. A focus for the many large farms and cattle-raising ranches surrounding it, the town, with a population of less than ten thousand, supports twelve churches and two restaurants. A movie house, though it has not shown a movie in ten years, still stands stark and cheerless on Main Street. There once was a hotel, too; but that also has been closed, and nowadays the only place a traveler can find shelter is the Prairie Motel.

The motel is clean, the rooms are well heated; that's about all you can say for it. A man named Jake Pepper has been living there for almost five years. He is fifty-eight, a widower with four grown sons. He is five-foot-ten, in top condition, and looks fifteen years younger than his age. He

has a handsome-homely face with periwinkle blue eyes and a
thin mouth that twitches into quirky shapes that are sometimes smiles and sometimes not. The secret of his boyish
appearance is not his lanky trimness, not his chunky ripe-
apple cheeks, nor his naughty mysterious grins; it's because of
his hair that looks like somebody's kid brother: dark blond,
clipped short, and so afflicted with cowlicks that he cannot
really comb it; he sort of wets it down.

Jake Pepper is a detective employed by the State Bureau
of Investigation. We had first met each other through a close
mutual friend, another detective in a different state. In 1972
he wrote a letter saying he was working on a murder case,
something that he thought might interest me. I telephoned
him and we talked for three hours. I was very interested in
what he had to tell me, but he became alarmed when I
suggested that I travel out there and survey the situation
myself; he said that would be premature and might endanger
his investigation, but he promised to keep me informed. For
the next three years we exchanged telephone calls every few
months. The case, developing along lines intricate as a rat's
maze, seemed to have reached an impasse. Finally I said:
Just let me come there and look around.

And so it was that I found myself one cold March night
sitting with Jake Pepper in his motel room on the wintry,
windblown outskirts of this forlorn little Western town.
Actually, the room was pleasant, cozy; after all, off and on, it
had been Jake's home for almost five years, and he had built
shelves to display pictures of his family, his sons and grandchildren, and to hold hundreds of books, many of them concerning the Civil War and all of them the selections of an
intelligent man: he was partial to Dickens, Melville, Trollope,
Mark Twain.

Jake sat crosslegged on the floor, a glass of bourbon beside him. He had a chessboard spread before him; absently he shifted the chessmen about.

TC: The amazing thing is, nobody seems to know anything about this case. It's had almost no publicity.

JAKE: There are reasons.

TC: I've never been able to put it into proper sequence. It's like a jigsaw puzzle with half the pieces missing.

JAKE: Where shall we begin?

TC: From the beginning.

JAKE: Go over to the bureau. Look in the bottom drawer. See that little cardboard box? Take a look at what's inside it.

(What I found inside the box was a miniature coffin. It was a beautifully made object, carved from light balsam wood. It was undecorated; but when one opened the hinged lid one discovered the coffin was not empty. It contained a photograph—a casual, candid snapshot of two middle-aged people, a man and a woman, crossing a street. It was not a posed picture; one sensed that the subjects were unaware that they were being photographed.)

That little coffin. I guess that's what you might call the beginning.

TC: And the picture?

JAKE: George Roberts and his wife. George and Amelia Roberts.

TC: Mr. and Mrs. Roberts. Of course. The first victims. He was a lawyer?

JAKE: He was a lawyer, and one morning (to be exact: the tenth of August 1970) he got a present in the mail. That little coffin. With the picture inside it. Roberts was a happy-go-lucky guy; he showed it to some people around the court-

house and acted like it was a joke. One month later George
and Amelia were two very dead people.

TC: How soon did you come on the case?

JAKE: Immediately. An hour after they found them I was on
my way here with two other agents from the Bureau. When
we got here the bodies were still in the car. And so were the
snakes. That's something I'll never forget. Never.

TC: Go back. Describe it exactly.

JAKE: The Robertses had no children. Nor enemies, either.
Everybody liked them. Amelia worked for her husband; she
was his secretary. They had only one car, and they always
drove to work together. The morning it happened was hot. A
sizzler. So I guess they must have been surprised when they
went out to get in their car and found all the windows rolled
up. Anyway, they each entered the car through separate
doors, and as soon as they were inside—*wam!* A tangle of
rattlesnakes hit them like lightning. We found nine big rattlers inside that car. All of them had been injected with
amphetamine; they were crazy, they bit the Robertses everywhere: neck, arms, ears, cheeks, hands. Poor people. Their
heads were huge and swollen like Halloween pumpkins
painted green. They must have died almost instantly. I hope
so. That's one hope I really hope.

TC: Rattlesnakes aren't that prevalent in these regions. Not
rattlesnakes of that caliber. They must have been brought
here.

JAKE: They were. From a snake farm in Nogales, Texas. But
now's not the time to tell you how I know that.

(Outside, crusts of snow laced the ground; spring was a
long way off—a hard wind whipping the window announced that winter was still with us. But the sound of
the wind was only a murmur in my head underneath the
racket of rattling rattlesnakes, hissing tongues. I saw the

car dark under a hot sun, the swirling serpents, the human heads growing green, expanding with poison. I listened to the wind, letting it wipe the scene away.)

JAKE: 'Course, we don't know if the Baxters ever got a coffin. I'm sure they did; it wouldn't fit the pattern if they hadn't. But they never mentioned receiving a coffin, and we never found a trace of it.

TC: Perhaps it got lost in the fire. But wasn't there someone with them, another couple?

JAKE: The Hogans. From Tulsa. They were just friends of the Baxters who were passing through. The killer never meant to kill them. It was an accident.

See, what happened was: the Baxters were building a fancy new house, but the only part of it that was really finished was the basement. All the rest was still under construction. Roy Baxter was a well-to-do man; he could've afforded to rent this whole motel while his house was being built. But he chose to live in this underground basement, and the only entrance to it was through a trap door.

It was December—three months after the rattlesnake murders. All we know for certain is: the Baxters invited this couple from Tulsa to spend the night with them in their basement. And sometime just before dawn one humdinger of a fire broke out in that basement, and the four people were incinerated. I mean that literally: burned to ashes.

TC: But couldn't they have escaped through the trap door?

JAKE (twisting his lips, snorting): Hell, no. The arsonist, the murderer, had piled cement blocks on top of it. King Kong couldn't have budged it.

TC: But obviously there had to be some connection between the fire and the rattlesnakes.

JAKE: That's easy to say now. But damned if I could make any connection. We had five guys working this case; we knew

more about George and Amelia Roberts, about the Baxters
and the Hogans, than they ever knew about themselves. I'll
bet George Roberts never knew his wife had had a baby
when she was fifteen and had given it away for adoption.

'Course, in a place this size, everybody more or less
knows everybody else, at least by sight. But we could find
nothing that linked the victims. Or any motivations. There
was no reason, none that we could find, why anybody would
want to kill any of those people. (He studied his chessboard;
he lit a pipe and sipped his bourbon) The victims, all of them
were strangers to me. I'd never heard of them till they were
dead. But the next fellow was a friend of mine. Clem Anderson. Second-generation Norwegian; he'd inherited a ranch
here from his father, a pretty nice spread. We'd gone to
college together, though he was a freshman when I was a
senior. He married an old girl friend of mine, wonderful girl,
the only girl I've ever seen with lavender eyes. Like amethyst.
Sometimes, when I'd had a snootful, I used to talk about
Amy and her amethyst eyes, and my wife didn't think it was
one bit funny. Anyway, Clem and Amy got married and settled out here and had seven children. I had dinner at their
house the night before he got killed, and Amy said the only
regret she had in life was that she hadn't had more children.

But I'd been seeing a lot of Clem right along. Ever since
I came out here on the case. He had a wild streak, he drank
too much; but he was shrewd, he taught me a lot about this
town.

One night he called me here at the motel. He sounded
funny. He said he had to see me right away. So I said come
on over. I thought he was drunk, but it wasn't that—he was
scared. Know why?

TC: Santa Claus had sent him a present.

JAKE: Uh-huh. But you see, he didn't know what it was. What it meant. The coffin, and its possible connection to the rattlesnake murders, had never been made public. We were keeping that a secret. I had never mentioned the matter to Clem.

So when he arrived in this very room, and showed me a coffin that was an exact replica of the one the Robertses had received, I knew my friend was in great danger. It had been mailed to him in a box wrapped in brown paper; his name and address were printed in an anonymous style. Black ink.

TC: And was there a picture of him?

JAKE: Yes. And I'll describe it carefully because it is very relevant to the manner of Clem's death. Actually, I think the murderer meant it as a little joke, a sly hint as to how Clem was going to die.

In the picture, Clem is seated in a kind of jeep. An eccentric vehicle of his own invention. It had no top and it had no windshield, nothing to protect the driver at all. It was just an engine with four wheels. He said he'd never seen the picture before, and had no idea who had taken it or when.

Now I had a difficult decision. Should I confide in him, admit that the Roberts family had received a similar coffin before their deaths, and that the Baxters probably had as well? In some ways it might be better not to inform him: that way, if we kept close surveillance, he might lead us to the killer, and do it more easily by not being aware of his danger.

TC: But you decided to tell him.

JAKE: I did. Because, with this second coffin in hand, I was certain the murders were connected. And I felt that Clem must know the answer. He *must*.

But after I explained the significance of the coffin, he went into shock. I had to slap his face. And then he was like a child; he lay down on the bed and began to cry: "Somebody's going to kill me. Why? Why?" I told him: "Nobody's going to kill you. I can promise you that. But *think*, Clem! What do you have in common with these people who *did* die? There must be something. Maybe something very trivial." But all he could say was: "I don't know. I don't know." I forced him to drink until he was drunk enough to fall asleep. He spent the night here. In the morning he was calmer. But he still could not think of anything that connected him with the crimes, see how he in any way fitted into a pattern. I told him not to discuss the coffin with anyone, not even his wife; and I told him not to worry—I was importing an extra two agents just to keep an eye on him.

TC: And how long was it before the coffin-maker kept his promise?

JAKE: Oh, I think he must have been enjoying it. He teased it along like a fisherman with a trout trapped in a bowl. The Bureau recalled the extra agents, and finally even Clem seemed to shrug it off. Six months went by. Amy called and invited me out to dinner. A warm summer night. The air was full of fireflies. Some of the children chased about catching them and putting them into jars.

As I was leaving, Clem walked me out to my car. A narrow river ran along the path where it was parked, and Clem said: "About that connection business. The other day I suddenly thought of something. The river." I said what river; and he said that river, the one flowing past us. "It's kind of a complicated story. And probably silly. But I'll tell you the next time I see you."

Of course I never saw him again. At least, not alive.

TC: It's almost as though he must have overheard you.

JAKE: Who?

TC: Santa Claus. I mean, isn't it curious that after all those months Clem Anderson mentions the river, and the very next day, before he can tell you why he suddenly remembered the river, the murderer kept his promise?

JAKE: How's your stomach?

TC: Okay.

JAKE: I'll show you some photographs. But better pour yourself a stiff one. You'll need it.

(The pictures, three of them, were glossy black-and-whites made at night with a flash camera. The first was of Clem Anderson's homemade jeep on a narrow ranch road, where it had overturned and was lying on its side, headlights still shining. The second photograph was of a headless torso sprawled across the same road: a headless man wearing boots and Levis and a sheepskin jacket. The last picture was of the victim's head. It could not have been more cleanly severed by a guillotine or a master surgeon. It lay alone among some leaves, as though a prankster had tossed it there. Clem Anderson's eyes were open, but they did not look dead, merely serene, and except for a jagged gash along the forehead, his face seemed as calm, as unmarked by violence as his innocent, pale Norwegian eyes. As I examined the photographs, Jake leaned over my shoulder, looking at them with me.)

JAKE: It was around dusk. Amy was expecting Clem home for supper. She sent one of their boys down to the main road to meet him. It was the boy who found him.

First he saw the overturned car. Then, a hundred yards farther on, he found the body. He ran back home, and his mother called me. I cursed myself up one row and down the other. But when we drove out there, it was one of my agents who discovered the head. It was quite a distance from the body. In fact, it was still lying where the wire had hit him.

TC: The wire, yes. I never have understood about the wire. It's so—

JAKE: Clever?

TC: More than clever. Preposterous.

JAKE: Nothing preposterous about it. Our friend had simply figured out a nice neat way to decapitate Clem Anderson. Kill him without any possibility of witnesses.

TC: I suppose it's the mathematical element. I'm always bewildered by anything involving mathematics.

JAKE: Well, the gentleman responsible for this certainly has a mathematical mind. At least he had a lot of very accurate measuring to do.

TC: He strung a wire between two trees?

JAKE: A tree and a telephone pole. A strong steel wire sharpened thin as a razor. Virtually invisible, even in broad daylight. But at dusk, when Clem turned off the highway and was driving in that crazy little wagon along that narrow road, he couldn't possibly have glimpsed it. It caught him exactly where it was supposed to: just under the chin. And, as you can see, sliced off his head as easily as a girl picking petals off a daisy.

TC: So many things could have gone *wrong*.

JAKE: What if they had? What's one failure? He would have tried again. And continued till he succeeded.

TC: *That's* what's so preposterous. He always does succeed.

JAKE: Yes and no. But we'll come back to that later.

> (Jake slipped the pictures in a manila envelope. He sucked on his pipe and combed his fingers through his cowlicked hair. I was silent, for I felt a sadness had overtaken him. Finally I asked if he was tired, would he rather I left him? He said no, it was only nine o'clock, he never went to bed before midnight.)

TC: Are you here all alone now?

JAKE: No, Christ, I'd go crazy. I take turns with two other agents. But I'm still the principal guy on the case. And I want it that way. I've got a real investment here. And I'm going to nail our chum if it's the last thing I ever do. He'll make a mistake. In fact, he's already made some. Though I can't say that the manner in which he disposed of Dr. Parsons was one of them.

TC: The coroner?

JAKE: The coroner. The skinny itsy-bitsy hunchbacked little coroner.

TC: Let's see, now. At first you thought that was a suicide?

JAKE: If you'd known Dr. Parsons, you'd have thought it was a suicide, too. There was a man who had every reason to kill himself. Or get himself killed. His wife's a beautiful woman, and he had her hooked on morphine; that's how he got her to marry him. He was a loan shark. An abortionist. At least a dozen dotty old women left him everything in their wills. A true-blue scoundrel, Dr. Parsons.

TC: So you didn't like him?

JAKE: Nobody did. But what I said before was wrong. I said Parsons was a guy who had every reason to kill himself. Actually, he had no reason at all. God was in His heaven, and the sun was shining on Ed Parsons right around the clock. The only thing bothering him was he had ulcers. And a kind of permanent indigestion. He always carried around these big bottles of Maalox. Polished off a couple of those a day.

TC: All the same, everyone was surprised when they heard Dr. Parsons had killed himself?

JAKE: Well, no. Because nobody thought he had killed himself. Not at first.

TC: Sorry, Jake. But I'm getting confused again.

(Jake's pipe had gone out; he dumped it in an ashtray

and unwrapped a cigar, which he did not light; it was an object to chew on, not to smoke. A dog with a bone.)

To begin with, how long was it between funerals? Between Clem Anderson's funeral and Dr. Parsons'?

JAKE: Four months. Just about.

TC: And did Santa send the doctor a gift?

JAKE: Wait. Wait. You're going too fast. The day Parsons died—well, we just thought he had died. Plain and simple. His nurse found him lying on the floor of his office. Alfred Skinner, another doctor here in town, said he'd probably had a heart attack; it would take an autopsy to find out for sure.

That same night I got a call from Parsons' nurse. She said Mrs. Parsons would like to talk to me, and I said fine, I'll drive out there now.

Mrs. Parsons received me in her bedroom, a room I gather she seldom leaves; confined there, I suppose, by the pleasures of morphine. Certainly she isn't an invalid, not in any ordinary sense. She's a lovely woman, and a quite healthy-looking one. Good color in her cheeks, though her skin is smooth and pale as pearls. But her eyes were too bright, the pupils dilated.

She was lying in bed, propped up by a pile of lace-covered pillows. I noticed her fingernails—so long and carefully varnished; and her hands were very elegant, too. But what she was holding in her hands wasn't very elegant.

TC: A gift?

JAKE: Exactly the same as the others.

TC: What did she say?

JAKE: She said "I think my husband was murdered." But she was very calm; she didn't seem upset, under any stress at all.

TC: Morphine.

JAKE: But it was more than that. She's a woman who has

already left life. She's looking back through a door—without regret.

TC: Did she realize the significance of the coffin?

JAKE: Not really, no. And neither would her husband. Even though he was the county coroner, and in theory was part of our team, we never confided in him. He knew nothing about the coffins.

TC: Then why did she think her husband had been murdered?

JAKE (chewing his cigar, frowning): *Because* of the coffin. She said her husband had shown it to her a few weeks ago. He hadn't taken it seriously; he thought it was just a spiteful gesture, something sent to him by one of his enemies. But *she* said—she said the moment she saw the coffin and saw the picture of him inside it—she felt "a shadow" had fallen. Strange, but I think she loved him. That beautiful woman. That bristling little hunchback.

When we said goodnight I took the coffin with me and impressed on her the importance of not mentioning it to anyone. After that, all we could do was wait for the autopsy report. Which was: Death by poisoning, probably self-administered.

TC: But *you* knew it was a murder.

JAKE: I knew. And Mrs. Parsons knew. But everybody else thought it was a suicide. Most of them still think so.

TC: And what brand of poison did our friend choose?

JAKE: Liquid nicotine. A very pure poison, fast and powerful, colorless, odorless. We don't know exactly how it was administered, but I suspect it was mixed together with some of the doctor's beloved Maalox. One good gulp, and down you go.

TC: Liquid nicotine. I've never heard of it.

JAKE: Well, it's not exactly a name brand—like arsenic.

Speaking of our friend, I came across something the other day, something by Mark Twain, that struck me as very appropriate. (After searching his bookshelves, and finding the volume he wanted, Jake paced the room, reading aloud in a voice unlike his own: a hoarse, angry voice) "Of all the creatures that were made, man is the most *detestable*. Of the entire brood he is the only one, the solitary one, that possesses malice. That is the basest of all instincts, passions, vices —the most hateful. He is the only creature that inflicts pain for sport, knowing it to *be* pain. Also in all the list, he is the only creature that has a nasty mind." (Jake banged the book shut and threw it on the bed) Detestable. Malicious. A nasty mind. Yessir, that describes Mr. Quinn perfectly. Not the whole of him. Mr. Quinn is a man of varied talents.

TC: You never told me his name before.

JAKE: I've only known it myself the last six months. But that's it. Quinn.

(Again and again Jake slammed a hard fist into a cupped hand, like an angry prisoner too long confined, frustrated. Well, he had now been imprisoned by this case for many years; great fury, like great whiskey, requires long fermentation.)

Robert Hawley Quinn, Esquire. A most esteemed gentleman.

TC: But a gentleman who makes mistakes. Otherwise, you wouldn't know his name. Or rather, you wouldn't know he *was* our friend.

JAKE: (Silence; he's not listening)

TC: Was it the snakes? You said they came from a Texas snake farm. If you know that, then you must know who bought them.

JAKE (anger gone; yawning): What?

TC: Incidentally, why were the snakes injected with amphetamine?

JAKE: Why do you think? To stimulate them. Increase their ferocity. It was like throwing a lighted match into a gasoline tank.

TC: I wonder, though. I wonder how he managed to inject the snakes, and install them in that car, all without getting bitten himself.

JAKE: He was taught how to do it.

TC: By whom?

JAKE: By the woman who sold him the snakes.

TC: A *woman*?

JAKE: The snake farm in Nogales, it's owned by a woman. You think that's funny? My oldest boy married a girl who works for the Miami police department; she's a professional deep-sea diver. The best car mechanic I know is a woman—

> (The telephone interrupted; Jake glanced at his wrist-watch and smiled, and his smile, so real and relaxed, told me not only that he knew who the caller was, but that it was someone whose voice he'd been happily expecting to hear.)

Hello, Addie. Yeah, he's here. He says it's spring in New York; I said he should've stayed there. Naw, nothin'. Just knocking off some drinks and discussing you-know-what. Is tomorrow Sunday? I thought it was Thursday. Maybe I'm losing my marbles. Sure, we'd love to come to dinner. Addie —don't *worry* about it. He'll like anything you cook. You're the greatest cook either side of the Rockies, east or west. So don't make a big deal out of it. Yeah, well, maybe that raisin pie with the apple crust. Lock your doors. Sleep tight. Yes, I do. You know I do. *Buenas noches.*

> (After he'd hung up, his smile remained, broadened. At last he lit the cigar, puffed on it with pleasure. He pointed at the phone, chuckled.)

That was the mistake Mr. Quinn made. Adelaide Mason. She invited us to dinner tomorrow.

TC: And who is Mrs. Mason?

JAKE: *Miss* Mason. She's a terrific cook.

TC: But other than that?

JAKE: Addie Mason was what I had been waiting for. My big break.

You know, my wife's dad was a Methodist minister. She was very serious about the whole family going to church. I used to get out of it as much as I could, and after she died I never went at all. But about six months ago the Bureau was ready to close shop on this case. We'd spent a lot of time and a lot of money. And we had nothing to show for it; no case at all. Eight murders, and not a single clue that would link the victims together to produce some semblance of a motive. Nothing. Except those three little handcarved coffins.

I said to myself: No! No, it can't be! There's a *mind* behind all this, a reason. I started going to church. There's nothing to do here on Sunday anyway. Not even a golf course. And I prayed: Please, God, don't let this sonofabitch get away with it!

Over on Main Street there's a place called the Okay Café. Everybody knows you can find me there just about any morning between eight and ten. I have my breakfast in the corner booth, and then just hang around reading the papers and talking to the different guys, local businessmen, that stop by for a cup of coffee.

Last Thanksgiving Day, I was having breakfast there as usual. I had the place pretty much to myself, it being a holiday and all; and I was in low spirits anyway—the Bureau was putting the final pressure on me to close this case and clear out. Christ, it wasn't that I didn't want to dust off this damn town! I sure as hell did. But the idea of quitting, of leaving that devil to dance on all those graves, made me sick to my guts. One time, thinking about it, I did vomit. I actually did.

Well, suddenly Adelaide Mason walked into the café. She came straight to my table. I'd met her many times, but I'd never really talked to her. She's a schoolteacher, teaches first grade. She lives here with her sister, Marylee, a widow. Addie Mason said: "Mr. Pepper, surely you're not going to spend Thanksgiving in the Okay Café? If you haven't other plans, why don't you take dinner at our house? It's just my sister and myself." Addie isn't a nervous woman, but despite her smiles and cordiality, she seemed, hmnn, distracted. I thought: Maybe she considers it not quite proper for an unmarried lady to invite an unmarried man, a mere acquaintance, to her home. But before I could say yes or no, she said: "To be truthful, Mr. Pepper, I have a problem. Something I need to discuss with you. This will give us the chance. Shall we say noon?"

I've never eaten better food—and instead of turkey they served squabs with wild rice and a good champagne. All during the meal Addie kept the conversation moving in a very amusing manner. She didn't appear nervous at all, but her sister did.

After dinner we sat down in the living room with coffee and brandy. Addie excused herself from the room, and when she came back she was carrying—

TC: Two guesses?

JAKE: She handed it to me, and said: "This is what I wanted to discuss with you."

> (Jake's thin lips manufactured a smoke ring, then another. Until he sighed, the only sound in the room was the meowing wind clawing at the window.)

You've had a long trip. Maybe we ought to call it a night.

TC: You mean you're going to leave me hanging out here?

JAKE (seriously, but with one of his mischievously ambiguous grins): Just until tomorrow. I think you should hear Addie's story from Addie herself. Come along; I'll walk you to your room.

(Oddly, sleep struck me as though I'd been hit by a thief's blackjack; it *had* been a long journey, my sinus was troubling me, I was tired. But within minutes I was awake; or, rather, I entered some sphere between sleep and wakefulness, my mind like a crystal lozenge, a suspended instrument that caught the reflections of spiraling images: a man's head among leaves, the windows of a car streaked with venom, the eyes of serpents sliding through heat-mist, fire flowing from the earth, scorched fists pounding at a cellar door, taut wire gleaming in the twilight, a torso on a roadway, a head among leaves, fire, fire, fire flowing like a river, river, river. Then a telephone rings.)

MAN'S VOICE: How about it? Are you going to sleep all day?

TC (the curtains are drawn, the room is dark, I don't know where I am, who I am): Hello?

MAN'S VOICE: Jake Pepper speaking. Remember him? Mean guy? With mean blue eyes?

TC: Jake! What time is it?

JAKE: A little after eleven. Addie Mason's expecting us in about an hour. So jump under the shower. And wear something warm. It's snowing outside.

(It was a heavy snow, thick flakes too heavy to float; it fell to the ground and covered it. As we drove away from the motel in Jake's car, he turned on his windshield wipers. Main Street was grey and white and empty, lifeless except for a solitary traffic light winking its colors. Everything was closed, even the Okay Café. The somberness, the gloomy snow-silence, infected us; neither of us spoke. But I sensed that Jake was in a good mood, as though he was anticipating pleasant events. His healthy face was shiny, and he smelled, a bit too sharply, of after-shave lotion. Though his hair was rumpled as ever, he was carefully dressed—but not as though he was headed for church. The red tie he wore was appropriate for a more festive occasion. A suitor en route to a rendezvous? The possibility had occurred to me last night when I'd heard him talking to Miss Mason; there was a tone, a timbre, an intimacy.

But the instant I met Adelaide Mason, I crossed the thought right out of my mind. It didn't matter how bored and lonely Jake might be, the woman was simply too plain. That, at least, was my initial impression. She was somewhat younger than her sister, Marylee Connor, who was a woman in her late forties; her face was a nice face, amiable, but too strong, masculine—cosmetics would only have underlined this quality, and very wisely she wore none. Cleanliness was her most attractive physical feature—her brown bobbed hair, her fingernails, her skin: it was as though she bathed in some special spring rain. She and her sister were fourth-generation natives of the town, and she had been teaching school there since she left college; one wondered why—with her intelligence, her character and general sophistication, it was surprising that she hadn't sought a vaster auditorium for her abilities than a schoolroom full of six-year-olds. "No," she told me, "I'm very happy. I'm doing what I enjoy. Teaching first grade. To be there at the beginning, that's what I like. And with first-graders, you see, I get to teach all subjects. That includes manners. Manners are very important. So few of my children ever learn any at home."

The rambling old house that the sisters shared, a family inheritance, reflected, in its warm soothing comfort, its civilized solid colors and atmospheric "touches," the personality of the younger woman, for Mrs. Connor, agreeable as she was, lacked Adelaide Mason's selective eye, imagination.

The living room, mostly blue and white, was filled with flowering plants, and contained an immense Victorian birdcage, the residence of a half-dozen musical canaries. The dining room was yellow and white and green, with pine-plank floors, bare and polished mirror-bright; logs blazed in a big fireplace. Miss Mason's culinary gifts were even greater than Jake had claimed. She served an extraordinary Irish stew, an amazing apple and raisin pie; and there was red wine, white wine, champagne. Mrs. Connor's husband had left her well-off.

It was during dinner that my original impression of our younger hostess began to change. Yes, very definitely an understanding existed between Jake and this lady. They were lovers. And watching her more attentively, seeing her, as it were, through Jake's eyes, I began to appreciate his unmistakable sensual interest. True, her face was flawed, but her figure, displayed in a close-fitting grey jersey dress, was adequate, not bad really; and she *acted* as though it was *sensational*: a rival to the sexiest film star imaginable. The sway of her hips, the loose movements of her fruity breasts, her contralto voice, the fragility of her hand-gestures: all ultra seductive, ultra feminine without being effeminate. Her power resided in her attitude: she behaved as though she believed she was irresistible; and whatever her opportunities may have been, the style of the woman implied an erotic history complete with footnotes.

As dinner ended, Jake looked at her as if he'd like to march her straight into the bedroom: the tension between them was as taut as the steel wire that had severed Clem Anderson's head. However, he unwrapped a cigar, which Miss Mason proceeded to light for him. I laughed.)

JAKE: Eh?

TC: It's like an Edith Wharton novel. *The House of Mirth*— where ladies are forever lighting gentlemen's cigars.

MRS. CONNOR (defensively): That's quite the custom here. My mother always lighted our father's cigars. Even though she disliked the aroma. Isn't that so, Addie?

ADDIE: Yes, Marylee. Jake, would you like more coffee?

JAKE: Sit still, Addie. I don't want anything. It was a wonderful dinner, and it's time for you to quiet down. Addie? How do you feel about the aroma?

ADDIE (*almost* blushing): I'm very partial to the smell of a good cigar. If I smoked, I'd smoke cigars myself.

JAKE: Addie, let's go back to last Thanksgiving. When we were sitting around like we are now.

ADDIE: And I showed you the coffin?

JAKE: I want you to tell my friend your story. Just as you told it to me.

MRS. CONNOR (pushing back her chair): Oh, please! Must we talk about that? Always! Always! I have nightmares.

ADDIE (rising, placing an arm around her sister's shoulder): That's all right, Marylee. We won't talk about it. We'll move to the living room, and you can play the piano for us.

MRS. CONNOR: It's so *vile*. (Then, looking at me) I'm sure you think I'm a dreadful sissy. No doubt I am. In any event, I've had too much wine.

ADDIE: Darling, what you need is a nap.

MRS. CONNOR: A nap? Addie, how many times have I told you? *I* have *night*mares. (Now, recovering) Of course. A nap. If you'll excuse me.

(As her sister departed, Addie poured herself a glass of red wine, lifted it, letting the glow from the fireplace enhance its scarlet sparkle. Her eyes drifted from the fire to the wine to me. Her eyes were brown, but the various illuminations—firelight, candles on the table—colored them, made them cat-yellow. In the distance the caged canaries sang, and snow, fluttering at the windows like torn lace curtains, emphasized the comforts of the room, the warmth of the fire, the redness of the wine.)

ADDIE: My story. Ho-hum.

I'm forty-four, I've never married, I've been around the world twice, I try to go to Europe every other summer; but it's fair to say that except for a drunken sailor who went berserk and tried to rape me on a Swedish tramp steamer, nothing of a bizarre nature has ever happened to me until this year—the week before Thanksgiving.

My sister and I have a box at the post office; what they call a "drawer"—it's not that we have such a lot of correspondence, but we subscribe to so many magazines. Anyway, on my way home from school I stopped to pick up the mail, and in our drawer there was a package, rather large but very light. It was wrapped in old wrinkled brown paper that looked as if it had been used before, and it was tied with old twine. The postmark was local and it was addressed to me. My name was precisely printed in thick black ink. Even before I opened it I thought: What kind of rubbish is this? Of course, you know all about the coffins?

TC: I've seen one, yes.

ADDIE: Well, I knew nothing about them. No one did. That was a secret between Jake and his agents.

(She winked at Jake, and tilting her head back, swallowed all her wine in one swoop; she did this with astonishing grace, an agility that revealed a lovely throat. Jake, winking back, directed a smoke ring toward her, and the empty oval, floating through the air, seemed to carry with it an erotic message.)

Actually, I didn't open the package until quite late that night. Because when I got home I found my sister at the bottom of the stairs; she'd fallen and sprained an ankle. The doctor came. There was so much commotion. I forgot about the package until after I'd gone to bed. I decided: Oh well, it can wait until tomorrow. I wish I'd abided by that decision; at least I wouldn't have lost a night's sleep.

Because. Because it was *shocking*. I once received an anonymous letter, a truly atrocious one—especially upsetting because, just between us, a good deal of what the writer wrote happened to be true. (Laughing, she replenished her glass) It wasn't really the coffin that shocked me. It was the snapshot inside—a quite recent picture of me, taken on the steps outside the post office. It seemed such an intrusion, a theft—having one's picture made when one is unaware of it. I can sympathize with those Africans who run away from cameras, fearing the photographer intends to steal their spirit. I was shocked, but not frightened. It was my sister who was frightened. When I showed her my little gift, she said: "You don't suppose it has anything to do with that other business?" By "other business" she meant what's been happening here the past five years—murders, accidents, suicides, whatever: it depends on who you're talking to.

I shrugged it off, put it in a category with the anonymous letter; but the more I thought about it—perhaps my sister had stumbled on to something. That package had not been sent to me by some jealous woman, a mere mischief-making ill-wisher. This was the work of a man. A man had whittled that coffin. A man with strong fingers had printed my name on that package. And the whole thing was meant as a threat. But why? I thought: Maybe Mr. Pepper will know.

I'd met Mr. Pepper. Jake. Actually, I had a crush on him.

JAKE: Stick to the story.

ADDIE: I am. I only used the story to lure you into my lair.

JAKE: That's not true.

ADDIE (sadly, her voice in dull counterpoint to the canaries' chirping serenades): No, it isn't true. Because by the time I decided to speak to Jake, I had concluded that someone did indeed intend to kill me; and I had a fair notion who it was, even though the motive was so improbable. Trivial.

JAKE: It's neither improbable nor trivial. Not after you've studied the style of the beast.

ADDIE (ignoring him; and impersonally, as if she were reciting the multiplication table to her students): Everybody knows everybody else. That's what they say about small-town people. But it isn't true. I've never met the parents of some of my pupils. I pass people every day who are virtual strangers. I'm a Baptist, our congregation isn't all that large; but we have some members—well, I couldn't tell you their names if you held a revolver to my head.

The point is: when I began to think about the people who had died, I realized I had known them all. Except the couple from Tulsa who were staying with Ed Baxter and his wife—

JAKE: The Hogans.

ADDIE: Yes. Well, they're not part of this anyway. Bystanders —who got caught in an inferno. Literally.

Not that any of the victims were close friends—except,

perhaps, Clem and Amy Anderson. I'd taught all their children in school.

But I knew the others: George and Amelia Roberts, the Baxters, Dr. Parsons. I knew them rather well. And for only one reason. (She gazed into her wine, observed its ruby flickerings, like a gypsy consulting clouded crystal, ghostly glass) The river. (She raised the wineglass to her lips, and again drained it in one long luxuriously effortless gulp) Have you seen the river? Not yet? Well, now is not the time of year. But in the summer it is very nice. By far the prettiest thing around here. We call it Blue River; it is blue—not Caribbean blue, but very clear all the same and with a sandy bottom and deep quiet pools for swimming. It originates in those mountains to the north and flows through the plains and ranches; it's our main source of irrigation, and it has two tributaries—much smaller rivers, one called Big Brother and the other Little Brother.

The trouble started because of these tributaries. Many ranchers, who were dependent on them, felt that a diversion should be created in Blue River to enlarge Big Brother and Little Brother. Naturally, the ranchers whose property was nourished by the main river were against this proposition. None more so than Bob Quinn, owner of the B.Q. Ranch, through which the widest and deepest stretches of Blue River travels.

JAKE (spitting into the fire): Robert Hawley Quinn, Esquire.

ADDIE: It was a quarrel that had been simmering for decades. Everyone knew that strengthening the two tributaries, even at the expense of Blue River (in terms of power and sheer beauty), was the fair and logical thing to do. But the Quinn family, and others among the rich Blue River ranchers, had always, through various tricks, prevented any action from being taken.

Then we had two years of drought, and that brought the situation to a head. The ranchers whose survival depended upon Big Brother and Little Brother were raising holy hell. The drought had hit them hard; they'd lost a lot of cattle, and now they were out full-force demanding their share of Blue River.

Finally the town council voted to appoint a special committee to settle the matter. I have no idea how the members of the committee were chosen. Certainly I had no particular qualification; I remember old Judge Hatfield—he's retired now, living in Arizona—phoned me and asked if I would serve; that's all there was to it. We had our first meeting in the Council Room at the courthouse, January 1970. The other members of the committee were Clem Anderson, George and Amelia Roberts, Dr. Parsons, the Baxters, Tom Henry, and Oliver Jaeger—

JAKE (to me): Jaeger. He's the postmaster. A crazy sonofabitch.

ADDIE: He's not really crazy. You only say that because—

JAKE: Because he's really crazy.

(Addie was disconcerted. She contemplated her wineglass, moved to refill it, found the bottle empty, and then produced from a small purse, conveniently nestling in her lap, a pretty little silver box filled with blue pills: Valiums; she swallowed one with a sip of water. And Jake had said that Addie was not a nervous woman?)

TC: Who's Tom Henry?

JAKE: Another nut. Nuttier than Oliver Jaeger. He owns a filling station.

ADDIE: Yes, there were nine of us. We met once a week for about two months. Both sides, those for and those against, sent in experts to testify. Many of the ranchers appeared themselves—to talk to us, to present their own case.

But not Mr. Quinn. Not Bob Quinn—we never heard a word from him, even though, as the owner of the B.Q. Ranch, he stood to lose the most if we voted to divert "his" river. I figured: He's too high and mighty to bother with us and our silly little committee; Bob Quinn, he's been busy talking to the governor, the congressmen, the senators; he thinks he's got all those boys in his hip pocket. So whatever we might decide didn't matter. His big-shot buddies would veto it.

But that's not how it turned out. We voted to divert Blue River at exactly the point where it entered Quinn's property; of course, that didn't leave him without a river—he just wouldn't have the hog's share he'd always had before.

The decision would have been unanimous if Tom Henry hadn't gone against us. You're right, Jake. Tom Henry *is* a nut. So the vote stood eight to one. And it proved such a popular decision, a verdict that really harmed no one and benefited many, there wasn't much Quinn's political cronies could do about it, not if they wanted to stay in office.

A few days after the vote I ran into Bob Quinn at the post office. He made a tremendous point of tipping his hat, smiling, asking after my welfare. Not that I expected him to spit on me; still, I'd never met with so much courtesy from him before. One would never have supposed he was resentful. Resentful? Insane!

TC: What does he look like—Mr. Quinn?

JAKE: *Don't tell him!*

ADDIE: Why not?

JAKE: Just because.

(Standing, he walked over to the fireplace and offered what remained of his cigar to the flames. He stood with his back to the fire, legs slightly apart, arms folded: I'd never thought of Jake as vain, but clearly he was posing a bit—trying, successfully, to look attractive. I laughed.) Eh?

TC: Now it's a Jane Austen novel. In her novels, sexy gentlemen are always warming their fannies at fireplaces.

ADDIE (laughing): Oh, Jake, it's true! It's true!

JAKE: I never read female literature. Never have. Never will.

ADDIE: Just for that, I'm going to open another bottle of wine, and drink it all myself.

(Jake returned to the table and sat down next to Addie; he took one of her hands in one of his and entwined their fingers. The effect upon her was embarrassingly visible— her face flushed, splashes of red blotched her neck. As for him, he seemed unaware of her, unaware of what he was doing. Rather, he was looking at me; it was as if we were alone together.)

JAKE: Yes, I know. Having heard what you have, you're thinking: Well, now the case is solved. Mr. Quinn did it.

That's what I thought. Last year, after Addie told me what she told you, I lit out of here like a bear with a bumblebee up his ass. I drove straight to the city. Thanksgiving or no Thanksgiving, that very night we had a meeting of the whole Bureau. I laid it on the line: this is the motive, this is the guy. Nobody said boo!—except the chief, and he said: "Slow down, Pepper. The man you're accusing is no flyweight. And where's your case? This is all speculation. Guesswork." Everybody agreed with him. Said: "Where's the evidence?"

I was so mad I was shouting; I said: "What the hell do you think I'm here for? We've all got to pull together and build the evidence. I know Quinn did it." The chief said: "Well, I'd be careful who you said that to. Christ, you could get us all fired."

ADDIE: That next day, when he came back here, I wish I'd taken Jake's picture. In the line of duty I've had to paddle many boys, but none of them ever looked as sad as you, Jake.

JAKE: I wasn't too happy. That's the fact of that.

The Bureau backed me; we began checking out the life of Robert Hawley Quinn from the year one. But we had to move on tiptoe—the chief was jittery as a killer on Death Row. I wanted a warrant to search the B.Q. Ranch, the houses, the whole property. Denied. He wouldn't even let me question the man—

TC: Did Quinn know you suspected him?

JAKE (snorting): Right off the bat. Someone in the governor's office tipped him off. Probably the governor himself. And guys in our own Bureau—they probably told him, too. I don't trust nobody. Nobody connected with this case.

ADDIE: The whole town knew before you could say Rumpelstiltskin.

JAKE: Thanks to Oliver Jaeger. *And* Tom Henry. That's my fault. Since they had both been on the River Committee, I felt I had to take them into my confidence, discuss Quinn, warn them about the coffins. They both promised me they would keep it confidential. Well, telling them, I might as well have had a town meeting and made a speech.

ADDIE: At school, one of my little boys raised his hand and said: "My daddy told my mama somebody sent you a coffin, like for the graveyard. Said Mr. Quinn done it." And I said: "Oh, Bobby, your daddy was just teasing your mama, telling her fairy tales."

JAKE: One of Oliver Jaeger's fairy tales! That bastard called everybody in Christendom. And you say he isn't crazy?

ADDIE: You think he's crazy because he thinks *you're* crazy. He sincerely believes that you're mistaken. That you're persecuting an innocent man. (Still looking at Jake, but addressing me) Oliver would never win any contest, neither for charm nor brains. But he's a rational man—a gossip, but good-hearted. He's related to the Quinn family; Bob Quinn is his second cousin. That may be relevant to the violence of his opinions. It's Oliver's contention, and one that is shared by most people, that even if some connection exists between the decision of the Blue River Committee and the deaths that have occurred here, why point the finger at Bob Quinn? He's not the only Blue River rancher that might bear a grievance. What about Walter Forbes? Jim Johanssen? The Throby family. The Millers. The Rileys. Why pick on Bob Quinn? What are the special circumstances that single him out?

JAKE: He did it.

ADDIE: Yes, he did. We know that. But you can't even prove he bought the rattlesnakes. And even if you could—

JAKE: I'd like a whiskey.

ADDIE: You shall have it, sir. Anybody else?

JAKE (after Addie left on her errand): She's right. We can't prove he bought the snakes, even though we know he did. See, I always figured those snakes came from a professional source; breeders who breed for the venom—they sell it to medical laboratories. The major suppliers are Florida and Texas, but there are snake farms all across the country. Over the last few years we sent inquiries to most of them—and never received a single reply.

But in my heart I knew those rattlers came from the Lone Star State. It was only logical—why would a man go all the way to Florida when he could find what he wanted more or less next door? Well, as soon as Quinn entered the picture, I decided to zero in on the snake angle—an angle we'd never concentrated on to the degree we should have, mainly because it required personal investigation and traveling expenses. When it comes to getting the chief to spend money—hell, it's easier to crack walnuts with store-bought teeth. But I know this fellow, an old-time investigator with the Texas Bureau; he owed me a favor. So I sent him some material: pictures of Quinn I'd managed to collect, and photographs of the rattlers themselves—nine of them hanging on a washline after we'd killed them.

TC: How did you kill them?

JAKE: Shotguns. Blasted their heads off.

TC: I killed a rattler once. With a garden hoe.

JAKE: I don't think you could've killed these bastards with any hoe. Even put a dent in them. The smallest one was seven feet long.

TC: There were nine snakes. And nine members of the Blue River Committee. Nice quaint coincidence.

JAKE: Bill, my Texas friend, he's a determined guy; he covered Texas from border to border, spent most of his vacation visiting snake farms, talking to the breeders. Now, about a month ago, he called and said he thought he had located my party: a Mrs. Garcia, a Tex-Mex lady who owned a snake farm near Nogales. That's about a ten-hour drive from here. If you're driving a State car and doing ninety miles an hour. Bill promised to meet me there.

Addie went with me. We drove overnight, and had breakfast with Bill at a Holiday Inn. Then we visited Mrs. Garcia. Some of these snake farms are tourist attractions; but her place was nothing like that—it was way off the highway, and quite a small operation. But she sure had some impressive specimens. All the time we were there she kept hauling out these huge rattlers, wrapping them around her neck, her arms: laughing; she had almost solid gold-teeth. At first I thought she was a man; she was built like Pancho Villa, and she was wearing cowboy britches with a zipper fly.

She had a cataract in one eye; and the other didn't look too sharp. But she wasn't hesitant about identifying Quinn's picture. She said he had visited her place in either June or July 1970 (the Robertses died 5 September 1970), and that he had been accompanied by a young Mexican; they arrived in a small truck with a Mexican license plate. She said she never spoke to Quinn; according to her, he never said a word —simply listened while she dealt with the Mexican. She said it was not her policy to question a customer as to his reasons for purchasing her merchandise; but, she told us, the Mexican volunteered the information—he wanted a dozen adult rattlers to use in a religious ceremony. That didn't surprise her; she said people often bought snakes for ritualistic usage. But the Mexican wanted her to guarantee that the snakes he bought would attack and kill a bull weighing a thousand pounds. She said yes, that was possible—provided the snakes had been injected with a drug, an amphetamine stimulant, before being put in contact with the bull.

She showed him how to do it, with Quinn observing. She showed us, too. She used a pole, about twice the length of a riding crop and limber as a willow wand; it had a leather loop attached to the end of it. She caught the head of the snake in the loop, dangled him in the air, and jabbed a syringe into the belly. She let the Mexican run a few practice sessions; he did just fine.

TC: Had she ever seen the Mexican before?

JAKE: No. I asked her to describe him, and she described any border-town Mexicali Rose between twenty and thirty. He paid her; she packed the snakes in individual containers, and away they went.

Mrs. Garcia was a very obliging lady. Very cooperative. Until we asked her the important question: would she give us

a sworn affidavit that Robert Hawley Quinn was one of two
men who had bought a dozen rattlesnakes from her on a
certain summer day in 1970? She sure turned sour then. Said
she wouldn't sign nothing.

I told her those snakes had been used to murder two
people. You should have seen her face then. She walked in
the house and locked the doors and pulled down the shades.

TC: An affidavit from her. That wouldn't have carried much
legal weight.

JAKE: It would have been something to confront him with:
an opening gambit. More than likely, it was the Mexican who
put the snakes into Roberts' car; of course, Quinn hired him
to do it. Know what? I'll bet that Mexican is dead, buried out
there on the lone prairie. Courtesy of Mr. Quinn.

TC: But surely, somewhere in Quinn's history, there must be
something to indicate that he was capable of psychotic violence?

(Jake nodded, nodded, nodded.)

JAKE: The gentleman was well acquainted with homicide.

(Addie returned with the whiskey. He thanked her, and
kissed her on the cheek. She sat down next to him, and
again their hands met, their fingers mingled.)

The Quinns are one of the oldest families here. Bob Quinn is
the eldest of three brothers. They all own a share of the B.Q.
Ranch, but he's the boss.

ADDIE: No, his wife's the boss. He married his first cousin,
Juanita Quinn. Her mother was Spanish, and she has the
temper of a hot tamale. Their first child died in childbirth,
and she refused to ever have another. It's generally known,
though, that Bob Quinn does have children. By another
woman in another town.

JAKE: He was a war hero. A colonel in the marines during

the Second World War. He never refers to it himself, but to
hear other people tell it, Bob Quinn single-handedly slaugh-
tered more Japanese than the Hiroshima bomb.

But right after the war he did a little killing that wasn't
quite so patriotic. Late one night he called the sheriff to come
out to the B.Q. Ranch and collect a couple of corpses. He
claimed he'd caught two men rustling cattle and had shot
them dead. That was his tale, and nobody challenged it, at
least not publicly. But the truth is those two guys weren't
cattle rustlers; they were gamblers from Denver and Quinn
owed them a stack of money. They'd traveled down to B.Q.
for a promised payoff. What they got was a load of buckshot.

TC: Have you ever questioned him about that?

JAKE: Questioned who?

TC: Quinn.

JAKE: Strictly speaking, I've never *questioned* him at all.

> (His quirky cynical smile bent his mouth; he tinkled the
> ice in his whiskey, drank some, and chuckled—a deep
> rough chuckle, like a man trying to bring up phlegm.)

Just lately, I've talked to him plenty. But during the five years
I'd been on the case, I'd never met the man. I'd seen him.
Knew who he was.

ADDIE: But now they're like two peas in a pod. Real buddies.

JAKE: Addie!

ADDIE: Oh, Jake. I'm only teasing.

JAKE: That's nothing to tease about. It's been pure torture
for me.

ADDIE (squeezing his hand): I know. I'm sorry.

> (Jake drained his glass, banged it on the table.)

JAKE: Looking at him. Listening to him. Laughing at his
dirty jokes. I hate him. He hates me. We both know that.

ADDIE: Let me sweeten you up with another whiskey.

JAKE: Sit still.

ADDIE: Perhaps I ought to peek in on Marylee. See if she's all right.

JAKE: Sit still.

(But Addie wanted to escape the room, for she was uncomfortable with Jake's anger, the numb fury inhabiting his face.)

ADDIE (glancing out the window): It's stopped snowing.

JAKE: The Okay Café is always crowded Monday mornings. After the weekend everybody has to stop by to catch up on the news. Ranchers, businessmen, the sheriff and his gang, people from the courthouse. But on this particular Monday— the Monday after Thanksgiving—the place was packed; guys were squatting on each other's laps, and everybody was yakking like a bunch of sissy old women.

You can guess what they were yakking about. Thanks to Tom Henry and Oliver Jaeger, who'd spent the weekend spreading the word, saying that guy from the Bureau, that Jake Pepper fella, was accusing Bob Quinn of murder. I sat in my booth pretending not to notice. But I couldn't help but notice when Bob Quinn himself walked in; you could hear the whole café hold its breath.

He squeezed into a booth next to the sheriff; the sheriff hugged him, and laughed, and let out a cowboy holler. Most of the crowd mimicked him, yelled wahoo, Bob! hiya, Bob! Yessir, the Okay Café was one hundred percent behind Bob Quinn. I had the feeling—a feeling that even if I could prove dead-certain this man was a murderer many times over, they'd lynch me before I could arrest him.

ADDIE (pressing a hand to her forehead, as though she had a headache): He's right. Bob Quinn has the whole town on his side. That's one reason my sister doesn't like to hear us talk about it. She says Jake's wrong, Mr. Quinn's a fine fellow. It's her theory that Dr. Parsons was responsible for these crimes, and that's why he committed suicide.

TC: But Dr. Parsons was dead long before you received the coffin.

JAKE: Marylee's sweet but not too bright. Sorry, Addie, but that's how it is.

(Addie removed her hand from Jake's: an admonishing gesture, but not a severe one. Anyway, it left Jake free to stand up and pace the floor, which he did. His footsteps echoed on the polished pine planks.)

So back to the Okay Café. As I was leaving, the sheriff reached out and grabbed my arm. He's a fresh Irish bastard. And crooked as the devil's toes. He said: "Hey, Jake. I wantcha to meet Bob Quinn. Bob, this is Jake Pepper. From the Bureau." I shook Quinn's hand. Quinn said: "I heard plenty about you. I hear you're a chess player. I don't find too many games. How about us getting together?" I said sure, and he said: "Tomorrow okay? Come by around five. We'll have a drink and play a couple of games."

That's how I started. I went to the B.Q. Ranch the next afternoon. We played for two hours. He's a better player than I am, but I won often enough to make it interesting. He's garrulous, he'll talk about anything: politics, women, sex, trout fishing, bowel movements, his trip to Russia, cattle versus wheat, gin versus vodka, Johnny Carson, his safari in Africa, religion, the Bible, Shakespeare, the genius of General MacArthur, bear hunting, Reno whores versus Las Vegas whores, the stock market, venereal diseases, cornflakes versus Shredded Wheat, gold versus diamonds, capital punishment (he's all for it), football, baseball, basketball—*anything*. Anything except why I'm stuck in this town.

TC: You mean he won't discuss the case?

JAKE (halting in his pacing): It's not that he won't discuss

the case. He simply behaves as though it doesn't exist. I
discuss it, but he never reacts. I showed him the Clem Anderson photographs: I hoped I could shock him into some response. *Some* comment. But he only looked back at the
chessboard, made a move, and told me a dirty joke.

So Mr. Quinn and I have been playing our games within
a game several afternoons a week for the last few months. In
fact, I'm going there later today. And you—(Cocking a finger
in my direction) are going with me.

TC: Am I welcome?

JAKE: I called him this morning. All he asked was: Does he
play chess?

TC: I do. But I'd rather watch.

(A log collapsed, and its crackling drew my attention to
the fireplace. I stared into the purring flames, and wondered why he had forbidden Addie to describe Quinn, tell
me what he looked like. I tried to imagine him; I couldn't.
Rather, I remembered the passage from Mark Twain that
Jake had read aloud: "Of all the creatures that were
made, man is the most detestable . . . the only one, the
solitary one, that possesses malice . . . he is the only
creature that has a nasty mind." Addie's voice rescued me
from my queasy reverie.)

ADDIE: Oh, dear. It's snowing again. But lightly. Just floating.
(Then, as though the resumption of the snow had prompted
thoughts of mortality, the evaporation of time) You know, it's
been almost five months. That's quite long for him. He usually doesn't wait that long.

JAKE (vexed): Addie, what is it now?

ADDIE: My coffin. It's been almost five months. And as I say,
he doesn't usually wait that long.

JAKE: Addie! I'm here. Nothing is going to happen to you.

ADDIE: Of course, Jake. I wonder about Oliver Jaeger. I wonder when he'll receive his coffin. Just think, Oliver is the postmaster. He'll be sorting the mail and—(Her voice was suddenly, startlingly quavery, vulnerable—wistful in a way that accentuated the canaries' carefree songfest) Well, it won't be very soon.

TC: Why not?

ADDIE: Because Quinn has to fill my coffin first.

It was after five when we left, the air was still, free of snow, and shimmering with the embers of a sunset and the first pale radiance of a moonrise: a full moon rolling on the horizon like a round white wheel, or a mask, a white featureless menacing mask peering at us through our car windows. At the end of Main Street, just before the town turns into prairie, Jake pointed at a filling station: "That's Tom Henry's place. Tom Henry, Addie, Oliver Jaeger; out of the original River Committee, they're the only three left. I said Tom Henry was a nut. And he is. But he's a lucky nut. He voted against the others. That leaves him in the clear. No coffin for Tom Henry."

TC: *A Coffin for Dimitrios.*

JAKE: What say?

TC: A book by Eric Ambler. A thriller.

JAKE: Fiction? (I nodded; he grimaced) You really read that junk?

TC: Graham Greene was a first-class writer. Until the Vatican grabbed him. After that, he never wrote anything as good as *Brighton Rock.* I like Agatha Christie, love her. And Raymond Chandler is a great stylist, a poet. Even if his plots are a mess.

JAKE: Junk. Those guys are just daydreamers—squat at a typewriter and jerk themselves off, that's all they do.

TC: So no coffin for Tom Henry. How about Oliver Jaeger?

JAKE: He'll get his. One morning he'll be shuffling around the post office, emptying out the incoming mail sacks, and there it will be, a brown box with his very own name printed on it. Forget the cousin stuff; forget that he's been hanging halos over Bob Quinn's head. Saint Bob isn't going to let him off with a few Hail Marys. Not if I know Saint Bob. Chances are, he's already used his whittling knife, made a little something, and popped Oliver Jaeger's picture inside it—

> (Jake's voice jolted to a stop, and as though it were a correlated action, his foot hit the brake pedal: the car skidded, swerved, straightened; we drove on. I knew what had happened. He had remembered, as I was remembering, Addie's pathetic complaint: ". . . Quinn will have to fill my coffin first." I tried to hold my tongue; it rebelled.)

TC: But that means—

JAKE: Better turn on my headlights.

TC: That means Addie is going to die.

JAKE: Hell, no! I just knew you were going to say that! (He slapped a flattened palm against the steering wheel) I've built a wall around Addie. I gave her a .38 Detective Special, and taught her how to use it. She can put a bullet between a man's eyes at a hundred yards. She's learned enough karate to split a plank with one hand-chop. Addie's smart; she won't be tricked. And I'm here. I'm watching her. I'm watching Quinn, too. So are other people.

> (Strong emotion, fears edging toward terror, can demolish the logic of even so logical a man as Jake Pepper —whose precautions had not saved Clem Anderson. I

wasn't prepared to argue the point with him, not in his present irrational humor; but why, since he assumed Oliver Jaeger was doomed, was he so certain Addie was not? That she would be spared? For if Quinn stayed true to his design, then absolutely he would have to dispatch Addie, remove her from the scene before he could start the last step of his task by addressing a package to his second cousin and staunch defender, the local post-master.)

TC: I know Addie's been around the world. But I think it's time she went again.

JAKE (truculently): She can't leave here. Not now.

TC: Oh? She doesn't strike me as suicidal.

JAKE: Well, for one thing, school. School's not out till June.

TC: Jake! My God! How can you talk about *school*?

(Dim though the light was, I could discern his ashamed expression; at the same time, he jutted his jaw.)

JAKE: We've discussed it. Talked about her and Marylee taking a long cruise. But she doesn't want to go anywhere. She said: "The shark needs bait. If we're going to hook the shark, then the bait has to be available."

TC: So Addie is a stakeout? A goat waiting for the tiger to pounce?

JAKE: Hold on. I'm not sure I like the way you put that.

TC: Then how would you put it?

JAKE: (Silence)

TC: (Silence)

JAKE: Quinn has Addie in his thoughts, he does indeed. He means to keep his promise. And that's when we'll nail him: in the attempt. Catch him when the curtain is up and all the lights are on. There's some risk, sure; but we have to take it. Because—well, to be goddamned honest, it's probably the only damn chance we're gonna get.

(I leaned my head against the window: saw Addie's pretty throat as she threw back her head and drank the dazzling red wine in one delicious swallow. I felt weak, feeble; and disgusted with Jake.)

TC: I like Addie. She's real; and yet there's mystery. I wonder why she never married.

JAKE: Keep this under your hat. Addie's going to marry me.

TC (my mental-eye was still elsewhere; still, in fact, watching Addie drink her wine): When?

JAKE: Next summer. When I get my vacation. We haven't told anybody. Except Marylee. So now do you understand? Addie's *safe*; I won't let anything happen to her; I love her; I'm going to marry her.

(Next summer: a lifetime away. The full moon, higher, whiter now, and celebrated by coyotes, rolled across the snow-gleaming prairies. Clumps of cattle stood in the cold snowy fields, bunched together for warmth. Some stood in pairs. I noticed two spotted calves huddled side by side, lending each other comfort, protection: like Jake, like Addie.)

TC: Well, congratulations. That's wonderful. I know you'll both be very happy.

Soon an impressive barbed-wire fence, like the high fences of a concentration camp, bordered both sides of the highway; it marked the beginnings of the B.Q. Ranch: ten thousand acres, or thereabouts. I lowered the window, and accepted a rush of icy air, sharp with the scent of new snow and old sweet hay. "Here we go," said Jake as we left the highway and drove through wooden swung-open gates. At the entrance, our headlights caught a handsomely lettered sign: *B.Q. /Ranch R. H. Quinn/Proprietor.* A pair of crossed tomahawks was painted underneath the proprietor's name; one wondered whether it was the ranch's logo or the family crest. Either way, an ominous set of tomahawks seemed suitable.

The road was narrow, and lined with leafless trees, dark except for a rare glitter of animal-eyes among the silhouetted branches. We crossed a wooden bridge that rumbled under our weight, and I heard the sound of water, deep-toned liquid tumblings, and I knew it must be Blue River, but I couldn't see it, for it was hidden by trees and snowdrifts; as we continued along the road, the sound followed, for the river was running beside us, occasionally eerily quiet, then abruptly bubbling with the broken music of waterfalls, cascades.

The road widened. Sprinklings of electric light pierced the trees. A beautiful boy, a child with bouncing yellow hair and riding a horse bareback, waved at us. We passed a row of bungalows, lamplit and vibrating with the racket of television voices: the homes of ranch hands. Ahead, standing in distinguished isolation, was the main house, Mr. Quinn's house. It was a large white clapboard two-storied structure with a covered veranda running its full length; it seemed abandoned, for all the windows were dark.

Jake honked the car horn. At once, like a fanfare of welcoming trumpets, a blaze of floodlights swept the veranda; lamps bloomed in downstairs windows. The front door opened; a man stepped out and waited to greet us.

My first introduction to the owner of the B.Q. Ranch failed to resolve the question of why Jake had not wanted Addie to describe him to me. Although he wasn't a man who would pass unnoticed, his appearance was not excessively unusual; and yet the sight of him startled me: *I knew Mr. Quinn.* I was positive, I would have sworn on my own heart-

beat that somehow, and undoubtedly long ago, I had encountered Robert Hawley Quinn, and that together we had,
in fact, shared an alarming experience, an adventure so disturbing, memory had kindly submerged it.

He sported expensive high-heel boots, but even without
them the man measured over six feet, and if he had stood
straight, instead of assuming a stooped, slope-shouldered posture, he would have presented a fine tall figure. He had long
simianlike arms; the hands dangled to his knees, and the
fingers were long, capable, oddly aristocratic. I recalled a
Rachmaninoff concert; Rachmaninoff's hands were like
Quinn's. Quinn's face was broad but gaunt, hollow-cheeked,
weather-coarsened—the face of a medieval peasant, the man
behind the plow with all the woes of the world lashed to his
back. But Quinn was no dumb, sadly burdened peasant. He
wore thin wire-rimmed glasses, and these professorial spectacles, and the grey eyes looming behind their thick lenses,
betrayed him: his eyes were alert, suspicious, intelligent,
merry with malice, complacently superior. He had a hos-
pitable, fraudulently genial laugh and voice. But he was not a
fraud. He was an idealist, an achiever; he set himself tasks,
and his tasks were his cross, his religion, his identity; no, not
a fraud—a fanatic; and presently, while we were still gathered on the veranda, my sunken memory surfaced: I remembered where and in what form I had met Mr. Quinn before.

He extended one of his long hands toward Jake; his other
hand plowed through a rough white-and-grey mane worn
pioneer-style—a length not popular with his fellow ranchers:
men who looked as though they visited the barber every
Saturday for a close clip and a talcum shampoo. Tufts of grey
hair sprouted from his nostrils and his ears. I noticed his belt

buckle; it was decorated with two crossed tomahawks made of gold and red enamel.

QUINN: Hey, Jake. I told Juanita, I said honey, that rascal's gonna chicken out. Account of the snow.

JAKE: You call this *snow*?

QUINN: Just pullin' your leg, Jake. (To me) You oughta see the snow we do get! Back in 1952 we had a whole week when the only way I could get out of the house was to climb through the attic window. Lost seven hundred head of cattle, all my Santa Gertrudis. Ha ha! Oh, I tell you that was a time. Well, sir, you play chess?

TC: Rather the way I speak French. *Un peu.*

QUINN (cackling, slapping his thighs with spurious mirth): Yeah, I know. You're the city slicker come to skin us country boys. I'll bet you could play me and Jake at the same time and beat us blindfolded.

(We followed him down a wide high hallway into an immense room, a cathedral stuffed with huge heavy Spanish furniture, armoires and chairs and tables and baroque mirrors commensurate with their spacious surroundings. The floor was covered with brick-red Mexican tiles and dotted with Navajo rugs. An entire wall had been composed from blocks of irregularly cut granite, and this granite cavelike wall housed a fireplace big enough to roast a brace of oxen; in consequence, the dainty fire ensconced there seemed as insignificant as a twig in a forest.

But the person seated near the hearth was not insignificant. Quinn introduced me to her: "My wife, Juanita." She nodded, but was not to be distracted from the television screen confronting her: the set was working with the sound turned off—she was watching the zany ditherings of muted images, some visually boisterous game show. The chair in which she sat may well have once decorated the throne room of an Iberian castle; she shared it with a shivering little Chihuahua dog and a yellow guitar, which lay across her lap.

Jake and our host settled themselves at a table furnished with a splendid ebony-and-ivory chess set. I observed the start of a game, listened to their easygoing badinage, and it was strange: Addie was right, they seemed real buddies, two peas in a pod. But eventually I wandered back to the fireplace, determined to further explore the quiet Juanita. I sat near her on the hearth and searched for some topic to start a conversation. The guitar? The quivering Chihuahua, now jealously yapping at me?)

JUANITA QUINN: Pepe! You stupid mosquito!

TC: Don't bother. I like dogs.

(She looked at me. Her hair, center-parted and too black to be true, was slicked to her narrow skull. Her face was like a fist: tiny features tightly bunched together. Her head was too big for her body—she wasn't fat, but she weighed more than she should, and most of the overweight was distributed between her bosom and her belly. But she had slender, nicely shaped legs, and she was wearing a pair of very prettily beaded Indian moccasins. The mosquito yap-yapped, but now she ignored him. The television regained her attention.)

I was just wondering: why do you watch without the sound?

(Her bored onyx eyes returned to me. I repeated the question.)

JUANITA QUINN: Do you drink tequila?

TC: Well, there's a little dump in Palm Springs where they make fantastic Margaritas.

JUANITA QUINN: A man drinks tequila straight. No lime. No salt. Straight. Would you like some?

TC: Sure.

JUANITA QUINN: So would I. Alas, we have none. We can't keep it in the house. If we did, I would drink it; my liver would dry up . . .

> (She snapped her fingers, signifying disaster. Then she touched the yellow guitar, strummed the strings, developed a tune, a tricky, unfamiliar melody that for a moment she happily hummed and played. When she stopped, her face retied itself into a knot.)

I used to drink every night. Every night I drank a bottle of tequila and went to bed and slept like a baby. I was never sick a day; I looked good, I felt good, I slept well. No more. Now I have one cold after the other, headaches, arthritis; and I can't sleep a wink. All because the doctor said I had to stop drinking tequila. But don't jump to conclusions. I'm not a drunk. You can take all the wine and whiskey in the world and dump it down the Grand Canyon. It's only that I like tequila. The dark yellow kind. I like that best. (She pointed at the television set) You asked why I have the sound off. The only time I have the sound on is to hear the weather report. Otherwise, I just watch and imagine what's being said. If I actually listen, it puts me right to sleep. But just imagining keeps me awake. And I have to stay awake—at least till midnight. Otherwise, I'd never get any sleep at all. Where do you live?

TC: New York, mostly.

JUANITA QUINN: We used to go to New York every year or two. The Rainbow Room: now there's a view. But it wouldn't be any fun now. Nothing is. My husband says you're an old friend of Jake Pepper's.

TC: I've known him ten years.

JUANITA QUINN: Why does he suppose my husband has any connection with this thing?

TC: Thing?

JUANITA QUINN (amazed): You *must* have heard about it. Well, why does Jake Pepper think my husband's involved?

TC: *Does* Jake think your husband's involved?

JUANITA QUINN: That's what some people say. My sister told me—

TC: But what do you think?

JUANITA QUINN (lifting her Chihuahua and cuddling him against her bosom): I feel sorry for Jake. He must be lonely. And he's mistaken; there's nothing here. It all ought to be forgotten. He ought to go home. (Eyes closed; utterly weary) Ah well, who knows? *Or* cares? Not I. Not I, said the Spider to the Fly. Not I.

Beyond us, there was a commotion at the chess table. Quinn, celebrating a victory over Jake, vociferously congratulated himself: "Sonofagun! Thought you had me trapped there. But the moment you moved your queen—it's hot beer and horse piss for the Great Pepper!" His hoarse baritone rang through the vaulted room with the *brio* of an opera star. "Now you, young man," he shouted at me. "I need a game. A bona-fide challenge. Old Pepper here ain't fit to lick my boots." I started to excuse myself, for the prospect of a chess game with Quinn was both intimidating and tiresome; I might have felt differently if I'd thought I could beat him, triumphantly invade that citadel of conceit. I had once won a prep-school chess championship, but that was eons ago; my knowledge of the game had long been stored in a mental attic. However, when Jake beckoned, stood up, and offered me his chair, I acquiesced, and leaving Juanita Quinn to the

silent flickerings of her television screen, seated myself opposite her husband; Jake stood behind my chair, an encouraging presence. But Quinn, assessing my faltering manner, the
indecision of my first moves, dismissed me as a walkover, and
resumed a conversation he'd been having with Jake, apparently concerning cameras and photography.

QUINN: The Krauts are good. I've always used Kraut cameras. Leica. Rolliflex. But the Japs are whippin' their ass. I
bought a new Jap number, no bigger than a deck of cards,
that will take five hundred pictures on a single roll of film.

TC: I know that camera. I've worked with a lot of photographers and I've seen some of them use it. Richard Avedon has
one. He says it's no good.

QUINN: To tell the truth, I haven't tried mine yet. I hope your
friend's wrong. I could've bought a prize bull for what that
doodad set me back.

> (I suddenly felt Jake's fingers urgently squeezing my
> shoulder, which I interpreted as a message that he wished
> me to pursue the subject.)

TC: Is that your hobby—photography?

QUINN: Oh, it comes and goes. Fits and starts. How I started
was, I got tired of paying so-called professionals to take
pictures of my prize cattle. Pictures I need to send round to
different breeders and buyers. I figured I could do just as
good, and save myself a nickel to boot.

> (Jake's fingers goaded me again.)

TC: Do you make many portraits?

QUINN: Portraits?

TC: Of people.

QUINN (scoffingly): I wouldn't call them *portraits*. Snapshots,
maybe. Aside from cattle, mostly I do nature pictures. Land-

scapes. Thunderstorms. The seasons here on the ranch. The wheat when it's green and then when it's gold. My river—I've got some dandy pictures of my river in full flood.

> (The river. I tensed as I heard Jake clear his throat, as though he were about to speak; instead, his fingers prodded me even more firmly. I toyed with a pawn, stalling.)

TC: Then you must shoot a lot of color.

QUINN (nodding): That's why I do my own developing. When you send your stuff off to those laboratories, you never know what the hell you're gonna get back.

TC: Oh, you have a darkroom?

QUINN: If you want to call it that. Nothing fancy.

> (Once more Jake's throat rumbled, this time with serious intent.)

JAKE: Bob? You remember the pictures I told you about? The coffin pictures. They were made with a fast-action camera.

QUINN: (Silence)

JAKE: A Leica.

QUINN: Well, it wasn't mine. My old Leica got lost in darkest Africa. Some nigger stole it. (Staring at the chessboard, his face suffused with a look of amused dismay) Why, you little rascal! Damn your hide. Look here, Jake. Your friend almost has me checkmated. *Almost . . .*

It was true; with a skill subconsciously resurrected, I had been marching my ebony army with considerable, though unwitting, competence, and had indeed managed to maneuver Quinn's king into a perilous position. In one sense I regretted my success, for Quinn was using it to divert the angle of Jake's inquiry, to revert from the suddenly sensitive topic of

photography back to chess; on the other hand, I was elated—
by playing flawlessly, I might now very well win. Quinn
scratched his chin, his grey eyes dedicated to the religious
task of rescuing his king. But for me the chessboard had
blurred; my mind was snared in a time warp, numbed by
memories dormant almost half a century.

It was summer, and I was five years old, living with
relatives in a small Alabama town. There was a river attached
to this town, too; a sluggish muddy river that repelled me, for
it was full of water moccasins and whiskered catfish. However, much as I disliked their ferocious snouts, I was fond of
captured catfish, fried and dripping with ketchup; we had a
cook who served them often. Her name was Lucy Joy,
though I've seldom known a less joyous human. She was a
hefty black woman, reserved, very serious; she seemed to live
from Sunday to Sunday, when she sang in the choir of some
pineywoods church. But one day a remarkable change came
over Lucy Joy. While I was alone with her in the kitchen she
began talking to me about a certain Reverend Bobby Joe
Snow, describing him with an excitement that kindled my
own imagination: he was a miracle-maker, a famous evangelist, and he was traveling soon to this very town; the Reverend Snow was due here next week, come to preach, to
baptize and save souls! I pleaded with Lucy to take me to see
him, and she smiled and promised she would. The fact was, it
was necessary that I accompany her. For the Reverend Snow
was a white man, his audiences were segregated, and Lucy
had figured it out that the only way she would be welcome
was if she brought along a little white boy to be baptized.
Naturally, Lucy did not let on that such an event was in store
for me. The following week, when we set off to attend the
Reverend's camp meeting, I only envisioned the drama of

watching a holy man sent from heaven to help the blind see
and the lame walk. But I began to feel uneasy when I realized we were headed toward the river; when we got there
and I saw hundreds of people gathered along the bank, country people, backwoods white trash stomping and hollering, I
hesitated. Lucy was furious—she pulled me into the swelter-
ing mob. Jingling bells, cavorting bodies; I could hear one
voice above the others, a chanting booming baritone. Lucy
chanted, too; moaned, shook. Magically, a stranger hoisted
me onto his shoulder and I got a quick view of the man with
the dominant voice. He was planted in the river with water
up to his white-robed waist; his hair was grey and white,
a drenched tangled mass, and his long hands, stretched sky-
ward, implored the humid noon sun. I tried to see his face,
for I knew this must be the Reverend Bobby Joe Snow, but
before I could, my benefactor dropped me back into the
disgusting confusion of ecstatic feet, undulating arms, trembling tambourines. I begged to go home; but Lucy, drunk
with glory, held me close. The sun churned; I tasted vomit in
my throat. But I didn't throw up; instead, I started to yell
and punch and scream: Lucy was pulling me toward the
river, and the crowd parted to create a path for us. I strug-
gled until we reached the river's bank; then stopped, silenced
by the scene. The white-robed man standing in the river
was holding a reclining young girl; he recited biblical scrip-
ture before rapidly immersing her underwater, then swoop-
ing her up again: shrieking, weeping, she stumbled to shore.
Now the Reverend's simian arms reached for me. I bit Lucy's
hand, fought free of her grip. But a redneck boy grabbed me
and dragged me into the water. I shut my eyes; I smelled the
Jesus hair, felt the Reverend's arms carrying me downward
into drowning blackness, then hours later lifting me into sun-
light. My eyes, opening, looked into his grey, manic eyes. His

face, broad but gaunt, moved closer, and he kissed my lips. I heard a loud laugh, an eruption like gunfire: "Checkmate!"

QUINN: Checkmate!

JAKE: Hell, Bob. He was just being polite. He let you win.

(The kiss dissolved; the Reverend's face, receding, was replaced by a face virtually identical. So it was in Alabama, some fifty years earlier, that I had first seen Mr. Quinn. At any rate, his counterpart: Bobby Joe Snow, evangelist.)

QUINN: How about it, Jake? You ready to lose another dollar?

JAKE: Not tonight. We're driving to Denver in the morning. My friend here has to catch a plane.

QUINN (to me): Shucks. That wasn't much of a visit. Come again soon. Come in the summer and I'll take you trout fishing. Not that it's like what it was. Used to be I could count on landing a six-pound rainbow with the first cast. Back before they ruined my river.

(We departed without saying goodnight to Juanita Quinn; she was sound asleep, snoring. Quinn walked with us to the car: "Be careful!" he warned, as he waved and waited until our taillights vanished.)

JAKE: Well, I learned one thing, thanks to you. Now I *know* he developed those pictures himself.

TC: So—why wouldn't you let Addie tell me what he looked like?

JAKE: It might have influenced your first impression. I wanted you to see him with a clear eye, and tell me what you saw.

TC: I saw a man I'd seen before.

JAKE: *Quinn?*

TC: No, not Quinn. But someone like him. His twin.

JAKE: Speak English.

(I described that summer day, my baptism—it was so clear to me, the similarities between Quinn and the Reverend Snow, the linking fibers; but I spoke too emotionally, metaphysically, to communicate what I felt, and I could sense Jake's disappointment: he had expected from me a series of sensible perceptions, pristine, pragmatic insights that would help clarify his own concept of Quinn's character, the man's motivations.

I fell silent, chagrined to have failed Jake. But as we arrived at the highway, and steered toward town, Jake let me know that, garbled, confused as my memoir must have seemed, he had partially deciphered what I had so poorly expressed.)

Well, Bob Quinn *does* think he's the Lord Almighty.

TC: Not think. Knows.

JAKE: Any doubts?

TC: No, no doubts. Quinn's the man who whittles coffins.

JAKE: And some day soon he'll whittle his own. Or my name ain't Jake Pepper.

Over the next few months I called Jake at least once a week, usually on Sundays when he was at Addie's house, which gave me a chance to talk with them both. Jake usually opened our conversations by saying: "Sorry, pardner. Nothing new to report." But one Sunday, Jake told me that he and Addie had settled on a wedding date: August 10. And Addie said: "We hope you can come." I promised I would, though the day conflicted with a planned three-week trip to Europe; well, I'd juggle my dates. However, in the end it was the bride and groom who had to alter schedules, for the Bureau agent who was supposed to replace Jake while he was on his honeymoon ("We're going to Honolulu!") had a hepatitis attack, and the wedding was postponed until the first of September. "That's rotten luck," I told Addie. "But I'll be back by then; I'll be there."

So, early in August, I flew Swissair to Switzerland, and lolled away several weeks in an Alpine village, sunbathing among the eternal snows. I slept, I ate, I reread the whole of Proust, which is rather like plunging into a tidal wave, destination unknown. But my thoughts too often revolved around Mr. Quinn; occasionally, while I slept, he knocked at the door and entered my dreams, sometimes as himself, his grey eyes glittering behind the wire-framed spectacles, but now and then he appeared guised as the white-robed Reverend Snow.

A brief whiff of Alpine air is exhilarating, but extended holidays in the mountains can become claustrophobic, arouse inexplicable depressions. Anyway, one day when one of these black moods descended, I hired a car and drove via the Grand St. Bernard pass into Italy and on to Venice. In Venice one is always in costume and wearing a mask; that is, you are not yourself, and not responsible for your behavior. It wasn't the real me who arrived in Venice at five in the afternoon and before midnight boarded a train bound for Istanbul. It all began in Harry's Bar, as so many Venetian escapades do. I had just ordered a martini when who should slam through the swinging doors but Gianni Paoli, an energetic journalist whom I had known in Moscow when he had been a correspondent for an Italian newspaper: together, aided by vodka, we had enlivened many a morose Russian restaurant. Gianni was in Venice en route to Istanbul; he was catching the Orient Express at midnight. Six martinis later he had talked me into going with him. It was a journey of two days and two nights; the train meandered through Jugoslavia and

Bulgaria, but our impressions of those countries were confined to what we glimpsed out the window of our wagon-lit
compartment, which we never left except to renew our sup-
ply of wine and vodka.

The room spun. Stopped. Spun. I stepped out of bed. My
brain, a hunk of shattered glass, painfully clinked inside my
head. But I could stand; I could walk; I even remembered
where I was: the Hilton Hotel in Istanbul. Gingerly, I made
my way toward a balcony overlooking the Bosphorus. Gianni
Paoli was basking there in the sunshine, eating breakfast and
reading the Paris *Herald Tribune*. Blinking, I glanced at the
newspaper's date. It was the first of September. Now, why
should that cause such severe sensations? Nausea; guilt; re-
morse. Holy smoke, I'd missed the wedding! Gianni couldn't
fathom why I was so upset (Italians are always upset; but
they never understand why anybody else should be); he
poured vodka into his orange juice, offered it to me, and said
drink, get drunk: "But first, send them a telegram." I took his
advice, all of it. The telegram said: *Unavoidably detained
but wish you every happiness on this wonderful day*. Later,
when rest and abstinence had steadied my hand, I wrote
them a short letter; I didn't lie, I simply didn't explain why I
had been "unavoidably detained"; I said I was flying to New
York in a few days, and would telephone them as soon as
they returned from their honeymoon. I addressed the letter to
Mr. and Mrs. Jake Pepper, and when I left it at the desk to
be mailed I felt relieved, exonerated; I thought of Addie with
a flower in her hair, of Addie and Jake walking at dusk along
Waikiki beach, the sea beside them, stars above them; I
wondered if Addie was too old to have children.

But I didn't go home; things happened. I encountered an
old friend in Istanbul, an archeologist who was working on a

"dig" on the Anatolia coast in southern Turkey; he invited me
to join him, he said I would enjoy it, and he was right, I did.
I swam every day, learned to dance Turkish folk dances,
drank ouzo and danced outdoors all night every night at the
local bistro; I stayed two weeks. Afterward I traveled by boat
to Athens, and from there took a plane to London, where I
had a suit fitted. It was October, almost autumn, before I
turned the key that opened the door of my New York apartment.

A friend, who had been visiting the apartment to water
the plants, had arranged my mail in orderly stacks on the
library table. There were a number of telegrams, and I leafed
through those before taking off my coat. I opened one; it
was an invitation to a Halloween party. I opened another; it
was signed Jake: *Call me urgent.* It was dated August 29, six
weeks ago. Hurriedly, not allowing myself to believe what I
was thinking, I found Addie's telephone number and dialed
it; no answer. Then I placed a person-to-person call to the
Prairie Motel: No, Mr. Pepper was not at present registered
there; yes, the operator thought he could be contacted
through the State Bureau of Investigation. I called it; a man
—an ornery bastard—informed me that Detective Pepper
was on a leave of absence, and no, he couldn't tell me his
whereabouts ("That's against the rules"); and when I gave
him my name and told him I was calling from New York he
said oh yeah and when I said listen, please, this is very important the sonofabitch hung up.

I needed to take a leak; but the desire, which had been
insistent all during the ride from Kennedy airport, subsided,
disappeared as I stared at the letters piled on the library
table. Intuition attracted me to them. I flipped through the
stacks with the professional speed of a mail sorter, seeking a
sample of Jake's handwriting. I found it. The envelope was

postmarked September 10; it was on the official stationery of the Investigation Bureau, and had been sent from the state capital. It was a brief letter, but the firm masculine style of the penmanship disguised the author's anguish:

Your letter from Istanbul arrived today. When I read it I was sober. I'm not so sober now. Last August, the day Addie died, I sent a telegram asking you to call me. But I guess you were overseas. But that is what I had to tell you—Addie is gone. I still don't believe it, and I never will, not until I know what really happened. Two days before our wedding she and Marylee were swimming in Blue River. Addie drowned; but Marylee didn't see her drown. I can't write about it. I've got to get away. I don't trust myself. Wherever I go, Marylee Connor will know how to locate me. Sincerely . . .

MARYLEE CONNOR: Why, hello! Why, sure, I recognized your voice right off.

TC: I've been calling you every half-hour all afternoon.

MARYLEE: Where are you?

TC: New York.

MARYLEE: How's the weather?

TC: It's raining.

MARYLEE: Raining here, too. But we can use it. We've had such a dry summer. Can't get the dust out of your hair. You say you've been calling me?

TC: All afternoon.

MARYLEE: Well, I was home. But I'm afraid my hearing's not too good. And I've been down in the cellar and up in the attic. Packing. Now that I'm alone, this house is too much for me. We have a cousin—she's a widow, too—she bought a place in Florida, a condominium, and I'm going to live with her. Well, how are you? Have you spoken to Jake lately?

(I explained that I'd just returned from Europe, and had

not been able to contact Jake; she said he was staying with one of his sons in Oregon, and gave me the telephone number.)

Poor Jake. He's taken it all so hard. Somehow he seems to blame himself. Oh? Oh, you didn't *know*?

TC: Jake wrote me, but I didn't get the letter until today. I can't tell you how sorry . . .

MARYLEE (a catch in her voice): You didn't know about Addie?

TC: Not until today . . .

MARYLEE (suspiciously): What did Jake say?

TC: He said she drowned.

MARYLEE (defensively, as though we were arguing): Well, she did. And I don't care what Jake thinks. Bob Quinn was nowhere in sight. He *couldn't* have had anything to do with it.

(I heard her take a deep breath, followed by a long pause—as if, attempting to control her temper, she was counting to ten.)

If anybody's to blame, it's me. It was my idea to drive out to Sandy Cove for a swim. Sandy Cove doesn't even belong to Quinn. It's on the Miller ranch. Addie and I always used to go there; it's shady and you can hide from the sun. It's the safest part of Blue River; it has a natural pool, and it's where we learned to swim when we were little girls. That day we had Sandy Cove all to ourselves; we went into the water together, and Addie remarked how this time next week she'd be swimming in the Pacific Ocean. Addie was a strong swimmer, but I tire easily. So after I'd cooled off, I spread a towel under a tree and started reading through some of the magazines we'd brought along. Addie stayed in the water; I heard her say: "I'm going to swim around the bend and sit on the waterfall." The river flows out of Sandy Cove and sweeps around a bend; beyond the bend a rocky ridge runs across the river, creating a small waterfall—a short drop, not more than two feet. When we were children it was fun to sit on the ridge and feel the water rushing between our legs.

I was reading, not noticing the time until I felt a shiver and saw the sun was slanting toward the mountains; I wasn't worried—I imagined Addie was still enjoying the waterfall. But after a while I walked down to the river and shouted Addie! Addie! I thought: Maybe she's trying to tease me. So I climbed the embankment to the top of Sandy Cove; from there I could see the waterfall and the whole river moving north. There was no one there; no Addie. Then, just below the fall, I saw a white lily pad floating on the water, bobbing. But then I realized it wasn't a lily; it was a hand—with a diamond twinkling: Addie's engagement ring, the little diamond Jake gave her. I slid down the embankment and waded into the river and crawled along the waterfall ridge. The water was very clear and not too deep: I could see Addie's face under the surface and her hair tangled in the twigs of a tree branch, a sunken tree. It was hopeless—I grabbed her hand and pulled and pulled with all my strength but I couldn't budge her. Somehow, we'll never know how, she'd fallen off the ridge and the tree had caught her hair, held her down. *Accidental death by drowning.* That was the coroner's verdict. Hello?

TC: Yes, I'm here.

MARYLEE: My grandmother Mason never used the word "death." When someone died, especially someone she cared about, she always said that they had been "called back." She meant that they had not been buried, lost forever; but, rather, that the person had been "called back" to a happy childhood place, a world of living things. And that's how I feel about my sister. Addie was called back to live among the things she loves. Children. Children and flowers. Birds. The wild plants she found in the mountains.

TC: I'm so very sorry, Mrs. Connor. I . . .

MARYLEE: That's all right, dear.

TC: I wish there was something . . .

MARYLEE: Well, it was good to hear from you. And when you speak to Jake, remember to give him my love.

I showered, set a bottle of brandy beside my bed, climbed under the covers, took the telephone off the night table, nestled it on my stomach, and dialed the Oregon number that I had been given. Jake's son answered; he said his father was out, he wasn't sure where and didn't know when to expect him. I left a message for Jake to call as soon as he came home, no matter the hour. I filled my mouth with all the brandy it could hold, and rinsed it around like a mouthwash, a medicine to stop my teeth from chattering. I let the brandy trickle down my throat. Sleep, in the curving shape of a murmuring river, flowed through my head; in the end, it was always the river; everything returned to it. Quinn may have provided the rattlesnakes, the fire, the nicotine, the steel wire; but the river had inspired those deeds, and now it had claimed Addie, too. Addie: her hair, tangled in watery undergrowths, drifted, in my dream, across her wavering drowned face like a bridal veil.

An earthquake erupted; the earthquake was the telephone, rumbling on my stomach where it had still been resting when I dozed off. I knew it was Jake. I let it ring while I poured myself a guaranteed eye-opener.

TC: Jake?

JAKE: So you finally made it back stateside?

TC: This morning.

JAKE: Well, you didn't miss the wedding, after all.

TC: I got your letter. Jake—

JAKE: No. You don't have to make a speech.

TC: I called Mrs. Connor. Marylee. We had a long talk—

JAKE (alertly): Yeah?

TC: She told me everything that happened—

JAKE: Oh, no she didn't! Damned if she did!

TC (jolted by the harshness of his response): But, Jake, she said—

JAKE: *Yeah.* What did she say?

TC: She said it was an accident.

JAKE: You believed that?

> (The tone of his voice, grimly mocking, suggested Jake's expression: his eyes hard, his thin quirky lips twitching.)

TC: From what she told me, it seems the only explanation.

JAKE: She doesn't know what happened. She wasn't *there.* She was sitting on her butt reading magazines.

TC: Well, if it was Quinn—

JAKE: I'm listening.

TC: Then he must be a magician.

JAKE: Not necessarily. But I can't discuss it just now. Soon, maybe. A little something happened that might hasten matters. Santa Claus came early this year.

TC: Are we talking about Jaeger?

JAKE: Yessir, the postmaster got his package.

TC: When?

JAKE: Yesterday. (He laughed, not with pleasure but excitement, released energy) Bad news for Jaeger but good news for me. My plan was to stay up here till after Thanksgiving. But boy, I was going nuts. All I could hear was slamming doors. All I could think was: Suppose he doesn't go after Jaeger? Suppose he doesn't give me that one last chance?

Well, you can call me at the Prairie Motel tomorrow night. Because that's where I'll be.

TC: Jake, wait a minute. It has to have been an accident. Addie, I mean.

JAKE (unctuously patient, as though instructing a retarded aborigine): Now I'll leave you with something to sleep on.

Sandy Cove, where this "accident" occurred, is the property of a man named A. J. Miller. There are two ways to reach it. The shortest way is to take a back road that cuts across Quinn's place and leads straight to Miller's ranch. Which is what the ladies did.

Adios, amigo.

Naturally, the something he had left me to sleep on kept me sleepless until daybreak. Images formed, faded; it was as though I were mentally editing a motion picture.

Addie and her sister are in their car driving along the highway. They turn off the highway and onto a dirt road that is part of the B.Q. Ranch. Quinn is standing on the veranda of his house; or perhaps watching from a window: whenever, however, at some point he spies the trespassing car, recognizes its occupants, and guesses that they are headed for a swim at Sandy Cove. He decides to follow them. By car? or horseback? afoot? Anyway, he approaches the area where the women are bathing by a roundabout route. Once there, he conceals himself among the shady trees above Sandy Cove. Marylee is resting on a towel reading magazines. Addie is in the water. He hears Addie tell her sister: "I'm going to swim around the bend and sit on the waterfall." Ideal; now Addie will be unprotected, alone, out of her sister's view. Quinn waits until he is certain she is playfully absorbed at the waterfall. Presently, he slides down the embankment (the same embankment the searching Marylee later used). Addie doesn't hear him; the splashing waterfall covers the sound of his movements. But how can he avoid her eyes? For surely, the instant she sees him, she will acknowledge her danger, protest, scream. No, he obtains her silence with a gun. Addie hears something, looks up, sees Quinn swiftly striding across the ridge, revolver aimed—he shoves her off the waterfall, plunges after her, pulls her under, holds her there: a final baptism.

It was possible.

But daybreak, and the beginning noise of New York traffic, lessened my enthusiasm for fevered fantasizing, briskly dropped me deep into that discouraging abyss—reality. Jake was without choice: like Quinn, he had set himself a passionate task, and his task, his human duty, was to prove that Quinn was responsible for ten indecent deaths, particularly the death of a warm, companionable woman he had wanted to marry. But unless Jake had evolved a theory more convincing than my own imagination had managed, then I preferred to forget it; I was satisfied to fall asleep remembering the coroner's common-sense verdict: *Accidental death by drowning*.

An hour later I was wide awake, a victim of jet lag. Awake but weary, fretful; and hungry, starved. Of course, due to my prolonged absence, the refrigerator contained nothing edible. Soured milk, stale bread, black bananas, rotten eggs, shriveled oranges, withered apples, putrid tomatoes, a chocolate cake iced with fungus. I made a cup of coffee, added brandy to it, and with that to fortify me, examined my accumulated mail. My birthday had fallen on September 30, and a few well-wishers had sent cards. One of them was from

Fred Wilson, the retired detective and mutual friend who had first introduced me to Jake Pepper. I knew he was familiar with Jake's case, that Jake often consulted him, but for some reason we had never discussed it, an omission I now rectified by calling him.

TC: Hello? May I speak to Mr. Wilson, please?

FRED WILSON: Speaking.

TC: Fred? You sound like you have a helluva cold.

FRED: You bet. It's a real granddaddy.

TC: Thanks for the birthday card.

FRED: Aw, hell. You didn't have to spend your money just for that.

TC: Well, I wanted to talk to you about Jake Pepper.

FRED: Say, there must be something to this telepathy stuff. I was thinking about Jake when the phone rang. You know, his Bureau has him on leave. They're trying to force him off that case.

TC: He's back on it now.

(After I recounted the conversation I'd had with Jake the previous evening, Fred asked several questions, mostly about Addie Mason's death and Jake's opinions pertaining to it.)

FRED: I'm damned surprised the Bureau would let him go back there. Jake's the fairest-minded man I've ever met. There's nobody in our business I respect more than Pepper. But he's lost all judgment. He's been banging his head against a wall so long he's knocked all the sense out of it. Sure, it was terrible what happened to his girl friend. But it was an accident. She drowned. But Jake can't accept that. He's standing on rooftops shouting murder. Accusing this man Quinn.

TC (resentfully): Jake could be right. It's possible.

FRED: And it's also possible the man is one-hundred-percent innocent. In fact, that seems to be the general consensus. I've talked with guys in Jake's own Bureau, and they say you couldn't swat a fly with the evidence they've got. Said it was downright embarrassing. And Jake's own chief told me, said so far as he knew Quinn had never killed anybody.

TC: He killed two cattle rustlers.

FRED (chuckles, followed by a coughing fit): Well, sir. We don't exactly call that killin'. Not around these parts.

TC: Except they weren't cattle rustlers. They were two gamblers from Denver; Quinn owed them money. And what's more, I don't think Addie's death was an accident.

> (Defiantly, with astounding authority, I related the "murder" as I had imagined it; the surmises I had rejected at dawn now seemed not only plausible but vividly convincing: Quinn *had* trailed the sisters to Sandy Cove, hidden among the trees, slid down the embankment, threatened Addie with a gun, trapped her, drowned her.)

FRED: That's Jake's story.

TC: No.

FRED: It's just something you worked out by yourself?

TC: More or less.

FRED: All the same, that *is* Jake's story. Hang on, I gotta blow my honker.

TC: What do you mean—"that *is* Jake's story"?

FRED: Like I said, there must be something to this telepathy stuff. Give or take a lotta little details, and that *is* Jake's story. He filed a report, and sent me a copy. And in the report that's how he reconstructed events: Quinn saw the car, he followed them . . .

> (Fred continued. A hot wave of shame hit me; I felt like

a schoolboy caught cheating in an exam. Irrationally, instead of blaming myself, I blamed Jake; I was angry at him for not having produced a solid solution, crestfallen that his conjectures were no better than mine. I trusted Jake, the professional man, and was miserable when I felt that trust seesawing. But it was such a haphazard concoction—Quinn and Addie and the waterfall. Even so, regardless of Fred Wilson's destructive comments, I knew that the basic faith I had in Jake was justified.)

The Bureau's in a tough spot. They have to take Jake off this case. He's disqualified himself. Oh, he'll fight them! But it's for the sake of his own reputation. Safety, too. One night here, it was after he lost his girl friend, he rang me up around four in the morning. Drunker than a hundred Indians dancing in a cornfield. The gist of it was: he was gonna challenge Quinn to a duel. I checked on him the next day. Bastard, he didn't even remember calling me.

Anxiety, as any expensive psychiatrist will tell you, is caused by depression; but depression, as the same psychiatrist will inform you on a second visit and for an additional fee, is caused by anxiety. I rotated around in that humdrum circle all afternoon. By nightfall the two demons had combined; while anxiety copulated with depression, I sat staring at Mr. Bell's controversial invention, fearing the moment when I would have to dial the Prairie Motel and hear Jake admit that the Bureau was taking him off the case. Of course, a good meal might have helped; but I had already abolished my hunger by eating the chocolate cake with the fungus icing. Or I could have gone to a movie and smoked some grass. But when you're in that kind of sweat, the only lasting remedy is to ride with it: accept the anxiety, be depressed, relax, and let the current carry you where it will.

OPERATOR: Good evening. Prairie Motel. Mr. Pepper? Hey, Ralph, you seen Jake Pepper? In the bar? Hello, sir—your party's in the bar. I'm ringing.

TC: Thank you.

> (I remembered the Prairie Bar; unlike the motel, it had a certain comic-strip charm. Cowboy customers, rawhide walls decorated with girlie posters and Mexican sombreros, a rest room for BULLS, another for BELLES, and a jukebox devoted to the twangs of Country & Western music. A jukebox blast announced that the bartender had answered.)

BARTENDER: Jake Pepper! Somebody for you. Hello, mister. He wants to know who is it?

TC: A friend from New York.

JAKE'S VOICE (distantly; rising in volume as he approaches the phone): Sure I have friends in New York. Tokyo. Bombay. Hello, my friend from New York!

TC: You sound jolly.

JAKE: About as jolly as a beggar's monkey.

TC: Can you talk? Or should I call later?

JAKE: This is okay. It's so noisy nobody can hear me.

TC (tentative; wary of opening wounds): So. How's it going?

JAKE: Not so hotsy-totsy.

TC: Is it the Bureau?

JAKE (puzzled): The Bureau?

TC: Well, I thought they might be giving you trouble.

JAKE: They ain't giving *me* no trouble. But I'm giving them plenty. Buncha nitwits. No, it's that knucklehead Jaeger. Our beloved postmaster. He's chicken. He wants to skip the coop. And I don't know how to stop him. But I've got to.

TC: Why?

JAKE: "The shark needs bait."

TC: Have you talked to Jaeger?

JAKE: For hours. He's with me now. Sitting over there in the corner like a little white rabbit ready to jump down a hole.

TC: Well, I can sympathize with that.

JAKE: I can't afford to. I've got to hold on to this old sissy. But how? He's sixty-four; he's got a bundle of dough and a pension coming. He's a bachelor; his closest living relative is Bob Quinn! For Christ's sake. And get this: he still doesn't believe Quinn did it. He says yes, maybe somebody means to harm me, but it can't be Bob Quinn; he's my own flesh and blood. There's just one thing that gives him pause.

TC: Something to do with the package?

JAKE: Uh-huh.

TC: The handwriting? No, it can't be that. It must be the picture.

JAKE: Nice shot. This picture's different. It's not like the others. For one thing, it's about twenty years old. It was made at the State Fair; Jaeger is marching in a Kiwanis parade—he's wearing a Kiwanis hat. *Quinn took the picture.* Jaeger says he saw him take it; the reason he remembers is because he asked Quinn to give him a copy, and Quinn never did.

TC: That ought to make the postmaster think twice. I doubt that it would do much to a jury.

JAKE: Actually, it doesn't do much to the postmaster.

TC: But he's frightened enough to leave town?

JAKE: He's scared, sure. But even if he wasn't, there's nothing to keep him here. He says he always planned to spend the last years of his life traveling. My job is to delay the journey.

Indefinitely. Listen, I'd better not leave my little rabbit alone too long. So wish me luck. And keep in touch.

I wished him luck, but he was not lucky; within a week, both the postmaster and the detective had gone their separate ways: the former packed for global wanderings, the latter because the Bureau had removed him from the case.

The following notes are excerpted from my personal journals: 1975 through 1979.

20 October 1975: Spoke to Jake. Very bitter; spewing venom in all directions. He said "for two pins and a Confederate dollar" he'd quit, write in his resignation, go to Oregon and work on his son's farm. "But as long as I'm here with the Bureau, I've still got a whip to crack." Also, if he quit now, he could forfeit his retirement pension, a *beau geste* I'm sure he can't afford.

6 November 1975: Spoke to Jake. He said they were having a cattle-rustling epidemic in the northeast part of the state. Rustlers steal the cattle at night, load them into trucks, and drive them down into the Dakotas. He said that he and some other agents had spent the last few nights out on the open range, hiding among the cattle herds, waiting for rustlers who never showed up: "Man, it's cold out there! I'm too old for this tough-guy stuff." He mentioned that Marylee Connor had moved to Sarasota.

25 November 1975: Thanksgiving. Awoke this morning, and thought of Jake, and remembered it was just a year ago that he had got his "big break": that he had gone to Addie's for dinner and she had told him about Quinn and Blue River. I decided against calling him; it might aggravate, rather than alleviate, the painful ironies attached to this particular anniversary. Did call Fred Wilson and his wife, Alice, to wish

them *"bon appétit."* Fred asked about Jake; I said the last I heard he was busy chasing cattle rustlers. Fred said: "Yeah, they're workin' his ass off. Trying to keep his mind off that other deal, what the Bureau guys call 'The Rattlesnake Baby.' They've assigned a young fellow named Nelson to it; but that's just for appearance sake. Legally, the case is open; but for all practical purposes the Bureau has drawn a line through it."

5 December 1975: Spoke to Jake. The first thing he said was: "You'll be pleased to hear the postmaster is safe and sound in Honolulu. He's been mailing postcards to everybody. I'm sure he sent one to Quinn. Well, he got to go to Honolulu, and I didn't. Yessir, life is strange." He said he was still in the "cattle-rustling business. And damned sick of it. I ought to join the rustlers. They make a hundred times the money I do."

20 December 1975: Received a Christmas card from Marylee Connor. She wrote: "Sarasota is lovely! This is my first winter in a warm climate, and I can honestly say I don't miss home. Did you know that Sarasota is famous as a winter quarter for the Ringling Bros. Circus? My cousin and I often drive over to watch the performers practice. It's the best fun! We've become friendly with a Russian woman who trains acrobats. May God see you through the New Year, and please find enclosed a small gift." The gift was an amateurish family-album snapshot of Addie as a young girl, perhaps sixteen, standing in a flower garden, wearing a white summer dress with a matching hair ribbon, and cradling in her arms, as though it were as fragile as the surrounding foliage, a white kitten; the kitten is yawning. On the back of the picture, Marylee had written: *Adelaide Minerva Mason. Born 14 June 1939. Called Back 29 August 1975.*

1 January 1976: Jake called—"Happy New Year!" He

sounded like a gravedigger digging his own grave. He said he'd spent New Year's Eve in bed reading *David Copperfield*. "The Bureau had a big party. But I didn't go. I knew if I did I'd get drunk and knock some heads together. Maybe a lotta heads. Drunk or sober, whenever I'm around the chief it's all I can do not to throw a punch bang into his fat gut." I told him I'd received a card from Marylee at Christmas and described the picture of Addie accompanying it, and he said yes, Marylee had sent him a very similar picture: "But what does it mean? What she wrote—'Called Back'?" When I tried to interpret the phrase as I understood it, he stopped me with a grunt: it was too fanciful for him; and he remarked: "I love Marylee. I've always said she's a sweet woman. But simple. Just a mite simple."

5 February 1976: Last week I bought a frame for Addie's snapshot. I put it on a table in my bedroom. Yesterday I removed it to a drawer. It was too disturbing, alive—especially the kitten's yawn.

14 February 1976: Three valentines—one from an old schoolteacher, Miss Wood; another from my tax accountant; and a third signed Love, Bob Quinn. A joke, of course. Jake's idea of black comedy?

15 February 1976: Called Jake, and he confessed yes, he'd sent the valentine. I said well, you must have been drunk. He said: "I was."

20 April 1976: A short letter from Jake scribbled on Prairie Motel stationery: "Have been here two days collecting gossip, mostly at the Okay Café. The postmaster is still in Honolulu. Juanita Quinn had a pretty bad stroke. I like Juanita, so I was sorry to hear it. But her husband is fit as a fiddle. Which is the way I prefer it. I don't want anything to happen to Quinn until I have a final crack at him. The

Bureau may have forgotten this matter, but not me. I'll never give up. Sincerely . . ."

10 July 1976: Called Jake last night, not having heard from him for more than two months. The man I spoke to was a new Jake Pepper; or rather, the old Jake Pepper, vigorous, optimistic—it was as though he had at last emerged from an inebriated slumber, his rested muscles primed to prowl. I quickly learned what had roused him: "I've got a devil by the tail. A humdinger." The humdinger, though it contained one intriguing element, turned out to be a very ordinary murder; or so it struck me. A young man, aged twenty-two, lived alone on a modest farm with an elderly grandfather. Earlier in the spring the grandson killed the old man in order to inherit his property and steal money the victim had misered away under a mattress. Neighbors noticed the farmer's disappearance and saw that the young man was driving a flashy new car. The police were notified, and they soon discovered that the grandson, who had no explanation for his relative's sudden and complete absence, had bought the new car with old cash. The suspect would neither admit nor deny that he had murdered his grandfather, though the authorities were certain he had. The difficulty was: no corpse. Without a body they couldn't make an arrest. But search as they might, the victim remained invisible. The local constabulary requested aid from the State Bureau of Investigation, and Jake was assigned to the case. "It's fascinating. This kid is smart as hell. Whatever he did to that old man is diabolical. And if we can't find the body, he'll go scot-free. But I'm sure it's somewhere on that farm. Every instinct tells me he chopped Grandpa into mincemeat and buried the parts in different spots. All I need is the head. I'll find it if I have to plow the place up acre by acre. Inch by inch." After we'd hung up, I felt a surge of anger; and jealousy: not just a

twinge, but a mean jab, as though I'd recently learned of a lover's betrayal. In truth, I don't want Jake to be interested in any case other than the case that interests me.

20 July 1976: A telegram from Jake. *Have Head One Hand Two Feet Stop Gone Fishing Jake.* I wonder why he sent a telegram instead of calling? Can he imagine that I resent this success? I'm pleased, for I know his pride has been at least partially restored. I only hope that wherever he has "gone fishing," it is somewhere in the neighborhood of Blue River.

22 July 1976: Wrote Jake a congratulatory letter, and told him I was going abroad for three months.

20 December 1976: A Christmas card from Sarasota. "If you ever come this way, please stop by. God bless you. Marylee Connor."

22 February 1977: A note from Marylee: "I still subscribe to the hometown paper, and thought the enclosed clipping might interest you. I've written her husband. He sent me such a lovely letter at the time of Addie's accident." The clipping was Juanita Quinn's obituary; she had died in her sleep. Surprisingly, there was to be no service or burial, for the deceased had requested that she be cremated and her ashes scattered over Blue River.

23 February 1977: Called Jake. He said, rather sheepishly: "Hiya, pardner! You've been quite the stranger." In fact, I'd mailed him a letter from Switzerland, to which he had not replied; and though I'd failed to reach him, had twice phoned during the Christmas holidays. "Oh yeah, I was in Oregon." Then I came to the point: Juanita Quinn's obituary. Predictably, he said: "I'm suspicious"; and when I asked why, answered: "Cremations always make me suspicious." We talked another quarter-hour, but it was a self-conscious conversation, an effort on his part. Perhaps I remind him of

matters that, for all his moral strength, he is beginning to want to forget.

10 July 1977: Jake called, elated. Without preamble, he announced: "Like I told you, cremations always make me suspicious. Bob Quinn's a bridegroom! Well, everybody knew he had another family, a woman with four children fathered by Squire Quinn. He kept them hidden over in Appleton, a place about a hundred miles southwest. Last week he married the lady. Brought his bride and brood back to the ranch, proud as a rooster. Juanita would spin in her grave. If she *had* a grave." Stupidly, dazed by the speed of Jake's narrative, I asked: "How old are the children?" He said: "The youngest is ten and the oldest seventeen. All girls. I tell you, the town is in an uproar. Sure, they can handle murder, a couple of homicides don't faze them; but to have their shining knight, their big War Hero, show up with this brazen trollop and her four little bastards is too much for their Presbyterian eyebrows." I said: "I feel sorry for the children. The woman, too." Jake said: "I'll save my sorrow for Juanita. If there was a body to exhume, I'll bet the coroner would find a nice dose of nicotine inside it." I said: "I doubt that. He wouldn't hurt Juanita. She was an alcoholic. He was her savior. He loved her." Quietly, Jake said: "And I gather you don't think he had anything to do with Addie's 'accident'?" I said: "He meant to kill her. He would have, eventually. But then she drowned." Jake said: "Saving him the trouble! Okay. Explain Clem Anderson, the Baxters." I said: "Yes, that was all Quinn's work. He had to do it. He's a messiah with a task." Jake said: "Then why did he let the postmaster glide through his fingers?" I said: "Has he? My guess is that old Mr. Jaeger has an appointment in Samarra. Quinn will cross his path one day. Quinn can't rest until that happens. He's not sane,

you know." Jake hung up, but not before acrimoniously asking: "Are you?"

15 December 1977: Saw a black alligator wallet in a pawnshop window. It was in fine condition, and initialed J.P. I bought it, and because our last conversation had ended angrily (he was angry, I wasn't), I sent it to Jake as both a Christmas present and a peace offering.

22 December 1977: A Christmas card from the faithful Mrs. Connor: "I'm working for the circus! No, I'm not an acrobat. I'm a receptionist. It beats shuffleboard! All wishes for the New Year."

17 January 1978: A four-line scrawl from Jake thanking me for the wallet—curtly, inadequately. I'm receptive to hints. I won't write or call again.

20 December 1978: A Christmas card from Marylee Connor, just her signature; nothing from Jake.

12 September 1979: Fred Wilson and his wife were in New York last week, en route to Europe (their first trip), happy as honeymooners. I took them to dinner; all talk was limited to the excitements of their impending tour until, while selecting desserts, Fred said: "I notice you haven't mentioned Jake." I pretended surprise, and casually remarked that I hadn't heard from Jake in well over a year. Shrewdly, Fred asked: "You fellows have a falling out?" I shrugged: "Nothing quite so clean-cut. But we haven't always seen eye to eye." Then Fred said: "Jake's had bad health problems lately. Emphysema. He's retiring the end of this month. Now, it's none of my business, but I think it would be a nice gesture if you called him. Just now he needs a pat on the back."

14 September 1979: I shall always be grateful to Fred Wilson; he had made it easy for me to swallow my pride and

call Jake. We spoke this morning; it was as if we had talked yesterday, and the day before. One wouldn't believe that there had ever been an interruption in our friendship. He confirmed the news of his retirement: "Just sixteen days to go!"—and said that he planned to live with his son in Oregon. "But before that, I'm going to spend a day or two at the Prairie Motel. I've some unfinished chores in that town. There's some records in the courthouse I want to steal for my files. Hey, listen! Why don't we go together? Have a real reunion. I could meet you at Denver and drive you down." Jake did not have to pressure me; if he hadn't offered the invitation, I would have suggested it myself: I had often dreamed, while awake or asleep, of returning to that melancholy village, for I wanted to see Quinn again—meet and talk with him, just the two of us alone.

It was the second day of October.

Jake, declining an offer to accompany me, had lent me his car, and after lunch I left the Prairie Motel to keep an appointment at the B.Q. Ranch. I remembered the last time I had traveled this territory: the full moon, the fields of snow, the cutting cold, the cattle banded together, gathered in groups, their warm breath smoking the arctic air. Now, in October, the landscape was gloriously different: the macadam highway was like a skinny black sea dividing a golden continent; on either side, the sun-bleached stubble of threshed wheat flamed, rippled with yellow colors, sable shadows under a cloudless sky. Bulls pranced about these pastures; and cows, among them mothers with new calves, grazed, dozed.

At the entrance to the ranch, a young girl was leaning

against a sign, the one with the crossed tomahawks. She
smiled, and waved for me to stop.

YOUNG GIRL: Afternoon! I'm Nancy Quinn. My dad sent me
to meet you.

TC: Well, thanks.

NANCY QUINN (opening the car door, climbing in): He's fishing. I'll have to show you where he is.

> (She was a cheerful twelve-year-old snaggle-toothed tom-
> boy. Her tawny hair was chopped short, and she was
> splashed with freckles from top to bottom. She was wear-
> ing only an old bathing suit. One of her knees was
> wrapped in a dirty bandage.)

TC (referring to the bandage): Hurt yourself?

NANCY QUINN: Naw. Well, I got throwed.

TC: Throwed?

NANCY QUINN: Bad Boy throwed me. He's one mean horse.
That's how come they call him Bad Boy. He's throwed every
kid on the ranch. Most of the guys, too. I said well, I bet I
can ride him. And I did. For 'bout two seconds flat.

> You been here before?

TC: Once; years ago. But it was at night. I remember a
wooden bridge—

NANCY QUINN: That's it yonder!

> (We crossed the bridge: finally I saw Blue River; but it
> was a glimpse as swift and flurried as a hummingbird's
> flight, for overhanging trees, leafless when last seen,
> blazed with obscuring autumn-trimmed foliage.)

You ever been to Appleton?

TC: No.

NANCY QUINN: *Never?* That's funny. I never met nobody
that's never been to Appleton.

TC: Have I missed something?

NANCY QUINN: Oh, it's okay. We used to live there. But I like it here better. It's easier to get off by yourself and do the kinda stuff I like. Fish. Shoot coyotes. My dad said he'd give me a dollar for every coyote I shot down; but after he'd give me more'n two hundred dollars, he cut me down to a dime. Well, I don't need money. I'm not like my sisters. Always got their face stuck in a mirror.

I got three sisters, and I'll tell you they're not too happy here. They don't like horses; they hate most everything. Boys. That's all they've got on their mind. When we lived in Appleton, we didn't see so much of my dad. Maybe like once a week. So they put on perfume and lipstick and had plenty of boyfriends. That was okay with my mom. She's a lot like them, someways. She likes to fuss with herself and look pretty. But my dad is real strict. He won't let my sisters have any boyfriends. Or wear lipstick. One time some of their old boyfriends drove over from Appleton, and my dad met them at the door with a shotgun; he told them, said the next time he saw them on his property he'd blow their heads off. Wow, did those guys scoot! The girls cried themselves sick. But the whole thing gives me the biggest laugh.

See that fork in the road? Stop there.

(I stopped the car; we both got out. She pointed to an opening in the trees: a dark, leafy, downward-sloping path.)

Just follow that.

TC (suddenly afraid to be alone): You're not coming with me?

NANCY QUINN: My dad don't like anybody around when he talks business.

TC: Well, thanks again.

NANCY QUINN: My pleasure!

She walked away whistling.

Parts of the path were so overgrown that I had to bend branches, shield my face against brushing leaves. Briars, strange thorns caught at my trousers; high in the trees, crows cawed, screamed. I saw an owl; it's odd to see an owl in daylight; he blinked, but did not stir. Once, I almost stumbled into a beehive—an old hollow tree-stump swarming with wild black bees. Always I could hear the river, a slow soft churning roar; then, at a curve in the path, I saw it; and saw Quinn, too.

He was wearing a rubber suit, and holding aloft, as though it were a conductor's baton, a supple fishing rod. He stood waist-deep, his hatless head in profile; his hair was no longer flecked with grey—it was white as the water-foam circling his hips. I wanted to turn and run, for the scene was so strongly reminiscent of that other day, that long-ago time when Quinn's look-alike, the Reverend Billy Joe Snow, had waited for me in waist-high water. Suddenly I heard my name; Quinn was calling it, and beckoning to me as he waded toward shore.

I thought of the young bulls I had seen parading in the golden pastures; Quinn, glistening in his rubber suit, reminded me of them—vital, powerful, dangerous; except for his whiter hair, he hadn't aged an iota; indeed, he seemed years younger, a man of fifty in perfect health.

Smiling, he squatted on a rock, and motioned for me to join him. He displayed some trout he'd caught. "Kinda puny. But they'll eat good."

I mentioned Nancy. He grinned and said: "Nancy. Oh, yeah. She's a good kid." He left it at that. He didn't refer to his wife's death, or the fact that he had remarried: he assumed I was aware of his recent history.

He said: "I was surprised when you called me."

"Oh?"

"I don't know. Just surprised. Where you staying?"

"At the Prairie Motel. Where else?"

After a silence, and almost shyly, he asked: "Jake Pepper with you?"

I nodded.

"Somebody told me he was leaving the Bureau."

"Yes. He's going to live in Oregon."

"Well, I don't guess I'll ever see the old bastard again. Too bad. We could've been real friends. If he hadn't had all those suspicions. Damn his soul, he even thought I drowned poor Addie Mason!" He laughed; then scowled. "The way I look at it is: it was the hand of God." He raised his own hand, and the river, viewed between his spread fingers, seemed to weave between them like a dark ribbon. "God's work. His will."

III

Conversational
Portraits

One

❧

A Day's Work

Scene: A rainy April morning, 1979. I am walking along Second Avenue in New York City, carrying an oilcloth shopping satchel bulging with house-cleaning materials that belong to Mary Sanchez, who is beside me trying to keep an umbrella above the pair of us, which is not difficult as she is much taller than I am, a six-footer.

Mary Sanchez is a professional cleaning woman who works by the hour, at five dollars an hour, six days a week. She works approximately nine hours a day, and visits on the average twenty-four different domiciles between Monday and Saturday: generally her customers require her services just once a week.

Mary is fifty-seven years old, a native of a small South Carolina town who has "lived North" the past forty years.

Her husband, a Puerto Rican, died last summer. She has a married daughter who lives in San Diego, and three sons, one of whom is a dentist, one who is serving a ten-year sentence for armed robbery, a third who is "just gone, God knows where. He called me last Christmas, he sounded far away. I asked where are you, Pete, but he wouldn't say, so I told him his daddy was dead, and he said good, said that was the best Christmas present I could've given him, so I hung up the phone, slam, and I hope he never calls again. Spitting on Dad's grave that way. Well, sure, Pedro was never good to the kids. Or me. Just boozed and rolled dice. Ran around with bad women. They found him dead on a bench in Central Park. Had a mostly empty bottle of Jack Daniel's in a paper sack propped between his legs; never drank nothing but the best, that man. Still, Pete was way out of line, saying he was *glad* his father was dead. He owed him the gift of life, didn't he? And I owed Pedro something too. If it wasn't for him, I'd still be an ignorant Baptist, lost to the Lord. But when I got married, I married in the Catholic church, and the Catholic church brought a *shine* to my life that has never gone out, and never will, not even when I die. I raised my children in the Faith; two of them turned out fine, and I give the church credit for that more than me."

Mary Sanchez is muscular, but she has a pale round smooth pleasant face with a tiny upturned nose and a beauty mole high on her left cheek. She dislikes the term "black," racially applied. "I'm not black. I'm brown. A light-brown colored woman. And I'll tell you something else. I don't know many other colored people that like being called blacks. Maybe some of the young people. And those radicals. But not folks my age, or even half as old. Even people who really are black, they don't like it. What's wrong with Negroes? I'm a Negro, and a Catholic, and proud to say it."

I've known Mary Sanchez since 1968, and she has worked for me, periodically, all these years. She is conscientious, and takes far more than a casual interest in her clients, many of whom she has scarcely met, or not met at all, for many of them are unmarried working men and women who are not at home when she arrives to clean their apartments; she communicates with them, and they with her, via notes: "Mary, please water the geraniums and feed the cat. Hope this finds you well. Gloria Scotto."

Once I suggested to her that I would like to follow her around during the course of a day's work, and she said well, she didn't see anything wrong with that, and in fact, would enjoy the company: "This can be kind of lonely work sometimes."

Which is how we happen to be walking along together on this showery April morning. We're off to her first job: a Mr. Andrew Trask, who lives on East Seventy-third Street.

TC: What the hell have you got in this sack?

MARY: Here, give it to me. I can't have you cursing.

TC: No. Sorry. But it's heavy.

MARY: Maybe it's the iron.

TC: You iron their clothes? You never iron any of mine.

MARY: Some of these people just have no equipment. That's why I have to carry so much. I leave notes: get this, get that. But they forget. Seems like all my people are bound up in their troubles. Like this Mr. Trask, where we're going. I've had him seven, eight months, and I've never seen him yet. But he drinks too much, and his wife left him on account of it, and he owes bills everywhere, and if ever I answered his phone, it's somebody trying to collect. Only now they've turned off his phone.

(We arrive at the address, and she produces from a

shoulder-satchel a massive metal ring jangling with dozens of keys. The building is a four-story brownstone with a midget elevator.)

TC (after entering and glancing around the Trask establishment—one fair-sized room with greenish arsenic-colored walls, a kitchenette, and a bathroom with a broken, constantly flowing toilet): Hmm. I see what you mean. This guy has problems.

MARY (opening a closet crammed and clammy with sweat-sour laundry): Not a clean sheet in the house! And look at that bed! Mayonnaise! Chocolate! Crumbs, crumbs, chewing gum, cigarette butts. Lipstick! What kind of woman would subject herself to a bed like that? I haven't been able to change the sheets for weeks. Months.

(She turns on several lamps with awry shades; and while she labors to organize the surrounding disorder, I take more careful note of the premises. Really, it looks as though a burglar had been plundering there, one who had left some drawers of a bureau open, others closed. There's a leather-framed photograph on the bureau of a stocky swarthy macho man and a blond hoity-toity Junior League woman and three tow-headed grinning snaggle-toothed suntanned boys, the eldest about fourteen. There is another unframed picture stuck in a blurry mirror: another blonde, but definitely not Junior League—perhaps a pickup from Maxwell's Plum; I imagine it is her lipstick on the bed sheets. A copy of the December issue of *True Detective* magazine is lying on the floor, and in the bathroom, stacked by the ceaselessly churning toilet, stands a pile of girlie literature—*Penthouse, Hustler, Oui*; otherwise, there seems to be a total absence of cultural possessions. But there are hundreds of empty vodka bottles everywhere—the miniature kind served by airlines.)

TC: Why do you suppose he drinks only these miniatures?

MARY: Maybe he can't afford nothing bigger. Just buys what he can. He has a good job, if he can hold on to it, but I guess his family keeps him broke.

TC: What does he do?

MARY: Airplanes.

TC: That explains it. He gets these little bottles free.

MARY: Yeah? How come? He's not a steward. He's a pilot.

TC: Oh, my God.

(A telephone rings, a subdued noise, for the instrument is submerged under a rumpled blanket. Scowling, her hands soapy with dishwater, Mary unearths it with the finesse of an archeologist.)

MARY: He must have got connected again. Hello? (Silence) Hello?

A WOMAN'S VOICE: Who *is* this?

MARY: This is Mr. Trask's residence.

WOMAN'S VOICE: Mr. Trask's *residence*? (Laughter; then, hoity-toity) To whom am I speaking?

MARY: This is Mr. Trask's maid.

WOMAN'S VOICE: So Mr. Trask has a maid, has he? Well, that's more than *Mrs.* Trask has. Will Mr. Trask's maid please tell Mr. Trask that Mrs. Trask would like to speak to him?

MARY: He's not home.

MRS. TRASK: Don't give me that. Put him on.

MARY: I'm sorry, Mrs. Trask. I guess he's out flying.

MRS. TRASK (bitter mirth): Out flying? He's always flying, dear. Always.

MARY: What I mean is, he's at work.

MRS. TRASK: Tell him to call me at my sister's in New Jersey. Call the instant he comes in, if he knows what's good for him.

MARY: Yes, ma'am. I'll leave that message. (She hangs up)

Mean woman. No wonder he's in the condition he's in. And now he's out of a job. I wonder if he left me my money. Uh-huh. That's it. On top of the fridge.

(Amazingly, an hour or so afterward she has managed to somewhat camouflage the chaos and has the room looking not altogether shipshape but reasonably respectable. With a pencil, she scribbles a note and props it against the bureau mirror: "Dear Mr. Trask yr. wive want you fone her at her sistar place sinsirly Mary Sanchez." Then she sighs and perches on the edge of the bed and from her satchel takes out a small tin box containing an assortment of roaches; selecting one, she fits it into a roach-holder and lights up, dragging deeply, holding the smoke down in her lungs and closing her eyes. She offers me a toke.)

TC: Thanks. It's too early.

MARY: It's never too early. Anyway, you ought to try this stuff. *Mucho cojones.* I get it from a customer, a real fine Catholic lady; she's married to a fellow from Peru. His family sends it to them. Sends it right through the mail. I never use it so's to get high. Just enough to lift the uglies a little. That heaviness. (She sucks on the roach until it all but burns her lips) Andrew Trask. Poor scared devil. He could end up like Pedro. Dead on a park bench, nobody caring. Not that I didn't care none for that man. Lately, I find myself remembering the good times with Pedro, and I guess that's what happens to most people if ever they've once loved somebody and lose them; the bad slips away, and you linger on the nice things about them, what made you like them in the first place. Pedro, the young man I fell in love with, he was a beautiful dancer, oh he could tango, oh he could rumba, he taught me to dance and danced me off my feet. We were regulars at the old Savoy Ballroom. He was clean, neat—even

when the drink got to him his fingernails were always
trimmed and polished. And he could cook up a storm. That's
how he made a living, as a short-order cook. I said he never
did anything good for the children; well, he fixed their lunch-
boxes to take to school. All kinds of sandwiches wrapped in
wax paper. Ham, peanut butter and jelly, egg salad, tuna fish,
and fruit, apples, bananas, pears, and a thermos filled with
warm milk mixed with honey. It hurts now to think of him
there in the park, and how I didn't cry when the police came
to tell me about it; how I never did cry. I ought to have. I
owed him that. I owed him a sock in the jaw, too.

I'm going to leave the lights on for Mr. Trask. No sense
letting him come home to a dark room.

(When we emerged from the brownstone the rain had
stopped, but the sky was sloppy and a wind had risen
that whipped trash along the gutters and caused pas-
sers-by to clutch their hats. Our destination was four
blocks away, a modest but modern apartment house with
a uniformed doorman, the address of Miss Edith Shaw, a
young woman in her mid-twenties who was on the edi-
torial staff of a magazine. "Some kind of news magazine.
She must have a thousand books. But she doesn't look
like no bookworm. She's a very healthy kind of girl, and
she has lots of boyfriends. Too many—just can't seem to
stay very long with one fellow. We got to be close because . . . Well, one time I came to her place and she was
sick as a cat. She'd come from having a baby murdered.
Normally I don't hold with that; it's against my beliefs.
And I said why didn't you marry this man? The truth
was, she didn't know who to marry; she didn't know who
the dad was. And anyway, the last thing she wanted was
a husband or a baby.")

MARY (surveying the scene from the opened front door of

Miss Shaw's two-room apartment): Nothing much to do here. A little dusting. She takes good care of it herself. Look at all those books. Ceiling to floor, nothing but library.

(Except for the burdened bookshelves, the apartment was attractively spare, Scandinavianly white and gleaming. There was one antique: an old roll-top desk with a typewriter on it; a sheet of paper was rolled into the machine; and I glanced at what was written on it:

"Zsa Zsa Gabor is
305 years old
I know
Because I counted
Her Rings"

And triple-spaced below that, was typed:

"Sylvia Plath, I hate you
And your damn daddy.
I'm glad, do you hear,
Glad you stuck your head
In a gas-hot oven!"

TC: Is Miss Shaw a poet?

MARY: She's always writing something. I don't know what it is. Stuff I see, sounds like she's on dope to me. Come here, I want to show you something.

(She leads me into the bathroom, a surprisingly large and sparkling chamber. She opens a cabinet door and points at an object on a shelf: a pink plastic vibrator molded in the shape of an average-sized penis.)

Know what that is?

TC: Don't you?

MARY: I'm the one asking.

TC: It's a dildo vibrator.

MARY: I know what a vibrator is. But I never saw one like that. It says "Made in Japan."

TC: Ah, Well. The Oriental mind.

MARY: Heathens. She's sure got some lovely perfumes. If you like perfume. Me, I only put a little vanilla behind my ears.

(Now Mary began to work, mopping the waxed carpetless floors, flicking the bookshelves with a feather duster; and while she worked she kept her roach-box open and her roach-holder filled. I don't know how much "heaviness" she had to lift, but the aroma alone was lofting me.)

MARY: You sure you don't want to try a couple of tokes? You're missing something.

TC: You twisted my arm.

(Man and boy, I've dragged some powerful grass, never enough to have acquired a habit, but enough to judge quality and know the difference between ordinary Mexican weed and luxurious contraband like Thai-sticks and the supreme Maui-Wowee. But after smoking the whole of one of Mary's roaches, and while halfway through another, I felt as though seized by a delicious demon, embraced by a mad marvelous merriment: the demon tickled my toes, scratched my itchy head, kissed me hotly with his red sugary lips, shoved his fiery tongue down my throat. Everything sparkled; my eyes were like zoom lenses; I could read the titles of books on the highest shelves: *The Neurotic Personality of Our Time by Karen Horney; Eimi by e.e. cummings; Four Quartets; The Collected Poems of Robert Frost.*)

TC: I despise Robert Frost. He was an evil, selfish bastard.

MARY: Now, if we're going to curse—

TC: Him with his halo of shaggy hair. An egomaniacal double-crossing sadist. He wrecked his whole family. Some of them. Mary, have you ever discussed this with your confessor?

MARY: Father McHale? Discussed what?

TC: The precious nectar we're so divinely devouring, my adorable chickadee. Have you informed Father McHale of this delectable enterprise?

MARY: What he don't know won't hurt him. Here, have a Life Saver. Peppermint. It makes that stuff taste better.

> (Odd, she didn't seem high, not a bit. I'd just passed Venus, and Jupiter, jolly old Jupiter, beckoned beyond in the lilac star-dazzled planetary distance. Mary marched over to the telephone and dialed a number; she let it ring a long while before hanging up.)

MARY: Not home. That's one thing to be grateful for. Mr. and Mrs. Berkowitz. If they'd been home, I couldn't have took you over there. On account of they're these real stuffy Jewish people. And you know how stuffy *they* are!

TC: Jewish people? Gosh, yes. Very stuffy. They all ought to be in the Museum of Natural History. All of them.

MARY: I've been thinking about giving Mrs. Berkowitz notice. The trouble is, Mr. Berkowitz, he was in garments, he's retired, and the two of them are always home. Underfoot. Unless they drive up to Greenwich, where they got some property. That's where they must have gone today. Another reason I'd like to quit them. They've got an old parrot— makes a mess everywhere. And stupid! All that dumb parrot can say is two things: "Holy cow!" and *"Oy vey!"* Every time you walk in the house it starts shouting *"Oy vey!"* Gets on my nerves something terrible. How about it? Let's toke another roach and blow this joint.

> (The rain had returned and the wind increased, a mixture that made the air look like a shattering mirror. The Berkowitzes lived on Park Avenue in the upper Eighties,

and I suggested we take a taxi, but Mary said no, what kind of sissy was I, we can walk it, so I realized that despite appearances, she, too, was traveling stellar paths. We walked along slowly, as though it were a warm tranquil day with turquoise skies, and the hard slippery streets ribbons of pearl-colored Caribbean beach. Park Avenue is not my favorite boulevard; it is rich with lack of charm; if Mrs. Lasker were to plant it with tulips all the way from Grand Central to Spanish Harlem, it would be of no avail. Still, there are certain buildings that prompt memories. We passed a building where Willa Cather, the American woman writer I've most admired, lived the last years of her life with her companion, Edith Lewis; I often sat in front of their fireplace and drank Bristol Cream and observed the firelight enflame the pale prairie-blue of Miss Cather's serene genius-eyes. At Eighty-fourth street I recognized an apartment house where I had once attended a small black-tie dinner given by Senator and Mrs. John F. Kennedy, then so young and insouciant. But despite the agreeable efforts of our hosts, the evening was not as enlightening as I had anticipated, because after the ladies had been dismissed and the men left in the dining room to savor their cordials and Havana cigars, one of the guests, a rather slope-chinned dressmaker named Oleg Cassini, overwhelmed the conversation with a travelogue account of Las Vegas and the myriad showgirls he'd recently auditioned there: their measurements, erotic accomplishments, financial requirements—a recital that hypnotized its auditors, none of whom was more chucklingly attentive than the future President.

When we reach Eighty-seventh street, I point out a window on the fourth floor at 1060 Park Avenue, and

inform Mary: "My mother lived there. That was her bedroom. She was beautiful and very intelligent, but she
didn't want to live. She had many reasons—at least she
thought she did. But in the end it was just her husband, my stepfather. He was a self-made man, fairly suc-
cessful—she worshipped him, and he really was a nice
guy, but he gambled, got into trouble and embezzled a
lot of money, and lost his business and was headed for
Sing Sing."

Mary shakes her head: "Just like my boy. Same as
him."

We're both standing staring at the window, the down-
pour drenching us. "So one night she got all dressed up
and gave a dinner party; everybody said she looked
lovely. But after the party, before she went to bed, she
took thirty Seconals and she never woke up."

Mary is angry; she strides rapidly away through the
rain: "She had no right to do that. I don't hold with that.
It's against my beliefs.")

SQUAWKING PARROT: Holy cow!

MARY: Hear that? What did I tell you?

PARROT: *Oy vey! Oy vey!*

(The parrot, a surrealist collage of green and yellow and
orange moulting feathers, is esconced on a mahogany
perch in the relentlessly formal parlor of Mr. and Mrs.
Berkowitz, a room suggesting that it had been entirely
made of mahogany: the parquet floors, the wall paneling,
and the furniture, all of it costly reproductions of grandi-
ose period-piece furniture—though God knows what
period, perhaps early Grand Concourse. Straight-back
chairs; settees that would have tested the endurance of
a posture professor. Mulberry velvet draperies swathed

the windows, which were incongruously covered with mustard-brown venetian blinds. Above a carved mahogany mantelpiece a mahogany-framed portrait of a jowly, sallow-skinned Mr. Berkowitz depicted him as a country squire outfitted for a fox hunt: scarlet coat, silk cravat, a bugle tucked under one arm, a riding crop under the other. I don't know what the remainder of this rambling abode looked like, for I never saw any of it except the kitchen.)

MARY: What's so funny? What you laughing at?

TC: Nothing. It's just this Peruvian tobacco, my cherub. I take it Mr. Berkowitz is an equestrian?

PARROT: *Oy vey! Oy vey!*

MARY: Shut up! Before I wring your damn neck.

TC: Now, if we're going to curse . . . (Mary mumbles; crosses herself) Does the critter have a name?

MARY: Uh-huh. Try and guess.

TC: Polly.

MARY (truly surprised): How'd you know that?

TC: So she's a female.

MARY: That's a girl's name, so she must be a girl. Whatever she is, she's a bitch. Just look at all that crap on the floor. All for me to clean it up.

TC: Language, language.

POLLY: Holy cow!

MARY: My nerves. Maybe we better have a little lift. (Out comes the tin box, the roaches, the roach-holder, matches) And let's see what we can locate in the kitchen. I'm feeling real munchie.

(The interior of the Berkowitz refrigerator is a glutton's fantasy, a cornucopia of fattening goodies. Small wonder the master of the house has such jowls. "Oh yes," confirms Mary, "they're both hogs. Her stomach. She looks like she's about to drop the Dionne quintuplets. And all his suits are tailor-made: nothing store-bought could fit him. Hmm, yummy, I sure do feel munchie. Those coconut cupcakes look desirable. And that mocha cake, I wouldn't mind a hunk of that. We could dump some ice cream on it." Huge soup bowls are found, and Mary masses them with cupcakes and mocha cake and fist-sized scoops of pistachio ice cream. We return to the parlor with this banquet and fall upon it like abused orphans. There's nothing like grass to grow an appetite. After finishing off the first helping, and fueling ourselves with more roaches, Mary refills the bowls with even heftier portions.)

MARY: How you feel?

TC: I feel good.

MARY: How good?

TC: Real good.

MARY: Tell me exactly how you feel.

TC: I'm in Australia.

MARY: Ever been to Austria?

TC: Not Austria. Australia. No, but that's where I am now. And everybody always said what a dull place it is. Shows what they know! Greatest surfing in the world. I'm out in the ocean on a surfboard riding a wave high as a, as a—

MARY: High as you. Ha-ha.

TC: It's made of melting emeralds. The wave. The sun is hot on my back, and the spray is salting my face, and there are hungry sharks all around me. *Blue Water, White Death.* Wasn't that a terrific movie? Hungry white man-eaters everywhere, but they don't worry me—frankly, I don't give a fuck . . .

MARY (eyes wide with fear): Watch for the sharks! They

got killer teeth. You'll be crippled for life. You'll be begging
on street corners.

TC: Music!

MARY: Music! That's the ticket.

(She weaves like a groggy wrestler toward a gargoyle
object that had heretofore happily escaped my attention:
a mahogany console combining television, phonograph,
and a radio. She fiddles with the radio until she finds a
station booming music with a Latin beat.

Her hips maneuver, her fingers snap, she is elegant
yet smoothly abandoned, as if recalling a sensuous youthful night, and dancing with a phantom partner some
remembered choreography. And it is magic, how her now-
ageless body responds to the drums and guitars, contours
itself to the subtlest rhythm: she is in a trance, the state
of grace saints supposedly achieve when experiencing
visions. And I am hearing the music, too; it is speeding
through me like amphetamine—each note ringing with
the separate clarity of cathedral chimings on a silent
winter Sunday. I move toward her, and into her arms,
and we match each other step for step, laughing, undulating, and even when the music is interrupted by an
announcer speaking Spanish as rapid as the rattle of cas-
tanets, we continue dancing, for the guitars are locked in
our heads now, as we are locked in our laughter, our
embrace: louder and louder, so loud that we are unaware
of a key clicking, a door opening and shutting. But the
parrot hears it.)

POLLY: Holy cow!

WOMAN'S VOICE: What is this? What's happening here?

POLLY: *Oy vey! Oy vey!*

MARY: Why, hello there, Mrs. Berkowitz. Mr. Berkowitz.
How ya doin'?

(And there they are, hovering in view like the Mickey and Minnie Mouse balloons in a Macy's Thanksgiving Day parade. Not that there's anything mousey about this twosome. Their infuriated eyes, hers hot behind harlequin spectacles with sequined frames, absorb the scene: our naughty ice-cream mustaches, the pungent roach smoke polluting the premises. Mr. Berkowitz stalks over and stops the radio.)

MRS. BERKOWITZ: Who is this man?

MARY: I din't think you was home.

MRS. BERKOWITZ: Obviously. I asked you: Who is this man?

MARY: He's just a friend of mine. Helping me out. I got so much work today.

MR. BERKOWITZ: You're drunk, woman.

MARY (deceptively sweet): How's that you say?

MRS. BERKOWITZ: He said you're drunk. I'm shocked. Truly.

MARY: Since we're speaking truly, what I have truly to say to you is: today is my last day of playing nigger around here— I'm giving you notice.

MRS. BERKOWITZ: You are giving *me* notice?

MR. BERKOWITZ: Get out of here! Before we call the police.

(Without ado, we gather our belongings. Mary waves at the parrot: "So long, Polly. You're okay. You're good girl. I was only kidding." And at the front door, where her former employers have sternly stationed themselves, she announces: "Just for the record, I've never touched a drop in my life."

Downstairs, the rain is still going. We trudge along Park Avenue, then cut across to Lexington.)

MARY: Didn't I tell you they were stuffy.

TC: Belong in a museum.

(But most of our buoyancy has departed; the power of the Peruvian foliage recedes, a letdown has set in, my surfboard is sinking, and any sharks sighted now would scare the piss out of me.)

MARY: I still got Mrs. Kronkite to do. But she's nice; she'll forgive me if I don't come till tomorrow. Maybe I'll head on home.

TC: Let me catch you a cab.

MARY: I hate to give them my business. Those taxi people don't like coloreds. Even when they're colored themselves. No, I can get the subway down here at Lex and Eighty-sixth.

(Mary lives in a rent-controlled apartment near Yankee Stadium; she says it was cramped when she had a family living with her, but now that she's by herself, it seems immense and dangerous: "I've got three locks on every door, and all the windows nailed down. I'd buy me a police dog if it didn't mean leaving him by himself so much. I know what it is to be alone, and I wouldn't wish it on a dog.")

TC: Please, Mary, let me treat you to a taxi.

MARY: The subway's a lot quicker. But there's someplace I want to stop. It's just down here a ways.

(The place is a narrow church pinched between broad buildings on a side street. Inside, there are two brief rows of pews, and a small altar with a plaster figure of a crucified Jesus suspended above it. An odor of incense and candle wax dominates the gloom. At the altar a woman is lighting a candle, its light fluttering like the sleep of a fitful spirit; otherwise, we are the only supplicants present. We kneel together in the last pew, and from the satchel Mary produces a pair of rosary beads— "I always carry a couple extra"—one for herself, the other for me, though I don't know quite how to handle it, never having used one before. Mary's lips move whisperingly.)

MARY: Dear Lord, in your mercy. Please, Lord, help Mr. Trask to stop boozing and get his job back. Please, Lord, don't leave Miss Shaw a bookworm and an old maid; she ought to bring your children into this world. And, Lord, I beg you to remember my sons and daughter and my grandchildren, each and every one. And please don't let Mr. Smith's family send him to that retirement home; he don't want to go, he cries all the time . . .

(Her list of names is more numerous than the beads on her rosary, and her requests in their behalf have the earnest shine of the altar's candle-flame. She pauses to glance at me.)

MARY: Are you praying?

TC: Yes.

MARY: I can't hear you.

TC: I'm praying for you, Mary. I want you to live forever.

MARY: Don't pray for me. I'm already saved. (She takes my hand and holds it) Pray for your mother. Pray for all those souls lost out there in the dark. Pedro. Pedro.

Two

✣

Hello, Stranger

Time: December 1977.

Place: A New York restaurant, The Four Seasons.

The man who had invited me to lunch, George Claxton, had suggested we meet at noon, and made no excuse for setting such an early hour. I soon discovered the reason, however; in the year or more since I had last seen him, George Claxton, heretofore a man moderately abstemious, had become a two-fisted drinker. As soon as we were seated he ordered a double Wild Turkey ("Just straight, please; no ice"), and within fifteen minutes requested an encore.

I was surprised, and not just by the urgency of his thirst. He had gained at least thirty pounds; the buttons of his pin-stripe vest seemed on the verge of popping loose, and his skin color, usually ruddy from jogging or tennis, had an alien pallor, as though he had just emerged from a penitentiary. Also, he was sporting dark glasses, and I thought: How theatrical! Imagine good old plain George Claxton, solidly entrenched Wall Street fellow living in Greenwich or Westport or wherever it was with a wife named Gertrude or Alice or whatever it was, with three or four or five children, imagine this guy chugging double Wild Turkeys and wearing dark glasses!

It was all I could do not to ask straight out: Well, what the hell happened to you? But I said: "How are you, George?"

GEORGE: Fine. Fine. Christmas. Jesus. Just can't keep up with it. Don't expect a card from me this year. I'm not sending any.

TC: Really? Your cards seemed such a tradition. Those family things, with dogs. And how is your family?

GEORGE: Growing. My oldest daughter just had her second baby. A girl.

TC: Congratulations.

GEORGE: Well, we wanted a boy. If it had been a boy, she would have named him after me.

TC (thinking: Why am I here? Why am I having lunch with this jerk? He bores me, he's always bored me): And Alice? How is Alice?

GEORGE: Alice?

TC: I mean Gertrude.

GEORGE (frowning, peevish): She's painting. You know our house is right there on the Sound. Have our own little beach. She stays locked in her room all day painting what she sees from the window. Boats.

TC: That's nice.

GEORGE: I'm not so sure. She was a Smith girl; majored in art. She did a little painting before we were married. Then she forgot about it. Seemed to. Now she paints all the time. *All the time*. Stays locked in her room. Waiter, could you send the maître d' over with a menu? And bring me another of these things. No ice.

TC: That's very British, isn't it? Neat whiskey without ice.

GEORGE: I'm having root-canal. Anything cold hurts my teeth. You know who I got a Christmas card from? Mickey Manolo. The rich kid from Caracas? He was in our class.

(Of course, I didn't remember Mickey Manolo, but I nodded and pretended yes, yes. Nor would I have re-membered George Claxton if he hadn't kept careful track of me for forty-odd years, ever since we had been students together at an especially abysmal prep school. He was a straight-arrow athletic kid from an upper-middle-class Pennsylvania family; we had nothing in common, but we stumbled into an alliance because in exchange for my writing all his book reports and English compositions, he did my algebra homework and during examinations slipped me the answers. As a result, I had been stuck for four decades with a "friendship" that demanded a duty lunch every year or two.)

TC: You very seldom see women in this restaurant.

GEORGE: That's what I like about it. Not a lot of gibbering broads. It has a nice masculine look. You know, I don't think I'll have anything to eat. My teeth. It hurts too much to chew.

TC: Poached eggs?

GEORGE: There's something I'd like to tell you. Maybe you could give me a little advice.

TC: People who take my advice usually regret it. However . . .

GEORGE: This started last June. Just after Jeffrey's graduation —he's my youngest boy. It was a Saturday and Jeff and I were down on our little beach painting a boat. Jeff went up to the house to get us some beer and sandwiches, and while he was gone I suddenly stripped down and went for a swim. The water was still too cold. You can't really swim in the Sound much before July. But I just felt like it.

I swam out quite a ways and was lying there floating on my back and looking at my house. It's really a great house—six-car garage, swimming pool, tennis courts; too bad we've never been able to get you out there. Anyway, I was floating on my back feeling pretty good about life when I noticed this bottle bobbing in the water.

It was a clear-glass bottle that had contained some kind of soda pop. Someone had stoppered it with a cork and sealed it with adhesive tape. But I could see there was a piece of paper inside, a note. It made me laugh; I used to do that when I was a kid—stuff messages in bottles and throw them in the water: *Help! Man Lost at Sea!*

So I grabbed the bottle and swam ashore. I was curious to see what was inside it. Well, it was a note dated a month earlier, and it was written by a girl who lived in Larchmont. It said: *Hello, stranger. My name is Linda Reilly and I am twelve years old. If you find this letter please write and let me know when and where you found it. If you do I will send you a box of homemade fudge.*

The thing is, when Jeff came back with our sandwiches I didn't mention the bottle. I don't know why, but I didn't. Now I wish I had. Maybe then nothing would have happened. But it was like a little secret I wanted to keep to myself. A joke.

TC: Are you sure you aren't hungry? I'm only having an omelette.

GEORGE: Okay. An omelette, very soft.

TC: And so you wrote this young lady, Miss Reilly?

GEORGE (hesitantly): Yes. Yes, I did.

TC: What did you say?

GEORGE: On Monday, when I was back in my office, I was checking through my briefcase and I found the note. I say "found" because I don't remember putting it there. It had vaguely crossed my mind I'd drop the kid a card—just a nice gesture, you know. But that day I had lunch with a client who likes martinis. Now, I never used to drink at lunch—nor much any other time, either. But I had two martinis, and I went back to the office feeling swivel-headed. So I wrote this little girl quite a long letter; I didn't dictate it, I wrote it in longhand and told her where I lived and how I'd found her bottle and wished her luck and said some dumb thing like that though I was a stranger, I sent her the affectionate wishes of a friend.

TC: A two-martini missive. Still, where's the harm?

GEORGE: Silver Bullets. That's what they call martinis. Silver Bullets.

TC: How about that omelette? Aren't you even going to touch it?

GEORGE: Jesus Christ! My teeth *hurt*.

TC: It's really quite good. For a restaurant omelette.

GEORGE: About a week later a big box of fudge arrived. Sent to my office. Chocolate fudge with pecans. I passed it around the office and told everybody my daughter had made it. One of the guys said: "Oh, yeah! I'll bet old George has a secret girl friend."

TC: And did she send a letter with the fudge?

GEORGE: No. But I wrote a thank-you note. Very brief. Have you got a cigarette?

TC: I stopped smoking years ago.

GEORGE: Well, I just started. I still don't buy them, though.

Just bum one now and then. Waiter, could you bring me a pack of cigarettes? Doesn't matter what brand, as long as it isn't menthol. And another Wild Turkey, please?

TC: I'd like some coffee.

GEORGE: But I got an answer to my thank-you note. A long letter. It really threw me. She enclosed a picture of herself. A color Polaroid. She was wearing a bathing suit and standing on a beach. She may have been twelve, but she looked sixteen. A lovely kid with short curly black hair and the bluest eyes.

TC: Shades of Humbert Humbert.

GEORGE: Who?

TC: Nothing. A character in a novel.

GEORGE: I never read novels. I hate to read.

TC: Yes, I know. After all, I used to do all your book reports. So what did Miss Linda Reilly have to say?

GEORGE (after pausing a full five seconds): It was very sad. Touching. She said she hadn't been living in Larchmont very long, and that she had no friends, and that she had tossed dozens of bottles into the water, but that I was the only person who had found one and answered. She said she was from Wisconsin, but that her father had died and her mother had married a man who had three daughters of his own and that none of them liked her. It was a ten-page letter, no misspellings. She said a lot of intelligent things. But she sounded really miserable. She said she hoped I'd write again, and maybe I could drive over to Larchmont and we could meet someplace. Do you mind listening to all this? If you do . . .

TC: Please. Go ahead.

GEORGE: I kept the picture. In fact, I put it in my wallet. Along with snaps of my other kids. See, because of the letter, I started to think of her as one of my own children. I couldn't get the letter out of my mind. And that night, when I took the train home, I did something I'd done only a very few times. I went into the club car and ordered myself a couple of stiff drinks and read the letter over and over. Memorized it, practically. Then when I got home I told my wife I had some office work to do. I shut myself in my den and started a letter to Linda. I wrote until midnight.

TC: Were you drinking all this time?

GEORGE (surprised): Why?

TC: It might have some bearing on what you wrote.

GEORGE: Yes, I was drinking, and I guess maybe it was a pretty emotional letter. But I felt so upset about this kid. I really wanted to help her. I wrote her about some of the troubles my own kids had had. About Harriet's acne and how she never had a single boyfriend. Not till she had her skin-peel. I told her about the hard times I'd had when I was growing up.

TC: Oh? I thought you'd enjoyed the ideal life of an ideal American youth.

GEORGE: I let people see what I wanted them to see. Inside was a different story.

TC: Had me fooled.

GEORGE: Around midnight my wife knocked on the door. She wanted to know if anything was wrong, and I told her to go back to bed, I had an urgent business letter to finish, and when it was finished I was going to drive down to the post office. She said why couldn't it wait until morning, it's after twelve. I lost my temper. Married thirty years, and I could count on ten fingers the times I've lost my temper with her. Gertrude is a wonderful, wonderful woman. I love her heart and soul. I do, goddamnit! But I shouted at her: No, it can't wait. It has to go tonight. It's very important.

(A waiter handed George a pack of cigarettes already

opened. He stuck one in his mouth, and the waiter lit it
for him, which was just as well, for his fingers were too
agitated to hold a match without endangering himself.)
And Jesus Christ, it *was* important. Because I felt if I didn't
mail the letter that night, I never would. Maybe, sober, I'd
think it was too personal or something. And here was this
lonely unhappy kid who'd shown me her heart: how would
she feel if she never heard one word from me? No. I got
in my car and drove down to the post office and as soon as I'd
mailed the letter, dropped it into the slot, I felt too tired to
drive home. I fell asleep in the car. It was dawn when I woke
up, but my wife was asleep and she didn't notice when I
came in.

I just about had time to shave and change my clothes
before rushing off to catch the train. While I was shaving,
Gertrude came into the bathroom. She was smiling; she
hadn't mentioned my little temper tantrum. But she had my
wallet in her hand, and she said, "George, I'm going to have
Jeff's graduation picture enlarged for your mother," and with
that she started shuffling through all the pictures in my
wallet. I didn't think anything about it until suddenly she
said: "Who is this girl?"

TC: And it was the young lady from Larchmont.

GEORGE: I should have told her the whole story right then.
But I . . . Anyway, I said it was the daughter of one of my
commuter friends. I said he'd been showing it to some of the
guys on the train, and he'd forgot and left it on the bar. So I'd
put it in my wallet to return the next time I saw him.

Garçon, un autre de Wild Turkey, s'il vous plaît.

TC (to the waiter): Make that a single.

GEORGE (in a tone unpleasantly pleasant): Are you telling me
I've had too much to drink?

TC: If you have to go back to the office, yes.

GEORGE: But I'm not going back to my office. I haven't been there since early November. I'm supposed to have had a nervous breakdown. Overwork. Exhaustion. I'm supposed to be resting quietly at home, tenderly cared for by my adoring wife. Who is locked in her room painting pictures of boats. A boat. The same damn boat over and over.

TC: George, I've got to take a leak.

GEORGE: Not running out on me? Not running out on your old school buddy that sneaked you all the algebra answers?

TC: And even so, I flunked! Be back in a jiffy.

> (I didn't need to take a leak; I needed to collect my thoughts. I didn't have the nerve to steal out of there and hide in a quiet movie somewhere, but I sure as hell didn't want to go back to that table. I washed my hands and combed my hair. Two men came in and stationed themselves at urinals. One said: "That guy that's so loaded. For a moment I thought it was somebody I know." His friend said: "Well, he's not a complete stranger. That's George Claxton." "You're kidding!" "I ought to know. He used to be my boss." "But my God! What happened?" "There are different stories." Then both men fell silent, perhaps out of deference to my presence. I returned to the dining room.)

GEORGE: So you *didn't* cut out?

> (Actually, he seemed more subdued, less intoxicated. He was able to strike a match and light a cigarette with reasonable competence.)

Are you ready to hear the rest of this?

TC: (Silent, but with an encouraging nod.)

GEORGE: My wife didn't say anything, just tucked the picture back in my wallet. I went on shaving, but cut myself twice. It had been so long since I'd had a real hangover, I'd forgotten what it was like. The sweat; my stomach—it felt like I was trying to shit razor blades. I stuffed a bottle of bourbon in my briefcase, and as soon as I got on the train I headed straight for the john. The first thing I did was to tear up the picture and drop it in the toilet. Then I sat down on the toilet and opened up that bottle. At first it made me gag. And it was hot as hell in there. Like Hades. But after a while I began to calm down, and to wonder: Well, what am I in such a stew about? I haven't done anything wrong. But when I stood up I saw that the torn-up Polaroid was still floating in the toilet bowl. I flushed it, and the pieces of the picture, her head and legs and arms, started churning around, and it made me dizzy: I felt like a killer who had taken a knife and cut her up.

By the time we got to Grand Central, I knew I was in no state to handle the office, so I walked over to the Yale Club and took a room. I called my secretary and said I had to go to Washington and wouldn't be in till the next day. Then I called home and told my wife that something had come up, a business thing, and I'd be staying overnight at the club. Then I got into bed, and thought: I'll sleep all day; I'll have one good long drink to relax me, stop the jitters, and go to sleep. But I couldn't—not until I'd downed the whole bottle. Boy, did I sleep then! Until around ten the next morning.

TC: About twenty hours.

GEORGE: About that. But I was feeling fairly okay when I woke up. They have a great masseur at the Yale Club, a German, hands strong as a gorilla's. That guy can really fix you up. So I had some sauna, a real storm-trooper massage, and fifteen minutes under a freezing shower. I stayed on and ate lunch at the club. No drinks, but boy, did I wolf it down. Four lamb chops, two baked potatoes, creamed spinach, corn-on-the-cob, a quart of milk, two deep-dish blueberry pies . . .

TC: I wish you'd eat something now.

GEORGE (a sharp bark, startlingly rude): Shut up!

TC: (Silence)

GEORGE: I'm sorry. I mean, it was like I was talking to myself. Like I'd forgotten you were here. And your voice . . .

TC: I understand. Anyway, you had a hearty lunch and you were feeling good.

GEORGE: Indeed. Indeed. The condemned man had a hearty lunch. Cigarette?

TC: I don't smoke.

GEORGE: That's right. Don't smoke. Haven't smoked for years.

TC: Here, I'll light that for you.

GEORGE: I'm perfectly capable of coping with a match without blowing up the place, thank you.

Well now, where were we? Oh yes, the condemned man was on his way to his office, subdued and shining.

It was Wednesday, the second week in July, a scorcher. I was alone in my office when my secretary rang through and said a Miss Reilly was on the phone. I didn't make the connection right off, and said: Who? What does she want? And my secretary said she says it's personal. The penny dropped. I said: Oh yes, put her on.

And I heard: "Mr. Claxton, this is Linda Reilly. I got your letter. It's the nicest letter I've ever had. I feel you really are a friend, and that's why I decided to take a chance on calling you. I was hoping you could help me. Because something has happened, and I don't know what I'll do if you can't help me." She had a sweet young-girl's voice, but was so breathless, so excited, that I had to ask her to speak more slowly. "I don't have much time, Mr. Claxton. I'm calling from upstairs and my mother might pick up the phone downstairs any minute. The thing is, I have a dog. Jimmy. He's six years old but frisky as can be. I've had him since I was a little girl, and he's the only thing I have. He's a real gent, just the cutest little dog you ever saw. But my mother is going to have him put to sleep. I'll die! I'll just die. Mr. Claxton, please, can you come to Larchmont and meet me in front of the Safeway? I'll have Jimmy with me, and you can take him away with you. Hide him until we can figure out what to do. I can't talk any more. My mother's coming up the stairs. I'll call you first chance I get tomorrow and we can make a date—"

TC: What did *you* say?

GEORGE: Nothing. She'd hung up.

TC: But what *would* you have said?

GEORGE: Well, as soon as she hung up, I decided that when she called back I'd say yes. Yes, I'd help the poor kid save her dog. That didn't mean I had to take it home with me. I could have put it in a kennel, or something. And if matters had turned out differently, that's what I would have done.

TC: I see. But she never called back.

GEORGE: Waiter, I'll have another one of these dark things. And a glass of Perrier, please. Yes, she called. And what she had to say was very brief. "Mr. Claxton, I'm sorry; I sneaked into a neighbor's house to phone, and I've got to hurry. My mother found your letters last night, the letters you wrote me. She's crazy, and her husband's crazy, too. They think all kinds of terrible things, and she took Jimmy away first thing this morning, but I can't talk any more; I'll try to call later."

But I didn't hear from her again—at least, not personally. My wife phoned a few hours later; I'd say it was about three in the afternoon. She said: "Darling, please come home as soon as you can," and her voice was so calm that I knew she was in extreme distress; I even half-knew why, although I acted surprised when she told me: "There are two policemen here. One from Larchmont and one from the village. They want to talk to you. They won't tell me why."

I didn't bother with the train. I hired a limousine. One of those limousines with a bar installed. It's not much of a drive, just over an hour, but I managed to knock down quite a few Silver Bullets. It didn't help much; I was really scared.

TC: Why, for Christ's sake? What had you done? Play Mr. Good Guy, Mr. Pen Pal.

GEORGE: If only it were that neat. That tidy. Anyway, when I got home the cops were sitting in the living room watching television. My wife was serving them coffee. When she offered to leave the room, I said no, I want you to stay and hear this, whatever it is. Both the cops were very young and embarrassed. After all, I was a rich man, a prominent citizen, a churchgoer, the father of five children. I wasn't frightened of them. It was Gertrude.

The Larchmont cop outlined the situation. His office had received a complaint from a Mr. and Mrs. Henry Wilson that their twelve-year-old daughter, Linda Reilly, had been receiving letters of a "suspicious nature" from a fifty-two-year-old man, namely, me, and the Wilsons intended to bring charges if I couldn't explain myself satisfactorily.

I laughed. Oh, I was just as jovial as Santa Claus. I told the whole story. About finding the bottle. Said I'd only answered it because I liked chocolate fudge. I had them grinning, apologizing, shuffling their big feet, and saying well, you know how parents get nutty ideas nowadays. The only one not taking it all as a dumb joke was Gertrude. In fact, without my realizing it, she'd left the room before I'd finished talking.

After the cops left, I knew where I'd find her. In that room, the one where she does her painting. It was dark and she was sitting there in a straight-back chair staring out at the darkness. She said: "The picture in your wallet. That was the girl." I denied it, and she said: "Please, George. You don't have to lie. You'll never have to lie again."

And she slept in that room that night, and every night ever since. Keeps herself locked in there painting boats. A boat.

TC: Perhaps you did behave a bit recklessly. But I can't see why she should be so unforgiving.

GEORGE: I'll tell you why. That wasn't our first visit from the police.

Seven years ago we had a sudden heavy snowstorm. I was driving my car, and even though I wasn't far from home, I lost my way several times. I asked directions from a number of people. One was a child, a young girl. A few days later the police came to the house. I wasn't there, but they talked to Gertrude. They told her that during the recent snowstorm a man answering my description and driving a Buick with my license plate had got out of his car and exposed himself to a young girl. Spoken lewdly to her. The girl said she had copied down the license number in the snow under a tree, and when the storm had stopped, it was still decipherable. There was no denying that it was my license number, but the story was untrue. I convinced Gertrude, and I convinced the police, that the girl was either lying or that she had made a mistake concerning the number.

But now the police have come a second time. About another young girl.

And so my wife stays in her room. Painting. Because she doesn't believe me. She believes that the girl who wrote the number in the snow told the truth. I'm innocent. Before God, on the heads of my children, I am innocent. But my wife locks her door and looks out the window. She doesn't believe me. Do you?

(George removed his dark glasses and polished them

with a napkin. Now I understood why he wore them. It wasn't because of the yellowed whites engraved with swollen red veins. It was because his eyes were like a pair of shattered prisms. I have never seen pain, a suffering, so permanently implanted, as if the slip of a surgeon's knife had left him forever disfigured. It was unbearable, and as he stared at me my own eyes flinched away.)

Do *you* believe me?

TC (reaching across the table and taking his hand, holding it for dear life): Of course, George. Of course I believe you.

Three

❧

Hidden Gardens

Scene: Jackson Square, named after Andrew Jackson—a three-hundred-year-old oasis complacently centered inside New Orleans' old quarter: a moderate-sized park dominated by the grey towers of St. Louis Cathedral, and the oldest, in some ways most somberly elegant, apartment houses in America, the Pontalba Buildings.

Time: 26 March 1979, an exuberant spring day. Bougainvillaea descends, azaleas thrust, hawkers hawk (peanuts, roses, horse-drawn carriage rides, fried shrimp in paper scoops), the horns of drifting ships hoot on the closeby Mississippi, and happy balloons, attached to giggling skipping children, bounce high in the blue silvery air.

"Well, I do declare, a boy sure do get around"—as my Uncle Bud, who was a traveling salesman when he could pry himself away from his porch swing and gin fizzes long enough to travel, used to complain. Yes, indeed, a boy sure do get around; in just the last several months I've been in Denver, Cheyenne, Butte, Salt Lake City, Vancouver, Seattle, Portland, Los Angeles, Boston, Toronto, Washington, Miami. But if somebody asked, I'd probably say, and really think: Why, I haven't been anywhere, I've just been in New York all winter.

Still, a boy do get around. And now here I am back in New Orleans, my birthplace, my old hometown. Sunning myself on a park bench in Jackson Square, always, since schoolboy days, a favorite place to stretch my legs and look and listen, to yawn and scratch and dream and talk to myself. Maybe you're one of those people who never talk to themselves. Aloud, I mean. Maybe you think only crazies do that. Personally, I consider it's a healthy thing. To keep yourself company that way: nobody to argue back, free to rant along, getting a lot of stuff out of your system.

For instance, take those Pontalba Buildings over there. Pretty fancy places, with their grillwork façades and tall dark French-shuttered windows. The first apartment houses ever built in the U.S.A.; relatives of the original occupants of those high airy aristocratic rooms are still living in them. For a long time I had a grudge against the Pontalba. Here's why. Once, when I was nineteen or so, I had an apartment a few blocks away on Royal Street, an insignificant, decrepit, roach-heaven apartment that erupted into earthquake shivers every time a streetcar clickety-clacked by on the narrow street outside. It was unheated; in the winter one dreaded getting out of bed, and during the swampy summers it was like swimming inside a bowl of tepid consommé. My constant fantasy was that one excellent day I would move out of that dump and into the celestial confines of the Pontalba. But even if I had been able to afford it, it could never have happened. The usual way of acquiring a place there is if a tenant dies and wills it to you; or, if an apartment should become vacant, generally it is the custom of the city of New Orleans to offer it to a distinguished local citizen for a very nominal fee.

A lot of fey folk have strolled about this square. Pirates. Lafitte himself. Bonnie Parker and Clyde Barrow. Huey Long. Or, moseying under the shade of a scarlet parasol, the Countess Willie Piazza, the proprietress of one of the ritzier *maisons de plaisir* in the red-light neighborhood: her house was famous for an exotic refreshment it offered—fresh cherries boiled in cream sweetened with absinthe and served stuffed inside the vagina of a reclining quadroon beauty. Or another lady, so unlike the Countess Willie: Annie Christmas, a female keelboat operator who was seven feet tall and was often observed toting a hundred-pound barrel of flour under either arm. And Jim Bowie. And Mr. Neddie Flanders, a dapper gentleman in his eighties, maybe nineties, who, until recent years, appeared in the square each evening, and accompanying himself on a harmonica, tap-danced from midnight until dawn in the most delicate, limber-puppet way. The *characters*. I could list hundreds.

Uh-oh. What's this I hear across the way? Trouble. A ruckus. A man and a woman, both black: the man is heavy-set, bull-necked, smartly coiffed but withal weak-mannered; she is thin, lemon-colored, shrill, but almost pretty.

HER: Sombitch. What you mean—hold out bread?! I ain't hold out no bread. Sombitch.

HIM: Hush, woman. I seen you. I counted. Three guys. Makes sixty bucks. You onna gimme thirty.

HER: Damn you, nigger. I oughta take a razor on your ear. I oughta cut out your liver and feed the cats. I oughta fry your eyes in turpentine. Listen, nigger. Let me hear you call me a liar again.

HIM (placating): Sugar—

HER: *Sugar.* I'll sugar you.

HIM: Miss Myrtle, now I knows what I seen.

HER (slowly: a serpentine drawl): Bastard. Nigger bastard. Fact is, you never had no mother. You was born out of a dog's ass.

> (She slaps him. Hard. Turns and walks off, head high. He doesn't follow, but stands with a hand rubbing his cheek.)

For a while I watch the prancing spring-spry balloon children and see them greedily gather around a pushcart salesman selling a concoction known as Sweetmouth: scoops of flaked ice flavored with a rainbow-variety of colored syrups. Suddenly I recognize that I am hungry, too, and thirsty. I consider walking over to the French Market and filling up on deep-fried doughnuts and that bitter delicious chicory-flavored coffee peculiar to New Orleans. It's better than anything on the menu at Antoine's—which, by the way, is a lousy restaurant. So are most of the city's famous eateries. Gallatoire's isn't bad, but it's too crowded; they don't accept reservations, you always have to wait in long lines, and it's not worth it, at least not to me. Just as I've decided to amble off to the Market, an interruption occurs.

Now, if there is one thing I hate, it's people who sneak up behind you and say—

VOICE (whiskey-husky, virile, but female): Two guesses. (Silence) Come on, Jockey. You know it's me. (Silence; then, removing her blindfolding hands, somewhat petulantly)

Jockey, you mean you didn't know it was *me*? Junebug?

TC: As I breathe—Big Junebug Johnson! *Comment ça va?*

BIG JUNEBUG JOHNSON (giggling with merriment): Oh, don't let me *commence*. Stand up, boy. Give old Junebug a hug. My, you're skinny. Like the first time I saw you. How much you weigh, Jockey?

TC: One twenty-five. Twenty-six.

(It is difficult to get my arms around her, for she weighs double that; more. I've known her going on forty years— ever since I lived alone at the gloomy Royal Street address and used to frequent a raucous waterfront bar she owned, and still does. If she had pink eyes, one might call her an albino, for her skin is white as calla lilies; so is her curly, skimpy hair. [Once she told me her hair had turned white overnight, before she was sixteen, and when I said "*Overnight?*" she said: "It was the roller-coaster ride and Ed Jenkins' peter. The two things coming so close together. See, one night I was riding on a roller- coaster out at the lake, and we were in the last car. Well, it came uncoupled, the car ran wild, we damn near fell off the track, and the next morning my hair had grey freckles. About a week later I had this experience with Ed Jenkins, a kid I knew. One of my girl friends told me that her brother had told her Ed Jenkins had the biggest peter anybody ever saw. He was nice-looking, but a scrawny fellow, not much taller than you, and I didn't believe it, so one day, joking him, I said, 'Ed Jenkins, I hear you have one helluva peter,' and he said, 'Yeah, I'll show you,' and he did, and I screamed; he said, 'And now I'm gonna put it in you,' and I said, 'Oh no you ain't!'—it was big as a baby's arm holding an apple. Lord's mercy! But he did. Put it in me. After a terrific tussle. And I was a virgin. Just about. Kind of. So you can imagine. Well, it wasn't long after that my hair went white like a witch."]

B.J.J. dresses stevedore-style: overalls, men's blue shirts rolled up to the elbow, ankle-high lace-up workman's boots, and no makeup to relieve her pallor. But she is womanly, a dignified figure for all her down-to-earth ways. And she wears expensive perfumes, Parisian smells bought at the Maison Blanche on Canal Street. Also, she has a glorious gold-toothed smile; it's like a heartening sunburst after a cold rainfall. You'd probably like her; most people do. Those who don't are mainly the proprietors of rival waterfront bars, for Big Junebug's is a popular hangout, if little known beyond the waterfront and that area's denizens. It contains three rooms—the big barroom itself with its mammoth zinc-topped bar, a second chamber furnished with three busy pool tables, and an alcove with a jukebox for dancing. It's open right around the clock, and is as crowded at dawn as it is at twilight. Of course, sailors and dockworkers go there, and the truck farmers who bring their produce to the French Market from outlying parishes, cops and firemen and hard-eyed gamblers and harder-eyed floozies, and around sunrise the place overflows with entertainers from the Bourbon Street tourist traps. Topless dancers, strippers, drag queens, B-girls, waiters, bartenders, and the hoarse-voiced doormen-barkers who so stridently labor to lure yokels into *vieux carré* sucker dives.

As for this "Jockey" business, it was a nickname I owed to Ginger Brennan. Forty-some years ago Ginger was the chief counterman at the old original all-night doughnuts-and-coffee café in the Market; that particular café is gone now, and Ginger was long ago killed by a bolt of lightning while fishing off a pier at Lake Pont-

chartrain. Anyway, one night I overheard another customer ask Ginger who the "little punk" was in the corner,
and Ginger, who was a pathological liar, bless his heart,
told him I was a professional jockey: "He's pretty hot
stuff out at the race track." It was plausible enough; I was
short and featherweight and could easily have posed as a
jockey; as it happened, it was a fantasy I cottoned to: I
liked the idea of people mistaking me for a wise-guy
race-track character. I started reading *Racing Form* and
learned the lingo. Word spread, and before you could
say Boo! everybody was calling me "The Jockey" and
soliciting tips on the horses.)

BIG JUNEBUG JOHNSON: I lost weight myself. Maybe fifty
pounds. Ever since I got married, I been losing weight. Most
ladies, they get the ring, then start swelling up. But after I
snagged Jim, I was so happy I stopped cleaning out my
icebox. The blues, that's what makes you fat.

TC: Big Junebug Johnson married? Nobody wrote me that. I
thought you were a devout bachelor.

BIG JUNEBUG JOHNSON: Can't a gal change her mind? Once
I got over the Ed Jenkins incident, once I got that view out of
my noggin, I was partial as the next lady for men. 'Course,
that took years.

TC: Jim? That's his name?

BIG JUNEBUG JOHNSON: Jim O'Reilly. Ain't Irish, though. He
comes from Plaquemine, and they're mostly Cajun, his people. I don't even know if that's his right name. I don't know a
whole lot about him. He's kind of quiet.

TC: But some lover. To catch you.

BIG JUNEBUG JOHNSON (eyes rotating): Oh, honey, don't let
me *commence*.

TC (laughs): That's one of the things I remember best about
you. No matter what anybody said, whether it was the

weather or whatever, you always said: "Oh, honey, don't let me *commence.*"

BIG JUNEBUG JOHNSON: Well. That kind of covers it all, wouldn't you say?

(Something I ought to have mentioned: she has a Brooklyn accent. If this sounds odd, it's not. Half the people in New Orleans don't sound Southern at all; close your eyes, and you would imagine you were listening to a taxi driver from Bensonhurst, a phenomenon that supposedly stems from the speech patterns idiosyncratic to a sector of the city known as the Irish Channel, a quarter predominantly populated by the descendants of Emerald Isle immigrants.)

TC: Just how long have you been Mrs. O'Reilly?

BIG JUNEBUG JOHNSON: Three years next July. Actually, I didn't have much choice. I was real confused. He's a lot younger than me, maybe twenty years. And good-looking, my goodness. Catnip to the ladies. But he was plain crazy about me, followed my every footstep, every minute begging me to hitch up, said he'd jump off the levee if I didn't. And presents every day. One time a pair of pearl earrings. Natural-born pearls: I bit them and they didn't crack. And a whole litter of kittens. He didn't know cats make me sneeze; make my eyes swell up, too. Everybody warned me he was only after my money. Why else would a cutie like him want an old hag like me? But that didn't altogether figure 'cause he has a real good job with the Streckfus Steamship Company. But they said he was broke, and in a lot of trouble with Red Tibeaux and Ambrose Butterfield and all those gamblers. I asked him, and he said it was a lie, but it could've been true, there was a lot I didn't know about him, and still don't. All I do know is he never asked me for a dime. I was so confused. So I went to Augustine Genet. You recall Madame Genet? Who could

read the spirits? I heard she was on her deathbed, so I rushed
right over there, and sure enough she was sinking. A hundred
if she was a day, and blind as a mole; couldn't hardly whis-
per, but she told me: Marry that man, he's a good man, and
he'll make you happy—marry him, promise me you will. So I
promised. So that's why I had no choice. I couldn't ignore a
promise made to a lady on her deathbed. And I'm soooo glad
I didn't. *I am happy.* I am a happy woman. Even if those cats
do make me sneeze. And you, Jockey. You feel good about
yourself?

TC: So-so.

BIG JUNEBUG JOHNSON: When was the last time you got to
Mardi Gras?

TC (reluctant to reply, not desiring to evoke Mardi Gras
memories: they were not amusing events to me, the streets
swirling with drunken, squalling, shrouded figures wearing
bad-dream masks; I always had nightmares after childhood
excursions into Mardi Gras melees): Not since I was a kid. I
was always getting lost in the crowds. The last time I got lost
they took me to the police station. I was crying there all night
before my mother found me.

BIG JUNEBUG JOHNSON: The damn police! You know we
didn't have any Mardi Gras this year 'cause the police went
on strike. Imagine, going on strike at a time like that. Cost
this town millions. Blackmail is all it was. I've got some good
police friends, good customers. But they're all a bunch of
crooks, the entire shebang. I've never had no respect for the
law around here, and how they treated Mr. Shaw finished me
off for good. That so-called District Attorney *Jim* Garrison.
What a sorry sonofagun. I hope the devil turns him on a
slooow spit. And he will. Too bad Mr. Shaw won't be there to
see it. From up high in *heaven*, where I know he is, Mr. Shaw
won't be able to see old Garrison rotting in hell.

(B.J.J. is referring to Clay Shaw, a gentle, cultivated architect who was responsible for much of the finer-grade historical restoration in New Orleans. At one time Shaw was accused by James Garrison, the city's abrasive, publicity-deranged D.A., of being the key figure in a purported plot to assassinate President Kennedy. Shaw stood trial twice on this contrived charge, and though fully acquitted both times, he was left more or less bankrupt. His health failed, and he died several years ago.)

TC: After his last trial, Clay wrote me and said: "I've always thought I was a little paranoid, but having survived this, I know I never was, and know now I never will be."

BIG JUNEBUG JOHNSON: What is it—paranoid?

TC: Well. Oh, nothing. Paranoia's nothing. As long as you don't take it seriously.

BIG JUNEBUG JOHNSON: I sure do miss Mr. Shaw. All during his trouble, there was one way you could tell who was and who wasn't a gentleman in this town. A gentleman, when he passed Mr. Shaw on the street, tipped his hat; the bastards looked straight ahead. (Chuckling) Mr. Shaw, he was a card. Every time he come in my bar, he kept me laughing. Ever hear his Jesse James story? Seems one day Jesse James was robbing a train out West. Him and his gang barged into a car with their pistols drawn, and Jesse James shouts: "Hands up! We're gonna rob all the women and rape all the men." So this one fellow says: "Haven't you got that wrong, sir? Don't you mean you're gonna rob all the men and rape all the women?" But there was this sweet little fairy on the train, and he pipes up: "Mind your own business! Mr. James knows how to rob a train."

(Two and three and four: the hour-bells of St. Louis Cathedral toll: . . . five . . . six . . . The toll is grave, like a gilded baritone voice reciting, echoing ancient episodes,

a sound that drifts across the park as solemnly as the on-
coming dusk: music that mingles with the laughing
chatter, the optimistic farewells of the departing, sugar-
mouthed, balloon-toting kids, mingles with the solitary
grieving howl of a far-off shiphorn, and the jangling
springtime bells of the syrup-ice peddler's cart. Redun-
dantly, Big Junebug Johnson consults her big ugly Rolex
wristwatch.)

BIG JUNEBUG JOHNSON: Lord save us. I ought to be halfway
home. Jim has to have his supper on the table seven sharp,
and he won't let anybody fix it for him 'cept me. Don't ask
why. I can't cook worth an owl's ass, never could. Only thing
I could ever do real good was draw beer. And . . . Oh hell,
that reminds me: I'm on duty at the bar tonight. Usually now
I just work days, and Irma's there the rest of the time. But
one of Irma's little boys took sick, and she wants to be home
with him. See, I forgot to tell you, but I got a partner now, a
widow gal with a real sense of fun, and hard-working, too.
Irma was married to a chicken farmer, and he up and died,
leaving her with five little boys, two of them twins, and her
not thirty yet. So she was scratching out a living on that
farm—raising chickens and wringing their necks and trucking
them into the market here. All by herself. And her just a mite
of a thing, but with a scrumptious figure, and natural straw-
berry hair, curly like mine. She could go up to Atlantic City
and win a beauty contest if she wasn't cockeyed: Irma, she's
so cockeyed you can't tell what she's looking at or who. She
started coming into the bar with some of the other gal truckers. First off I reckoned she was a dyke, same as most of those
gal truckers. But I was wrong. She likes men, and they dote
on her, cockeyes and all. Truth is, I think my guy's got a
sneaker for her; I tease him about it, and it makes him *soooo*
mad. But if you want to know, I have more than a slight

notion that Irma gets a real tingle when Jim's around. You
can tell who she's looking at *then*. Well, I won't live forever,
and after I'm gone, if they want to get together, that's fine by
me. I'll have had my happiness. And I know Irma will take
good care of Jim. She's a wonderful kid. That's why I talked
her into coming into business with me. Say now, it's great to
see you again, Jockey. Stop by later. We've got a lot to catch
up on. But I've got to get my old bones rattling now.

Six . . . six . . . six . . .: the voice of the hour-bell tarries in
the greening air, shivering as it subsides into the sleep of
history.

Some cities, like wrapped boxes under Christmas trees,
conceal unexpected gifts, secret delights. Some cities will always remain wrapped boxes, containers of riddles never to be
solved, nor even to be seen by vacationing visitors, or, for
that matter, the most inquisitive, persistent travelers. To
know such cities, to unwrap them, as it were, one has to have
been born there. Venice is like that. After October, when
Adriatic winds sweep away the last American, even the last
German, carry them off and send their luggage flying after
them, another Venice develops: a clique of Venetian *élé-
gants*, fragile dukes sporting embroidered waistcoats, spindly
contessas supporting themselves on the arms of pale, elon-
gated nephews; Jamesian creations, D'Annunzio romantics
who would never consider emerging from the mauve shadows
of their palazzos on a summer's day when the foreigners are
abroad, emerge to feed the pigeons and stroll under the Piazza
San Marco's arcades, sally forth to take tea in the lobby of the
Danieli (the Gritti having closed until spring), and most
amusing, to swill martinis and chew grilled-cheese sandwiches
within the cozy confines of Harry's American Bar, so lately

and exclusively the watering hole of loud-mouthed hordes from across the Alps and the seas.

Fez is another enigmatic city leading a double life, and Boston still another—we all understand that intriguing tribal rites are acted out beyond the groomed exteriors and purple-tinged bow windows of Louisburg Square, but except for what some literary, chosen-few Bostonians have divulged, we don't know what these coded rituals are, and never will. However, of all secret cities, New Orleans, so it seems to me, is the most secretive, the most unlike, in reality, what an outsider is permitted to observe. The prevalence of steep walls, of obscuring foliage, of tall thick locked iron gates, of shuttered windows, of dark tunnels leading to overgrown gardens where mimosa and camellias contrast colors, and laz-ing lizards, flicking their forked tongues, race along palm fronds—all this is not accidental décor, but architecture de-liberately concocted to camouflage, to mask, as at a Mardi Gras Ball, the lives of those born to live among these protec-tive edifices: two cousins, who between them have a hundred other cousins spread throughout the city's entangling, inter-tangling familial relationships, whispering together as they sit under a fig tree beside the softly spilling fountain that cools their hidden garden.

A piano is playing. I can't decide where it's coming from: strong fingers playing a striding, riding-it-on-out piano: "I want, I want . . ." That's a black man singing; he's good—"I want, I want a mama, a big fat mama, I want a big fat mama with the meat shakin' on her, yeah!"

Footfalls. High-heeled feminine footsteps that approach and stop in front of me. It is the thin, almost pretty, high-yeller who earlier in the afternoon I'd overheard having a fuss with her "manager." She smiles, then winks at me, just one eye, then the other, and her voice is no longer angry. She sounds the way bananas taste.

HER: How you doin'?

TC: Just taking it easy.

HER: How you doin' for time?

TC: Let's see. I think it's six, a little after.

HER (laughs): I mean how you doin' for *time*? I got a place just around the corner here.

TC: I don't think so. Not today.

HER: You're cute.

TC: Everybody's entitled to their opinion.

HER: I'm not playing you. I mean it. You're cute.

TC: Well, thanks.

HER: But you don't look like you're having any fun. Come on. I'll show you a good time. We'll have fun.

TC: I don't think so.

HER: What's the matter? You don't like me?

TC: No. I like you.

HER: Then what's wrong? Give me a reason.

TC: There's a lot of reasons.

HER: Okay. Give me one, just one.

TC: Oh, honey, don't let me *commence*.

Four

❦

Derring-do

Time: November, 1970.

Place: Los Angeles International Airport.

I am sitting inside a telephone booth. It is a little after eleven in the morning, and I've been sitting here half an hour, pretending to make a call. From the booth I have a good view of Gate 38, from which TWA's nonstop noon flight to New York is scheduled to depart. I have a seat booked on that flight, a ticket bought under an assumed name, but there is every reason to doubt that I will ever board the plane. For one thing, there are two tall men standing at the gate, tough guys with snap-brim hats, and I know both of them. They're detectives from the San Diego Sheriff's Office, and they have a warrant for my arrest. That's why I'm hiding in the phone booth. The fact is, I'm in a real predicament.

The cause of my predicament had its roots in a series of conversations I'd conducted a year earlier with Robert M., a slender, slight, harmless-looking young man who was then a prisoner on Death Row at San Quentin, where he was await-ing execution, having been convicted of three slayings: his mother, a sister, both of whom he had beaten to death, and a fellow prisoner, a man he had strangled while he was in jail awaiting trial for the two original homicides. Robert M. was an intelligent psychopath; I got to know him fairly well, and he discussed his life and crimes with me freely—with the understanding that I would not write about or repeat any-thing that he told me. I was doing research on the subject of multiple murderers, and Robert M. became another case his-tory that went into my files. As far as I was concerned, that was the end of it.

Then, two months prior to my incarceration in a swelter-ing telephone booth at Los Angeles airport, I received a call from a detective in the San Diego Sheriff's Office. He had called me in Palm Springs, where I had a house. He was courteous and pleasant-voiced; he said he knew about the many interviews I'd conducted with convicted murderers, and that he'd like to ask me a few questions. So I invited him to drive down to the Springs and have lunch with me the following day.

The gentleman did not arrive alone, but with three other San Diego detectives. And though Palm Springs lies deep in the desert, there was a strong smell of fish in the air. How-ever, I pretended there was nothing odd about suddenly hav-ing four guests instead of one. But they were not interested in my hospitality; indeed, they declined lunch. All they wanted to talk about was Robert M. How well did I know him? Had he ever admitted to me any of his killings? Did I have any records of our conversations? I let them ask their questions, and avoided answering them until I asked my own question: Why were they so interested in my acquaintance with Robert M.?

The reason was this: due to a legal technicality, a federal court had overruled Robert M.'s conviction and ordered the state of California to grant him a new trial. The starting date for the retrial had been set for late November—in other words, approximately two months hence. Then, having delivered these facts, one of the detectives handed me a slim but exceedingly legal-looking document. It was a subpoena ordering me to appear at Robert M.'s trial, presumably as a witness for the prosecution. Okay, they'd tricked me, and I was mad as hell, but I smiled and nodded, and they smiled and said what a good guy I was and how grateful they were that my testimony would help send Robert M. straight to the gas chamber. That homicidal lunatic! They laughed, and said goodbye: "See ya in court."

I had no intention of honoring the subpoena, though I was aware of the consequences of not doing so: I would be arrested for contempt of court, fined, and sent to jail. I had no high opinion of Robert M., or any desire to protect him; I knew he was guilty of the three murders with which he was charged, and that he was a dangerous psychotic who ought never to be allowed his freedom. But I also knew that the state had more than enough hard evidence to reconvict him without my testimony. But the main point was that Robert M. had confided in me on my sworn word that I would not use or repeat what he told me. To betray him under these circumstances would have been morally despicable, and would have proven to Robert M., and the many men like him whom I'd interviewed, that they had placed their trust in a police informer, a stool pigeon plain and simple.

I consulted several lawyers. They all gave the same advice: honor the subpoena or expect the worst. Everyone sympathized with my quandary, but no one could see any solution —*unless I left California*. Contempt of court was not an extraditable offense, and once I was out of the state, there was nothing the authorities could do to punish me. Yes, there was one thing: I could never *return* to California. That didn't strike me as a severe hardship, although, because of various property matters and professional commitments, it was difficult to depart on such short notice.

I lost track of time, and was still tarrying in Palm Springs the day the trial began. That morning my housekeeper, a devoted friend named Myrtle Bennett, rushed into the house hollering: "Hurry up! It's all on the radio. They've got a warrant out for your arrest. They'll be here any minute."

Actually, it was twenty minutes before the Palm Springs police arrived full-force and with handcuffs at the ready (an overkill scene, but believe me, California law enforcement is not an institution one toys with lightly). However, though they dismantled the garden and searched the house stem to stern, all they found was my car in the garage and the loyal Mrs. Bennett in the living room. She told them I'd left for New York the previous day. They didn't believe her, but Mrs. Bennett was a formidable figure in Palm Springs, a black woman who had been a distinguished and politically influential member of the community for forty years, so they didn't question her further. They simply sent out an all-points alarm for my arrest.

And where *was* I? Well, I was tooling along the highway in Mrs. Bennett's old powder-blue Chevrolet, a car that couldn't do fifty miles an hour the day she bought it. But we figured I'd be safer in her car than my own. Not that I was safe anywhere; I was jumpy as a catfish with a hook in its mouth. When I got to Palm Desert, which is about thirty minutes out of Palm Springs, I turned off the highway and onto the lonely curving careening little road that leads away from the desert and up into the San Jacinto mountains. It had been hot in the desert, over a hundred, but as I climbed higher in the desolate mountains the air became cool, then cold, then colder. Which was okay, except that the old Chevy's heater wouldn't work, and all I had to wear were the clothes I had on when Mrs. Bennett had rushed into the house with her panic-stricken warnings: sandals, white linen slacks, and a light polo sweater. I'd left with just that and my wallet, which contained credit cards and about three hundred dollars.

Still, I had a destination in mind, and a plan. High in the San Jacinto mountains, midway between Palm Springs and San Diego, there's a grim little village named Idylwyld. In the summer, people from the desert travel there to escape the heat; in the winter it's a ski resort, though the quality of both the snow and the runs is threadbare. But now, out of season, this grim collection of mediocre motels and fake chalets would be a good place to lie low, at least until I could catch my breath.

It was snowing when the old car grunted up the last hill into Idylwyld: one of those young snows that suffuses the air but dissolves as it falls. The village was deserted, and most of the motels closed. The one I finally stopped at was called Eskimo Cabins. God knows, the accommodations were icy as igloos. It had one advantage: the proprietor, and apparently the only human on the premises, was a semi-deaf octogenarian far more interested in the game of solitaire he was playing than he was in me.

I called Mrs. Bennett, who was very excited: "Oh, honey, they're looking for you everywhere! It's all on the TV!" I decided it was better not to let her know where I was, but assured her I was all right and would call again tomorrow. Then I telephoned a close friend in Los Angeles; he was excited, too: "Your picture is in the *Examiner!*" After calming him down, I gave specific instructions: buy a ticket for a "George Thomas" on a nonstop flight to New York, and expect me at his house by ten o'clock the next morning.

I was too cold and hungry to sleep; I left at daybreak, and reached Los Angeles around nine. My friend was waiting for me. We left the Chevrolet at his house, and after wolfing down some sandwiches and as much brandy as I could safely contain, we drove in his car to the airport, where we said goodbye and he gave me the ticket for the noon flight he had booked for me on TWA.

So that's how I happen now to be huddled in this forsaken telephone booth, sitting here contemplating my predicament. A clock above the departure gate announces the hour: 11:35. The passenger area is crowded; soon the plane will be ready for boarding. And there, standing on either side of the gate through which I must pass, are two of the gentlemen who had visited me in Palm Springs, two tall watchful detectives from San Diego.

I considered calling my friend, asking him to return to the airport and pick me up somewhere in the parking lot. But he'd already done enough, and if we were caught, he could be accused of harboring a fugitive. That held true for all the many friends who might be willing to assist me. Perhaps it would be wisest to surrender myself to the guardians at the gate. Otherwise, what? Only a miracle, to coin a phrase, was going to save me. And we don't believe in miracles, do we?

Suddenly a miracle occurs.

There, striding past my tiny glass-doored prison, is a haughty, beautiful black Amazon wearing a zillion dollars' worth of diamonds and golden sable, a star surrounded by a giddy, chattering entourage of gaudily dressed chorus boys. And who is this dazzling apparition whose plumage and presence are creating such a commotion among the passersby? A friend! An old, old friend!

TC (opening the booth's door; shouting): *Pearl!* Pearl Bailey! (A miracle! She *hears* me. All of them do, her whole entourage) Pearl! Please come here ...

PEARL (squinting at me, then erupting into a radiant grin): Why, baby! What you doing hiding in there?

TC (beckoning her to come closer; whispering): Pearl, listen. I'm in a terrific jam.

PEARL (immediately serious, for she is a very intelligent woman, and at once understood that whatever this was, it wasn't funny): Tell it to me.

TC: Are you on that plane to New York?

PEARL: Yeah, we all are.

TC: I've got to get on it, Pearl. I have a ticket. But there're two guys waiting at the gate to stop me.

PEARL: Which guys? (I pointed them out) How can they stop you?

TC: They're detectives. Pearl, I haven't got time to explain all this ...

PEARL: You don't have to explain nothing.

(She surveyed her troupe of handsome young black chorus boys; she had a half-dozen—Pearl, I remembered, always liked to travel with a lot of company. She motioned to one of them to join us; he was a sleek number sporting a yellow cowboy hat, a sweatshirt that said SUCK DAMMIT, DONT BLOW, a white leather windbreaker with an ermine lining, yellow jitterbug pants [circa 1940], and yellow wedgies.)

This is Jimmy. He's a little bigger than you, but I think it'll all fit. Jimmy, take my friend here to the men's room and change clothes with him. Jimmy, don't flap your yap, just do like Pearlie-Mae say. We'll wait right here for you. Now hurry up! Ten more minutes and we'll miss that plane.

(The distance between the telephone booth and the men's room was a ten-yard dash. We locked ourselves into a pay toilet and started our wardrobe exchange. Jimmy thought it was a riot: he was giggling like a schoolgirl who's just puffed her first joint. I said: "Pearl! That really was a miracle. I've never been so happy to see someone. Never." Jimmy said: "Oh, Miss Bailey's got spirit. She's all heart, know what I mean? All heart."

There was a time when I would have disagreed with him, a time when I would have described Pearl Bailey as a heartless bitch. That was when she was playing the part of Madame Fleur, the principal role in *House of Flowers*, a musical play for which I had written the book and, with Harold Arlen, co-authored the lyrics. There were many gifted men attached to that endeavor: the director was Peter Brook; the choreographer, George Balanchine; Oliver Messel was responsible for the legendarily enchanting décor and costumes. But Pearl Bailey was so strong, so determined to have her way, that she dominated the entire production, much to its ultimate detriment. However, live and learn, forgive and forget, and by the time the play ended its Broadway run, Pearl and I were friends again. Aside from her skill as a performer, I'd come to respect her character; it might occasionally be unpleasant to deal with, but certainly she had it: she was a woman of character—one knew who she was and where she stood.

As Jimmy was squeezing into my trousers, which were embarrassingly too tight for him, and as I was slip-

ping on his white leather ermine-lined windbreaker, there
was an agitated knock at the door.)

MAN'S VOICE: Hey! What's goin' on in there?

JIMMY: And just *who* are *you*, pray tell?

MAN'S VOICE: I'm the attendant. And don't sass me. What's
goin' on in there is against the law.

JIMMY: No shit?

ATTENDANT: I see four feet in there. I see clothes comin' off.
You think I'm too stupid I don't know what's goin' on? It's
against the law. It's against the law for two men to lock
themselves in the same toilet at the same time.

JIMMY: Aw, shove it up your ass.

ATTENDANT: I'll get the cops. They'll hand you an L and L.

JIMMY: What the hell's an L and L?

ATTENDANT: Lewd and lascivious conduct. Yessir. I'll get the
cops.

TC: Jesus, Joseph, and Mary—

ATTENDANT: Open that door!

TC: You've got it all wrong.

ATTENDANT: I know what I see. I see four feet.

TC: We're changing our costumes for the next scene.

ATTENDANT: Next scene what?

TC: The movie. We're getting ready to shoot the next scene.

ATTENDANT (curious and impressed): They're making a
movie out there?

JIMMY (catching on): With Pearl Bailey. She's the star. Marlon Brando, he's in it, too.

TC: Kirk Douglas.

JIMMY (biting his knuckles to keep from laughing): And
Shirley Temple. She's making her comeback.

ATTENDANT (believing, yet not believing): Yeah, well, who
are you?

TC: We're just extras. That's why we don't have a dressing room.

ATTENDANT: I don't care. Two men, four feet. It's against the law.

JIMMY: Look outside. You'll see Pearl Bailey in person. Marlon Brando. Kirk Douglas. Shirley Temple. Mahatma Gandhi —she's in it, too. Just a cameo.

ATTENDANT: Who?

JIMMY: Mamie Eisenhower.

TC (opening the door, having completed the transference of clothing; my stuff doesn't look too bad on Jimmy, but I suspect that his outfit, as worn by me, will produce a galvanizing effect, and the expression on the attendant's face, a bristling short black man, confirms this expectation): Sorry. We didn't realize we were doing anything against the rules.

JIMMY (regally sweeping past the attendant, who seems too befuddled to budge): Follow us, sweetheart. We'll introduce you to the gang. You can get some autographs.

(At last we were in the corridor, and an unsmiling Pearl wrapped her sable-soft arms around me; her companions closed about us in a concealing circle. There were no jokes or jesting. My nerves sizzled like a cat just hit by lightning, and as for Pearl, the qualities about her that had once alarmed me—that strength, that self-will— were flowing through her like power from a waterfall.)

PEARL: From now on keep quiet. Whatever I say, don't you say anything. Tuck the hat more over your face. Lean on me like you're weak and sick. Lean your face against my shoulder. Close your eyes. Let me lead you.

All right. We're moving now toward the counter. Jimmy has all the tickets. They've already announced the last boarding call, so there aren't too many people around. Those gumshoes haven't moved an inch, but they seem tired and kind of disgusted. They're looking at us now. Both of them. When we pass between them the boys will distract them and start jabbering. Here comes somebody. Lean closer, groan a little— it's one of those VIP guys from TWA. Watch Mama go into her act . . . (Changing voice, impersonating her theatrical self, simultaneously droll and drawling and slightly flaky) Mr. Calloway? Like in Cab? Well, aren't you just an angel to help us out. And we surely could use some help. We need to get on that plane just as fast as possible. My friend here—he's one of my musicians—he's feeling something terrible. Can't hardly walk. We've been playing Vegas, and maybe he got too much sun. Sun can addle your brain and your stomach both. Or maybe it's his diet. Musicians eat funny. Piano players in particular. He won't eat hardly anything but hot dogs. Last night he ate ten hot dogs. Now, that's just not healthy. I'm not surprised he feels poisoned. Are you surprised, Mr. Calloway? Well, I don't suppose very much surprises you, being in the airplane business. All this hijacking that's going on. Criminals afoot all over the place. Soon as we get to New York, I'm taking my friend straight to the doctor. I'm going to tell the doctor to tell him to stay out of the sun and stop eating hot dogs. Oh, thank you, Mr. Calloway. No, I'll take the aisle. We'll put my friend in the window seat. He'll be better off by the window. All that fresh air.

Okay, Buster. You can open your eyes now.

TC: I think I'll keep them closed. It makes it seem more like a dream.

PEARL (relaxed, chuckling): Anyway, we made it. Your friends never even saw you. As we went by, Jimmy goosed one, and Billy stomped on the other guy's toes.

TC: Where is Jimmy?

PEARL: All the kids go economy. Jimmy's duds do something

for you. Pep you up. I like the wedgies especially—just love 'em.

STEWARDESS: Good morning, Miss Bailey. Would you care for a glass of champagne?

PEARL: No, honey. But maybe my friend could use something.

TC: Brandy.

STEWARDESS: I'm sorry, sir, but we only serve champagne until after takeoff.

PEARL: The man wants brandy.

STEWARDESS: I'm sorry, Miss Bailey. It's not permitted.

PEARL (in a smooth yet metallic tone familiar to me from *House of Flowers* rehearsals): Bring the man his brandy. The whole bottle. Now.

> (The stewardess brought the brandy, and I poured myself a hefty dose with an unsteady hand: hunger, fatigue, anxiety, the dizzying events of the last twenty-four hours were presenting their bill. I treated myself to another drink and began to feel a bit lighter.)

TC: I suppose I ought to tell you what this is all about.

PEARL: Not necessarily.

TC: Then I won't. That way you'll have a free conscience. I'll just say that I haven't done anything a sensible person would classify as criminal.

PEARL (consulting a diamond wristwatch): We should be over Palm Springs by now. I heard the door close ages ago. Stewardess!

STEWARDESS: Yes, Miss Bailey?

PEARL: What's going on?

STEWARDESS: Oh, there's the captain now—

CAPTAIN'S VOICE (over loudspeaker): Ladies and gentlemen, we regret the delay. We should be departing shortly. Thank you for your patience.

TC: Jesus, Joseph, and Mary.

PEARL: Have another slug. You're shaking. You'd think it was a first night. I mean, it can't be *that* bad.

TC: It's worse. And I can't stop shaking—not till we're in the air. Maybe not till we land in New York.

PEARL: You still living in New York?

TC: Thank God.

PEARL: You remember Louis? My husband?

TC: Louis Bellson. Sure. The greatest drummer in the world. Better than Gene Krupa.

PEARL: We both work Vegas so much, it made sense to buy a house there. I've become a real homebody. I do a lot of cooking. I'm writing a cookbook. Living in Vegas is just like living anywhere else, as long as you stay away from the undesirables. *Gamblers.* Unemployeds. Any time a man says to me he'd work if he could find a job, I always tell him to look in the phone book under G. G for gigolo. He'll find work. In Vegas, anyways. That's a town of desperate women. I'm lucky; I found the right man and had the sense to know it.

TC: Are you going to work in New York?

PEARL: Persian Room.

CAPTAIN'S VOICE: I'm sorry, ladies and gentlemen, but we'll be delayed a few minutes longer. Please remain seated. Those who care to smoke may do so.

PEARL (suddenly stiffening): I don't like this. They're opening the door.

TC: What?

PEARL: *They're opening the door.*

TC: Jesus, Joseph—

PEARL: I don't like this.

TC: Jesus, Joseph—

PEARL: Slump down in the seat. Pull the hat over your face.

TC: I'm scared.

PEARL (gripping my hand, squeezing it): Snore.

TC: Snore?

PEARL: Snore!

TC: I'm strangling. I *can't* snore.

PEARL: You'd better start trying, 'cause our friends are coming through that door. Looks like they're gonna roust the joint. Clean-tooth it.

TC: Jesus, Joseph—

PEARL: Snore, you rascal, snore.

(I snored, and she increased the pressure of her hold on my hand; at the same time she began to hum a low sweet lullaby, like a mother soothing a fretful child. All the while another kind of humming surrounded us: human voices concerned with what was happening on the plane, the purpose of the two mysterious men who were pacing up and down the aisles, pausing now and again to scrutinize a passenger. Minutes elapsed. I counted them off: six, seven. Tickticktick. Eventually Pearl stopped crooning her maternal melody, and withdrew her hand from mine. Then I heard the plane's big round door slam shut.)

TC: Have they gone?

PEARL: Uh-huh. But whoever it is they're looking for, they sure must want him bad.

They did indeed. Even though Robert M.'s retrial ended exactly as I had predicted, and the jury brought in a verdict of guilty on three counts of first-degree murder, the California courts continued to take a harsh view of my refusal to cooperate with them. I was not aware of this; I thought that in due time the matter would be forgotten. So I did not hesitate to return to California when a year later something came up that required at least a brief visit there. Well, sir, I had no sooner registered at the Bel Air Hotel than I was arrested, summoned before a hard-nosed judge who fined me five thousand dollars and gave me an indefinite sentence in the Orange County jail, which meant they could keep me locked up for weeks or months or years. However, I was soon released because the summons for my arrest contained a small but significant error: it listed me as a legal resident of California, when in fact I was a resident of New York, a fact which made my conviction and confinement invalid.

But all that was still far off, unthought of, undreamed of when the silver vessel containing Pearl and her outlaw friend swept off into an ethereal November heaven. I watched the plane's shadow ripple over the desert and drift across the Grand Canyon. We talked and laughed and ate and sang. Stars and the lilac of twilight filled the air, and the Rocky Mountains, shrouded in blue snow, loomed ahead, a lemony slice of new moon hovering above them.

TC: Look, Pearl. A new moon. Let's make a wish.

PEARL: What are you going to wish?

TC: I wish I could always be as happy as I am at this very moment.

PEARL: Oh, honey, that's like asking miracles. Wish for something real.

TC: But I believe in miracles.

PEARL: Then all I can say is: don't ever take up gambling.

Five

✤

Then It All
Came Down

Scene: A cell in a maximum-security cell block at San Quentin prison in California. The cell is furnished with a single cot, and its permanent occupant, Robert Beausoleil, and his visitor are required to sit on it in rather cramped positions. The cell is neat, uncluttered; a well-waxed guitar stands in one corner. But it is late on a winter afternoon, and in the air lingers a chill, even a hint of mist, as though fog from San Francisco Bay had infiltrated the prison itself.

Despite the chill, Beausoleil is shirtless, wearing only a pair of prison-issue denim trousers, and it is clear that he is satisfied with his appearance, his body particularly, which is lithe, feline, in well-toned shape considering that he has been incarcerated more than a decade. His chest and arms are a panorama of tattooed emblems: feisty dragons, coiled chrysanthemums, uncoiled serpents. He is thought by some to be exceptionally good-looking; he is, but in a rather hustlerish camp-macho style. Not surprisingly, he worked as an actor as a child and appeared in several Hollywood films; later, as a very young man, he was for a while the protégé of Kenneth Anger, the experimental film-maker (*Scorpio Rising*) and author (*Hollywood Babylon*); indeed, Anger cast him in the title role of *Lucifer Rising*, an unfinished film.

Robert Beausoleil, who is now thirty-one, is the real mystery figure of the Charles Manson cult; more to the point— and it's a point that has never been clearly brought forth in accounts of that tribe—he is the key to the mystery of the homicidal escapades of the so-called Manson family, notably the Sharon Tate–Lo Bianco murders.

It all began with the murder of Gary Hinman, a middle-aged professional musician who had befriended various members of the Manson brethren and who, unfortunately for him, lived alone in a small isolated house in Topanga Canyon, Los Angeles County. Hinman had been tied up and tortured for several days (among other indignities, one of his ears had been severed) before his throat had been mercifully and lastingly slashed. When Hinman's body, bloated and abuzz with August flies, was discovered, police found bloody graffiti on the walls of his modest house ("Death to Pigs!")— graffiti similar to the sort soon to be found in the households of Miss Tate and Mr. and Mrs. Lo Bianco.

However, just a few days prior to the Tate–Lo Bianco slayings, Robert Beausoleil, caught driving a car that had been the property of the victim, was under arrest and in jail, accused of having murdered the helpless Mr. Hinman. It was then that Manson and his chums, in the hopes of freeing Beausoleil, conceived the notion of committing a series of homicides similar to the Hinman affair; if Beausoleil was still incarcerated at the time of these killings, then how could he be guilty of the Hinman atrocity? Or so the Manson brood reasoned. That is to say, it was out of devotion to "Bobby" Beausoleil that Tex Watson and those cutthroat young ladies, Susan Atkins, Patricia Krenwinkel, Leslie Van Hooten, sallied forth on their satanic errands.

RB: Strange. Beausoleil. That's French. My name is French. It means Beautiful Sun. Fuck. Nobody sees much sun inside this resort. Listen to the foghorns. Like train whistles. Moan, moan. And they're worse in the summer. Maybe it must be there's more fog in summer than in winter. Weather. Fuck it, I'm not going anywhere. But just listen. Moan, moan. So what've you been up to today?

TC: Just around. Had a little talk with Sirhan.

RB (laughs): Sirhan B. Sirhan. I knew him when they had me up on the Row. He's a sick guy. He don't belong here. He ought to be in Atascadero. Want some gum? Yeah, well, you seem to know your way around here pretty good. I was watching you out on the yard. I was surprised the warden lets you walk around the yard by yourself. Somebody might cut you.

TC: Why?

RB: For the hell of it. But you've been here a lot, huh? Some of the guys were telling me.

TC: Maybe half a dozen times on different research projects.

RB: There's just one thing here I've never seen. But I'd like to see that little apple-green room. When they railroaded me on that Hinman deal and I got the death sentence, well, they had me up on the Row a good spell. Right up to when the court abolished the death penalty. So I used to wonder about the little green room.

TC: Actually, it's more like three rooms.

RB: I thought it was a little round room with a sort of glass-sealed igloo hut set in the center. With windows in the igloo so the witnesses standing outside can see the guys choking to death on that peach perfume.

TC: Yes, that's the gas-chamber room. But when the prisoner is brought down from Death Row he steps from the elevator directly into a "holding" room that adjoins the witness room. There are two cells in this "holding" room, two, in case it's a double execution. They're ordinary cells, just like this one, and the prisoner spends his last night there before his execution in the morning, reading, listening to the radio, playing cards with the guards. But the interesting thing I discovered was that there's a *third* room in this little suite. It's behind a closed door right next to the "holding" cell. I just opened the door and walked in and none of the guards that were with me tried to stop me. And it was the most haunting room I've ever seen. Because you know what's in it? All the leftovers, all the paraphernalia that the different condemned men had had with them in the "holding" cells. Books. Bibles and Western paperbacks and Erle Stanley Gardner, James Bond. Old brown newspapers. Some of them twenty years old. Unfinished crossword puzzles. Unfinished letters. Sweetheart snapshots. Dim, crumbling little Kodak children. Pathetic.

RB: You ever seen a guy gassed?

TC: Once. But he made it look like a lark. He was happy to go, he wanted to get it over with; he sat down in that chair like he was going to the dentist to have his teeth cleaned. But in Kansas, I saw two men hanged.

RB: Perry Smith? And what's his name—Dick Hickock? Well, once they hit the end of the rope, I guess they don't feel anything.

TC: So we're told. But after the drop, they go on living—

fifteen, twenty minutes. Struggling. Gasping for breath, the body still battling for life. I couldn't help it, I vomited.

RB: Maybe you're not so cool, huh? You seem cool. So, did Sirhan beef about being kept in Special Security?

TC: Sort of. He's lonesome. He wants to mix with the other prisoners, join the general population.

RB: He don't know what's good for him. Outside, somebody'd snuff him for sure.

TC: Why?

RB: For the same reason he snuffed Kennedy. Recognition. Half the people who snuff people, that's what they want: recognition. Get their picture in the paper.

TC: That's not why you killed Gary Hinman.

RB: (Silence)

TC: That was because you and Manson wanted Hinman to give you money and his car, and when he wouldn't—well . . .

RB: (Silence)

TC: I was thinking. I know Sirhan, and I knew Robert Kennedy. I knew Lee Harvey Oswald, and I knew Jack Kennedy. The odds against that—one person knowing all four of those men—must be astounding.

RB: Oswald? You knew Oswald? Really?

TC: I met him in Moscow just after he defected. One night I was having dinner with a friend, an Italian newspaper correspondent, and when he came by to pick me up he asked me if I'd mind going with him first to talk to a young American defector, one Lee Harvey Oswald. Oswald was staying at the Metropole, an old Czarist hotel just off Kremlin Square. The Metropole has a big gloomy lobby full of shadows and dead palm trees. And there he was, sitting in the dark under a dead palm tree. Thin and pale, thin-lipped, starved-looking. He was wearing chinos and tennis shoes and a lumberjack shirt. And right away he was angry—he was grinding his teeth, and his eyes were jumping every which way. He was boiling over about everything: the American ambassador; the Russians—he was mad at them because they wouldn't let him stay in Moscow. We talked to him for about half an hour, and my Italian friend didn't think the guy was worth filing a story about. Just another paranoid hysteric; the Moscow woods were rampant with those. I never thought about him again, not until many years later. Not until after the assassination when I saw his picture flashed on television.

RB: Does that make you the only one that knew both of them, Oswald and Kennedy?

TC: No. There was an American girl, Priscilla Johnson. She worked for U.P. in Moscow. She knew Kennedy, and she met Oswald around the same time I did. But I can tell you something else almost as curious. About some of those people your friends murdered.

RB: (Silence)

TC: I knew them. At least, out of the five people killed in the Tate house that night, I knew four of them. I'd met Sharon Tate at the Cannes Film Festival. Jay Sebring cut my hair a couple of times. I'd had lunch once in San Francisco with Abigail Folger and her boyfriend, Frykowski. In other words, I'd known them independently of each other. And yet one night there they were, all gathered together in the same house waiting for your friends to arrive. Quite a coincidence.

RB (lights a cigarette; smiles): Know what I'd say? I'd say you're not such a lucky guy to know. Shit. Listen to that. Moan, moan. I'm cold. You cold?

TC: Why don't you put on your shirt?

RB: (Silence)

TC: It's odd about tattoos. I've talked to several hundred men convicted of homicide—multiple homicide, in most cases. The only common denominator I could find among them was tattoos. A good eighty percent of them were heavily tattooed. Richard Speck. York and Latham. Smith and Hickock.

RB: I'll put on my sweater.

TC: If you weren't here, if you could be anywhere you wanted to be, doing anything you wanted to do, where would you be and what would you be doing?

RB: Tripping. Out on my Honda chugging along the Coast road, the fast curves, the waves and the water, plenty of sun. Out of San Fran, headed Mendocino way, riding through the redwoods. I'd be making love. I'd be on the beach by a bonfire making love. I'd be making music and balling and sucking some great Acapulco weed and watching the sun go down. Throw some driftwood on the fire. Good gash, good hash, just tripping right along.

TC: You can get hash in here.

RB: And everything else. Any kind of dope—for a price. There are dudes in here on everything but roller skates.

TC: Is that what your life was like before you were arrested? Just tripping? Didn't you ever have a job?

RB: Once in a while. I played guitar in a couple of bars.

TC: I understand you were quite a cocksman. The ruler of a virtual seraglio. How many children have you fathered?

RB: (Silence—but shrugs, grins, smokes)

TC: I'm surprised you have a guitar. Some prisons don't allow it because the strings can be detached and used as weapons. A garrote. How long have you been playing?

RB: Oh, since I was a kid. I was one of those Hollywood kids. I was in a couple of movies. But my folks were against it. They're real straight people. Anyway, I never cared about the acting part. I just wanted to write music and play it and sing.

TC: But what about the film you made with Kenneth Anger—*Lucifer Rising*?

RB: Yeah.

TC: How did you get along with Anger?

RB: Okay.

TC: Then why does Kenneth Anger wear a picture locket on a chain around his neck? On one side of the locket there is a picture of you; on the other there is an image of a frog with an inscription: "Bobby Beausoleil changed into a frog by Kenneth Anger." A voodoo amulet, so to say. A curse he put on you because you're supposed to have ripped him off. Left in the middle of the night with his car—and a few other things.

RB (narrowed eyes): Did he tell you that?

TC: No, I've never met him. But I was told it by a number of other people.

RB (reaches for guitar, tunes it, strums it, sings): "This is my song, this is my song, this is my dark song, my dark song . . ." Everybody always wants to know how I got together with Manson. It was through our music. He plays some, too. One night I was driving around with a bunch of my ladies. Well, we came to this old roadhouse, beer place, with a lot of cars outside. So we went inside, and there was Charlie with some of his ladies. We all got to talking, played some together; the next day Charlie came to see me in my van, and we all, his people and my people, ended up camping out together. Brothers and sisters. A family.

TC: Did you see Manson as a leader? Did you feel influenced by him right away?

RB: Hell, no. He had his people, I had mine. If anybody was influenced, it was him. By me.

TC: Yes, he was attracted to you. Infatuated. Or so he says. You seem to have had that effect on a lot of people, men and women.

RB: Whatever happens, happens. It's all good.

TC: Do you consider killing innocent people a good thing?

RB: Who said they were innocent?

TC: Well, we'll return to that. But for now: What is your own sense of morality? How do you differentiate between good and bad?

RB: Good and bad? It's *all* good. If it happens, it's got to be good. Otherwise, it wouldn't be *happening*. It's just the way life flows. Moves together. I move with it. I don't question it.

TC: In other words, you don't question the act of murder. You consider it "good" because it "happens." Justifiable.

RB: I have my own justice. I live by my own law, you know. I don't respect the laws of this society. Because society doesn't respect its own laws. I make my own laws and live by them. I have my own sense of justice.

TC: And what is your sense of justice?

RB: I believe that what goes around comes around. What goes up comes down. That's how life flows, and I flow with it.

TC: You're not making much sense—at least to me. And I don't think you're stupid. Let's try again. In your opinion, it's all right that Manson sent Tex Watson and those girls into that house to slaughter total strangers, innocent people—

RB: I said: Who says they were innocent? They burned people on dope deals. Sharon Tate and that gang. They picked up kids on the Strip and took them home and whipped them. Made movies of it. Ask the cops; they found the movies. Not that they'd tell you the truth.

TC: The truth is, the Lo Biancos and Sharon Tate and her friends were killed to protect you. Their deaths were directly linked to the Gary Hinman murder.

RB: I hear you. I hear where you're coming from.

TC: Those were all imitations of the Hinman murder—to prove that you couldn't have killed Hinman. And thereby get you out of jail.

RB: To get me out of jail. (He nods, smiles, sighs—complimented) None of that came out at any of the trials. The girls got on the stand and tried to really tell how it all came down, but nobody would listen. People couldn't believe anything except what the media said. The media had them programmed to believe it all happened because we were out to start a race war. That it was mean niggers going around hurting all these good white folk. Only—it was like you say. The media, they called us a "family." And it was the only true thing they said. We *were* a family. We were mother, father, brother, sister, daughter, son. If a member of our family was in jeopardy, we didn't abandon that person. And so for the love of a brother, a brother who was in jail on a murder rap, all those killings came down.

TC: And you don't regret that?

RB: No. If my brothers and sisters did it, then it's good. Everything in life is good. It all flows. It's all good. It's all music.

TC: When you were up on Death Row, if you'd been forced to flow down to the gas chamber and whiff the peaches, would you have given that your stamp of approval?

RB: If that's how it came down. Everything that happens is good.

TC: War. Starving children. Pain. Cruelty. Blindness. Prisons. Desperation. Indifference. All good?

RB: What's that look you're giving me?

TC: Nothing. I was noticing how your face changes. One moment, with just the slightest shift of angle, you look so boyish, entirely innocent, a charmer. And then—well, one can see you as a sort of Forty-second Street Lucifer. Have you ever seen *Night Must Fall*? An old movie with Robert Montgomery? No? Well, it's about an impish, innocent-looking delightful young man who travels about the English countryside charming old ladies, then cutting off their heads and carrying the heads around with him in leather hat-boxes.

RB: So what's that got to do with me?

TC: I was thinking—if it was ever remade, if someone Americanized it, turned the Montgomery character into a young drifter with hazel eyes and a smoky voice, you'd be very good in the part.

RB: Are you trying to say I'm a psychopath? I'm not a nut. If I have to use violence, I'll use it, but I don't believe in killing.

TC: Then I must be deaf. Am I mistaken, or didn't you just tell me that it didn't matter what atrocity one person committed against another, it was good, all good?

RB: (Silence)

TC: Tell me, Bobby, how do you view yourself?

RB: As a convict.

TC: But beyond that.

RB: As a man. A *white* man. And everything a white man stands for.

TC: Yes, one of the guards told me you were the ringleader of the Aryan Brotherhood.

RB (hostile): What do *you* know about the Brotherhood?

TC: That it's composed of a bunch of hard-nosed white guys. That it's a somewhat fascist-minded fraternity. That it started in California, and has spread throughout the American prison system, north, south, east, and west. That the prison authorities consider it a dangerous, troublemaking cult.

RB: A man has to defend himself. We're outnumbered. You got no idea how rough it is. We're all more scared of each other than we are of the pigs in here. You got to be on your toes every second if you don't want a shiv in your back. The blacks and Chicanos, they got their own gangs. The Indians, too; or I should say the "Native Americans"—that's how these redskins call themselves: what a laugh! Yessir, *rough*. With all the racial tensions, politics, dope, gambling, and sex. The blacks really go for the young white kids. They like to shove those big black dicks up those tight white asses.

TC: Have you ever thought what you would do with your life if and when you were paroled out of here?

RB: That's a tunnel I don't see no end to. They'll never let Charlie go.

TC: I hope you're right, and I think you are. But it's very likely that you'll be paroled some day. Perhaps sooner than you imagine. Then what?

RB (strums guitar): I'd like to record some of my music. Get it played on the air.

TC: That was Perry Smith's dream. And Charlie Manson's, too. Maybe you fellows have more in common than mere tattoos.

RB: Just between us, Charlie doesn't have a whole lot of talent. (Strumming chords) "This is my song, my dark song, my dark song." I got my first guitar when I was eleven; I found it in my grandma's attic and taught myself to play it, and I've been nuts about music ever since. My grandma was a sweet woman, and her attic was my favorite place. I liked to lie up there and listen to the rain. Or hide up there when my dad came looking for me with his belt. Shit. You hear that? Moan, moan. It's enough to drive you crazy.

TC: Listen to me, Bobby. And answer carefully. Suppose, when you get out of here, somebody came to you—let's say Charlie—and asked you to commit an act of violence, kill a man, would you do it?

RB (after lighting another cigarette, after smoking it half through): I might. It depends. I never meant to . . . to . . . hurt Gary Hinman. But one thing happened. And another. And then it all came down.

TC: And it was all good.

RB: It was all good.

Six

❧

A Beautiful Child

Time: 28 April 1955.

Scene: The chapel of the Universal Funeral Home at Lexington Avenue and Fifty-second Street, New York City. An interesting galaxy packs the pews: celebrities, for the most part, from an international arena of theatre, films, literature, all present in tribute to Constance Collier, the English-born actress who had died the previous day at the age of seventy-five.

Born in 1880, Miss Collier had begun her career as a music-hall Gaiety Girl, graduated from that to become one of England's principal Shakespearean actresses (and the long-time fiancée of Sir Max Beerbohm, whom she never married, and perhaps for that reason was the inspiration for the mischievously unobtainable heroine in Sir Max's novel *Zuleika*

Dobson). Eventually she emigrated to the United States, where she established herself as a considerable figure on the New York stage as well as in Hollywood films. During the last decades of her life she lived in New York, where she practiced as a drama coach of unique caliber; she accepted only professionals as students, and usually only professionals who were already "stars"—Katharine Hepburn was a permanent pupil; another Hepburn, Audrey, was also a Collier protégée, as were Vivien Leigh and, for a few months prior to her death, a neophyte Miss Collier referred to as "my special problem," Marilyn Monroe.

Marilyn Monroe, whom I'd met through John Huston when he was directing her in her first speaking role in *The Asphalt Jungle*, had come under Miss Collier's wing at my suggestion. I had known Miss Collier perhaps a half-dozen years, and admired her as a woman of true stature, physically, emotionally, creatively; and, for all her commanding manner, her grand cathedral voice, as an adorable person, mildly wicked but exceedingly warm, dignified yet *Gemütlich*. I loved to go to the frequent small lunch parties she gave in her dark Victorian studio in mid-Manhattan; she had a barrel of yarns to tell about her adventures as a leading lady opposite Sir Beerbohm Tree and the great French actor Coquelin, her involvements with Oscar Wilde, the youthful Chaplin, and Garbo in the silent Swede's formative days. Indeed she was a delight, as was her devoted secretary and companion, Phyllis Wilbourn, a quietly twinkling maiden lady who, after her employer's demise, became, and has remained, the companion of Katharine Hepburn. Miss Collier introduced me to many people who became friends: the Lunts, the Oliviers, and especially Aldous Huxley. But it was I who introduced her to Marilyn Monroe, and at first it was not an acquaintance she was too keen to acquire: her eyesight was faulty, she had seen none of Marilyn's movies, and really knew nothing about her except that she was some sort of platinum sex-explosion who had achieved global notoriety; in short, she seemed hardly suitable clay for Miss Collier's stern classic shaping. But I thought they might make a stimulating combination.

They did. "Oh yes," Miss Collier reported to me, "there is something there. She is a beautiful child. I don't mean that in the obvious way—the perhaps too obvious way. I don't think she's an actress at all, not in any traditional sense. What she has—this presence, this luminosity, this flickering intelligence —could never surface on the stage. It's so fragile and subtle, it can only be caught by the camera. It's like a hummingbird in flight: only a camera can freeze the poetry of it. But anyone who thinks this girl is simply another Harlow or harlot or whatever is *mad*. Speaking of mad, that's what we've been working on together: Ophelia. I suppose people would chuckle at the notion, but really, she could be the most exquisite Ophelia. I was talking to Greta last week, and I told her about Marilyn's Ophelia, and Greta said yes, she could believe that because she had seen two of her films, very bad and vulgar stuff, but nevertheless she had glimpsed Marilyn's possibilities. Actually, Greta has an amusing idea. You know that she wants to make a film of *Dorian Gray*? With her playing Dorian, of course. Well, she said she would like to have Marilyn opposite her as one of the girls Dorian seduces and destroys. Greta! So unused! Such a gift—and rather like Marilyn's, if you consider it. Of course, Greta is a consummate artist, an artist of the utmost control. This beautiful child is without any concept of discipline or sacrifice. Somehow I don't think she'll make old bones. Absurd of me to say, but somehow I feel she'll go young. I hope, I really pray, that

she survives long enough to free the strange lovely talent
that's wandering through her like a jailed spirit."

But now Miss Collier had died, and here I was loitering
in the vestibule of the Universal Chapel waiting for Marilyn;
we had talked on the telephone the evening before, and
agreed to sit together at the services, which were scheduled
to start at noon. She was now a half-hour late; she was *always*
late, but I'd thought just for once! For God's sake, goddamnit! Then suddenly there she was, and I didn't recognize
her until she said . . .

MARILYN: Oh, baby, I'm so sorry. But see, I got all made up,
and then I decided maybe I shouldn't wear eyelashes or lipstick or anything, so then I had to wash all that off, and I
couldn't imagine what to wear . . .

(What she had imagined to wear would have been appropriate for the abbess of a nunnery in private audience
with the Pope. Her hair was entirely concealed by a
black chiffon scarf; her black dress was loose and long
and looked somehow borrowed; black silk stockings
dulled the blond sheen of her slender legs. An abbess,
one can be certain, would not have donned the vaguely
erotic black high-heeled shoes she had chosen, or the
owlish black sunglasses that dramatized the vanilla-
pallor of her dairy-fresh skin.)

TC: You look fine.

MARILYN (gnawing an already chewed-to-the-nub thumbnail): Are you sure? I mean, I'm so jumpy. Where's the john?
If I could just pop in there for a minute—

TC: And pop a pill? No! Shhh. That's Cyril Ritchard's voice:
he's started the eulogy.

(Tiptoeing, we entered the crowded chapel and wedged

ourselves into a narrow space in the last row. Cyril Ritchard finished; he was followed by Cathleen Nesbitt, a
lifelong colleague of Miss Collier's, and finally Brian
Aherne addressed the mourners. Through it all, my date
periodically removed her spectacles to scoop up tears
bubbling from her blue-grey eyes. I'd sometimes seen
her without makeup, but today she presented a new visual experience, a face I'd not observed before, and at first
I couldn't perceive why this should be. Ah! It was because of the obscuring head scarf. With her tresses invisible, and her complexion cleared of all cosmetics, she
looked twelve years old, a pubescent virgin who has just
been admitted to an orphanage and is grieving over her
plight. At last the ceremony ended, and the congregation
began to disperse.)

MARILYN: Please, let's sit here. Let's wait till everyone's left.

TC: Why?

MARILYN: I don't want to have to talk to anybody. I never
know what to say.

TC: Then you sit here, and I'll wait outside. I've got to have a
cigarette.

MARILYN: You can't leave me alone! My God! Smoke here.

TC: *Here?* In the chapel?

MARILYN: Why not? What do you want to smoke? A reefer?

TC: Very funny. Come on, let's go.

MARILYN: Please. There's a lot of shutterbugs downstairs.
And I certainly don't want them taking my picture looking
like this.

TC: I can't blame you for that.

MARILYN: You said I looked fine.

TC: You do. Just perfect—if you were playing the Bride of
Frankenstein.

MARILYN: Now you're laughing at me.

TC: Do I look like I'm laughing?

MARILYN: You're laughing inside. And that's the worst kind of laugh. (Frowning; nibbling thumbnail) Actually, I could've worn makeup. I see all these other people are wearing makeup.

TC: I am. Globs.

MARILYN: Seriously, though. It's my hair. I need color. And I didn't have time to get any. It was all so unexpected, Miss Collier dying and all. See?

> (She lifted her kerchief slightly to display a fringe of
> darkness where her hair parted.)

TC: Poor innocent me. And all this time I thought you were a bona-fide blonde.

MARILYN: I am. But nobody's *that* natural. And incidentally, fuck you.

TC: Okay, everybody's cleared out. So up, up.

MARILYN: Those photographers are still down there. I know it.

TC: If they didn't recognize you coming in, they won't recognize you going out.

MARILYN: One of them did. But I'd slipped through the door before he started yelling.

TC: I'm sure there's a back entrance. We can go that way.

MARILYN: I don't want to see any corpses.

TC: Why would we?

MARILYN: This is a funeral parlor. They must keep them somewhere. That's all I need today, to wander into a room full of corpses. Be patient. I'll take us somewhere and treat us to a bottle of bubbly.

> (So we sat and talked and Marilyn said: "I hate funerals.
> I'm glad I won't have to go to my own. Only, I don't

want a funeral—just my ashes cast on waves by one of my kids, if I ever have any. I wouldn't have come today except Miss Collier cared about me, my welfare, and she was just like a granny, a tough old granny, but she taught me a lot. She taught me how to breathe. I've put it to good use, too, and I don't mean just acting. There *are* other times when breathing is a problem. But when I first heard about it, Miss Collier cooling, the first thing I thought was: Oh, gosh, what's going to happen to Phyllis?! Her whole life was Miss Collier. But I hear she's going to live with Miss Hepburn. Lucky Phyllis; she's going to have fun now. I'd change places with her pronto. Miss Hepburn is a terrific lady, no shit. I wish she was my friend. So I could call her up sometimes and . . . well, I don't know, just call her up."

We talked about how much we liked New York and loathed Los Angeles ("Even though I was born there, I still can't think of one good thing to say about it. If I close my eyes, and picture L.A., all I see is one big varicose vein"); we talked about actors and acting ("Everybody says I can't act. They said the same thing about Elizabeth Taylor. And they were wrong. She was great in *A Place in the Sun*. I'll never get the right part, anything I really want. My looks are against me. They're too specific"); we talked some more about Elizabeth Taylor, and she wanted to know if I knew her, and I said yes, and she said well, what is she like, what is she *really* like, and I said well, she's a little bit like you, she wears her heart on her sleeve and talks salty, and Marilyn said fuck you and said well, if somebody asked me what Marilyn Monroe was like, what was Marilyn Monroe *really* like, what would I say, and I said I'd have to think about that.)

TC: Now do you think we can get the hell out of here? You promised me champagne, remember?

MARILYN: I remember. But I don't have any money.

TC: You're always late and you never have any money. By any chance are you under the delusion that you're Queen Elizabeth?

MARILYN: Who?

TC: Queen Elizabeth. The Queen of England.

MARILYN (frowning): What's that cunt got to do with it?

TC: Queen Elizabeth never carries money either. She's not allowed to. Filthy lucre must not stain the royal palm. It's a law or something.

MARILYN: I wish they'd pass a law like that for me.

TC: Keep going the way you are and maybe they will.

MARILYN: Well, gosh. How does she pay for anything? Like when she goes shopping.

TC: Her lady-in-waiting trots along with a bag full of far-things.

MARILYN: You know what? I'll bet she gets everything free. In return for endorsements.

TC: Very possible. I wouldn't be a bit surprised. By Appointment to Her Majesty. Corgi dogs. All those Fortnum & Mason goodies. Pot. Condoms.

MARILYN: What would she want with condoms?

TC: Not her, dopey. For that chump who walks two steps behind. Prince Philip.

MARILYN: Him. Oh, yeah. He's cute. He looks like he might have a nice prick. Did I ever tell you about the time I saw Errol Flynn whip out his prick and play the piano with it? Oh well, it was a hundred years ago, I'd just got into modeling, and I went to this half-ass party, and Errol Flynn, so pleased with himself, he was there and he took out his prick and played the piano with it. Thumped the keys. He played *You*

Are My Sunshine. Christ! Everybody says Milton Berle has the biggest schlong in Hollywood. But who *cares?* Look, don't you have *any* money?

TC: Maybe about fifty bucks.

MARILYN: Well, that ought to buy us some bubbly.

(Outside, Lexington Avenue was empty of all but harmless pedestrians. It was around two, and as nice an April afternoon as one could wish: ideal strolling weather. So we moseyed toward Third Avenue. A few gawkers spun their heads, not because they recognized Marilyn as *the* Marilyn, but because of her funereal finery; she giggled her special little giggle, a sound as tempting as the jingling bells on a Good Humor wagon, and said: "Maybe I should always dress this way. Real anonymous."

As we neared P. J. Clarke's saloon, I suggested P.J.'s might be a good place to refresh ourselves, but she vetoed that: "It's full of those advertising creeps. And that bitch Dorothy Kilgallen, she's always in there getting bombed. What is it with these micks? The way they booze, they're worse than Indians."

I felt called upon to defend Kilgallen, who was a friend, somewhat, and I allowed as to how she could upon occasion be a clever funny woman. She said: "Be that as it may, she's written some bitchy stuff about me. But all those cunts hate me. Hedda. Louella. I know you're supposed to get used to it, but I just can't. It really hurts. What did I ever do to those hags? The only one who writes a decent word about me is Sidney Skolsky. But he's a guy. The guys treat me okay. Just like maybe I was a human person. At least they give me the benefit of the doubt. And Bob Thomas is a gentleman. And Jack O'Brian."

We looked in the windows of antique shops; one

contained a tray of old rings, and Marilyn said: "That's pretty. The garnet with the seed pearls. I wish I could wear rings, but I hate people to notice my hands. They're too fat. Elizabeth Taylor has fat hands. But with those eyes, who's looking at her hands? I like to dance naked in front of mirrors and watch my titties jump around. There's nothing wrong with them. But I wish my hands weren't so fat."

Another window displayed a handsome grandfather clock, which prompted her to observe: "I've never had a home. Not a real one with all my own furniture. But if I ever get married again, and make a lot of money, I'm going to hire a couple of trucks and ride down Third Avenue buying every damn kind of crazy thing. I'm going to get a dozen grandfather clocks and line them all up in one room and have them all ticking away at the same time. That would be real homey, don't you think?")

MARILYN: Hey! Across the street!

TC: What?

MARILYN: See the sign with the palm? That must be a fortunetelling parlor.

TC: Are you in the mood for that?

MARILYN: Well, let's take a look.

(It was not an inviting establishment. Through a smeared window we could discern a barren room with a skinny, hairy gypsy lady seated in a canvas chair under a hellfire-red ceiling lamp that shed a torturous glow; she was knitting a pair of baby-booties, and did not return our stares. Nevertheless, Marilyn started to go in, then changed her mind.)

MARILYN: Sometimes I want to know what's going to happen. Then I think it's better not to. There's two things I'd like to know, though. One is whether I'm going to lose weight.

TC: And the other?

MARILYN: That's a secret.

TC: Now, now. We can't have secrets today. Today is a day of sorrow, and sorrowers share their innermost thoughts.

MARILYN: Well, it's a man. There's something I'd like to know. But that's all I'm going to tell. It really *is* a secret.

    (And I thought: That's what you think; I'll get it out of you.)

TC: I'm ready to buy that champagne.

    (We wound up on Second Avenue in a gaudily decorated deserted Chinese restaurant. But it did have a well-stocked bar, and we ordered a bottle of Mumm's; it arrived unchilled, and without a bucket, so we drank it out of tall glasses with ice cubes.)

MARILYN: This is fun. Kind of like being on location—if you like location. Which I most certainly don't. *Niagara.* That stinker. Yuk.

TC: So let's hear about your secret lover.

MARILYN: (Silence)

TC: (Silence)

MARILYN: (Giggles)

TC: (Silence)

MARILYN: You know so many women. Who's the most attractive woman you know?

TC: No contest. Barbara Paley. Hands down.

MARILYN (frowning): Is that the one they call "Babe"? She sure doesn't look like any Babe to me. I've seen her in *Vogue* and all. She's so elegant. Lovely. Just looking at her pictures makes me feel like pig-slop.

TC: She might be amused to hear that. She's very jealous of you.

MARILYN: Jealous of *me*? Now there you go again, laughing.

TC: Not at all. She *is* jealous.

MARILYN: But why?

TC: Because one of the columnists, Kilgallen I think, ran a blind item that said something like: "Rumor hath it that Mrs. DiMaggio rendezvoused with television's toppest tycoon and it wasn't to discuss business." Well, she read the item and she believes it.

MARILYN: Believes *what?*

TC: That her husband is having an affair with you. William S. Paley. TV's toppest tycoon. He's partial to shapely blondes. Brunettes, too.

MARILYN: But that's batty. I've never met the guy.

TC: Ah, come on. You can level with me. This secret lover of yours—it's William S. Paley, *n'est-ce pas?*

MARILYN: No! It's a writer. He's a writer.

TC: That's more like it. Now we're getting somewhere. So your lover is a writer. Must be a real hack, or you wouldn't be ashamed to tell me his name.

MARILYN (furious, frantic): What does the "S" stand for?

TC: "S." What "S"?

MARILYN: The "S" in William S. Paley.

TC: Oh, *that* "S." It doesn't stand for anything. He sort of tossed it in there for appearance sake.

MARILYN: It's just an initial with no name behind it? My goodness. Mr. Paley must be a little insecure.

TC: He twitches a lot. But let's get back to our mysterious scribe.

MARILYN: Stop it! You don't understand. I have so much to lose.

TC: Waiter, we'll have another Mumm's, please.

MARILYN: Are you trying to loosen my tongue?

TC: Yes. Tell you what. We'll make an exchange. I'll tell you a story, and if you think it's interesting, then perhaps we can discuss your writer friend.

MARILYN (tempted, but reluctant): What's your story about?

TC: Errol Flynn.

MARILYN: (Silence)

TC: (Silence)

MARILYN (hating herself): Well, go on.

TC: Remember what you were saying about Errol? How pleased he was with his prick? I can vouch for that. We once spent a cozy evening together. If you follow me.

MARILYN: You're making this up. You're trying to trick me.

TC: Scout's honor. I'm dealing from a clean deck. (Silence; but I can see that she's hooked, so after lighting a cigarette . . .) Well, this happened when I was eighteen. Nineteen. It was during the war. The winter of 1943. That night Carol Marcus or maybe she was already Carol Saroyan, was giving a party for her best friend, Gloria Vanderbilt. She gave it in her mother's apartment on Park Avenue. Big party. About fifty people. Around midnight Errol Flynn rolls in with his alter ego, a swashbuckling playboy named Freddie McEvoy. They were both pretty loaded. Anyway, Errol started yakking with me, and he was bright, we were making each other laugh, and suddenly he said he wanted to go to El Morocco, and did I want to go with him and his buddy McEvoy. I said okay, but then McEvoy didn't want to leave the party and all those debutantes, so in the end Errol and I left alone. Only we didn't go to El Morocco. We took a taxi down to Gramercy Park, where I had a little one-room apartment. He stayed until noon the next day.

MARILYN: And how would you rate it? On a scale of one to ten.

TC: Frankly, if it hadn't been Errol Flynn, I don't think I would have remembered it.

MARILYN: That's not much of a story. Not worth mine—not by a long shot.

TC: Waiter, where is our champagne? You've got two thirsty people here.

MARILYN: And it's not as if you'd told me anything new. I've always known Errol zigzagged. I have a masseur, he's practically my sister, and he was Tyrone Power's masseur, and he told me all about the thing Errol and Ty Power had going. No, you'll have to do better than that.

TC: You drive a hard bargain.

MARILYN: I'm listening. So let's hear your best experience. Along those lines.

TC: The best? The most memorable? Suppose you answer the question first.

MARILYN: And *I* drive hard bargains! Ha! (Swallowing champagne) Joe's not bad. He can hit home runs. If that's all it takes, we'd still be married. I still love him, though. He's genuine.

TC: Husbands don't count. Not in this game.

MARILYN (nibbling nail; really thinking): Well, I met a man, he's related to Gary Cooper somehow. A stockbroker, and nothing much to look at—sixty-five, and he wears those very thick glasses. Thick as jellyfish. I can't say what it was, but—

TC: You can stop right there. I've heard all about him from other girls. That old swordsman really scoots around. His name is Paul Shields. He's Rocky Cooper's stepfather. He's supposed to be sensational.

MARILYN: He is. Okay, smart-ass. Your turn.

TC: Forget it. I don't have to tell you damn nothing. Because I know who your masked marvel is: Arthur Miller. (She lowered her black glasses: Oh boy, if looks could kill, wow!) I guessed as soon as you said he was a writer.

MARILYN (stammering): But how? I mean, nobody . . . I mean, hardly anybody—

TC: At least three, maybe four years ago Irving Drutman—

MARILYN: Irving *who?*

TC: Drutman. He's a writer on the *Herald Tribune*. He told me you were fooling around with Arthur Miller. Had a hangup on him. I was too much of a gentleman to mention it before.

MARILYN: Gentleman! You bastard. (Stammering again, but dark glasses in place) You don't understand. That was long ago. That ended. But this is new. It's all different now, and—

TC: Just don't forget to invite me to the wedding.

MARILYN: If you talk about this, I'll murder you. I'll have you bumped off. I know a couple of men who'd gladly do me the favor.

TC: I don't question that for an instant.

(At last the waiter returned with the second bottle.)

MARILYN: Tell him to take it back. I don't want any. I want to get the hell out of here.

TC: Sorry if I've upset you.

MARILYN: I'm not upset.

(But she was. While I paid the check, she left for the powder room, and I wished I had a book to read: her visits to powder rooms sometimes lasted as long as an elephant's pregnancy. Idly, as time ticked by, I wondered if she was popping uppers or downers. Downers, no doubt. There was a newspaper on the bar, and I picked it up; it was written in Chinese. After twenty minutes had passed, I decided to investigate. Maybe she'd popped a lethal dose, or even cut her wrists. I found the ladies' room, and knocked on the door. She said: "Come in." Inside, she was confronting a dimly lit mirror. I said: "What are you doing?" She said: "Looking at Her." In fact, she was coloring her lips with ruby lipstick. Also, she had removed the somber head scarf and combed out her glossy fine-as-cotton-candy hair.)

MARILYN: I hope you have enough money left.

TC: That depends. Not enough to buy pearls, if that's your idea of making amends.

MARILYN (giggling, returned to good spirits. I decided I wouldn't mention Arthur Miller again): No. Only enough for a long taxi ride.

TC: Where are we going—Hollywood?

MARILYN: Hell, no. A place I like. You'll find out when we get there.

(I didn't have to wait that long, for as soon as we had flagged a taxi, I heard her instruct the cabby to drive to the South Street Pier, and I thought: Isn't that where one takes the ferry to Staten Island? And my next conjecture was: She's swallowed pills on top of that champagne and now she's off her rocker.)

TC: I hope we're not going on any boat rides. I didn't pack my Dramamine.

MARILYN (happy, giggling): Just the pier.

TC: May I ask why?

MARILYN: I like it there. It smells foreign, and I can feed the seagulls.

TC: With what? You haven't anything to feed them.

MARILYN: Yes, I do. My purse is full of fortune cookies. I swiped them from that restaurant.

TC (kidding her): Uh-huh. While you were in the john I cracked one open. The slip inside was a dirty joke.

MARILYN: Gosh. Dirty fortune cookies?

TC: I'm sure the gulls won't mind.

(Our route carried us through the Bowery. Tiny pawn-shops and blood-donor stations and dormitories with fifty-cent cots and tiny grim hotels with dollar beds and bars for whites, bars for blacks, everywhere bums, bums, young, far from young, ancient, bums squatting curb-side, squatting amid shattered glass and pukey debris, bums slanting in doorways and huddled like penguins at street corners. Once, when we paused for a red light, a purple-nosed scarecrow weaved toward us and began swabbing the taxi's windshield with a wet rag clutched in a shaking hand. Our protesting driver shouted Italian obscenities.)

MARILYN: What is it? What's happening?

TC: He wants a tip for cleaning the window.

MARILYN (shielding her face with her purse): How horrible! I can't stand it. Give him something. Hurry. Please!

(But the taxi had already zoomed ahead, damn near knocking down the old lush. Marilyn was crying.)

I'm sick.

TC: You want to go home?

MARILYN: Everything's ruined.

TC: I'll take you home.

MARILYN: Give me a minute. I'll be okay.

(Thus we traveled on to South Street, and indeed the sight of a ferry moored there, with the Brooklyn skyline across the water and careening, cavorting seagulls white against a marine horizon streaked with thin fleecy clouds fragile as lace—this tableau soon soothed her soul.

As we got out of the taxi we saw a man with a chow on a leash, a prospective passenger, walking toward the ferry, and as we passed them, my companion stopped to pat the dog's head.)

THE MAN (firm, but not unfriendly): You shouldn't touch strange dogs. Especially chows. They might bite you.

MARILYN: Dogs never bite me. Just humans. What's his name?

THE MAN: Fu Manchu.

MARILYN (giggling): Oh, just like the movie. That's cute.

THE MAN: What's yours?

MARILYN: My name? Marilyn.

THE MAN: That's what I thought. My wife will never believe me. Can I have your autograph?

> (He produced a business card and a pen; using her purse to write on, she wrote: *God Bless You—Marilyn Monroe*)

MARILYN: Thank you.

THE MAN: Thank *you*. Wait'll I show this back at the office.

> (We continued to the edge of the pier, and listened to the water sloshing against it.)

MARILYN: I used to ask for autographs. Sometimes I still do. Last year Clark Gable was sitting next to me in Chasen's, and I asked him to sign my napkin.

> (Leaning against a mooring stanchion, she presented a profile: Galatea surveying unconquered distances. Breezes fluffed her hair, and her head turned toward me with an ethereal ease, as though a breeze had swiveled it.)

TC: So when do we feed the birds? I'm hungry, too. It's late, and we never had lunch.

MARILYN: Remember, I said if anybody ever asked you what I was like, what Marilyn Monroe was *really* like—well, how would you answer them? (Her tone was teaseful, mocking, yet earnest, too: she wanted an honest reply) I bet you'd tell them I was a slob. A banana split.

TC: Of course. But I'd also say . . .

> (The light was leaving. She seemed to fade with it, blend

with the sky and clouds, recede beyond them. I wanted to lift my voice louder than the seagulls' cries and call her back: Marilyn! Marilyn, why did everything have to turn out the way it did? Why does life have to be so fucking rotten?)

TC: I'd say . . .

MARILYN: I can't hear you.

TC: I'd say you are a beautiful child.

Seven

❦

Nocturnal Turnings, or How Siamese Twins Have Sex

TC: Shucks! Wide awake! Lawsamercy, we ain't been dozed off a minute. How long we been dozed off, honey?

TC: It's two now. We tried to go to sleep around midnight, but we were too tense. So you said why don't we jack off, and I said yes, that ought to relax us, it usually does, so we jacked off and went right to sleep. Sometimes I wonder: Whatever would we do without Mother Fist and her Five Daughters? They've certainly been a friendly bunch to us through the years. Real pals.

TC: A lousy two hours. Lawd knows when we'll shut our eyes agin. An' cain't do nothin' 'bout it. Cain't haf a lil old sip of sompin 'cause dats a naw-naw. Nor none of dem snoozy pills, dat bein' also a naw-naw.

TC: Come on. Knock off the Amos 'n' Andy stuff. I'm not in the mood tonight.

TC: You're never in the mood. You didn't even want to jack off.

TC: Be fair. Have I ever denied you that? When you want to jack off, I always lie back and let you.

TC: Y'all ain't got de choice, dat's why.

TC: I much prefer solitary satisfaction to some of the duds you've forced me to endure.

TC: 'Twas up to you, we'd never have sex with anybody except each other.

TC: Yes, and think of all the misery *that* would have saved us.

TC: But then, we would never have been in love with people other than each other.

TC: Ha ha ha ha ha. Ho ho ho ho ho. "Is it an earthquake, or only a shock? Is it the real turtle soup, or merely the mock? Is it the Lido I see, or Asbury Park?" Or is it at long last shit?

TC: You never could sing. Not even in the bathtub.

TC: You really are bitchy tonight. Maybe we could pass some time by working on your Bitch List.

TC: I wouldn't call it a *Bitch* List. It's more sort of what you might say is a Strong Dislike List.

TC: Well, who are we strongly disliking tonight? Alive. It's not interesting if they're not alive.

TC: Billy Graham
    Princess Margaret
    Billy Graham
    Princess Anne
    The Reverend Ike
    Ralph Nader
    Supreme Court Justice Byron "Whizzer" White
    Princess Z
    Werner Erhard
    The Princess Royal

Billy Graham
Madame Gandhi
Masters and Johnson
Princess Z
Billy Graham
CBSABCNBCNET
Sammy Davis, Jr.
Jerry Brown, Esq.
Billy Graham
Princess Z
J. Edgar Hoover
Werner Erhard

TC: One minute! J. Edgar Hoover is dead.

TC: No, he's not. They cloned old Johnny, and he's every-where. They cloned Clyde Tolson, too, just so they could go on goin' steady. Cardinal Spellman, cloned version, occasion-ally joins them for a partouze.

TC: Why harp on Billy Graham?

TC: Billy Graham, Werner Erhard, Masters and Johnson, Princess Z—they're all full of horse manure. But the Rev-erend Billy is just *so* full of it.

TC: The fullest of anybody thus far?

TC: No, Princess Z is more fully packed.

TC: How so?

TC: Well, after all, she *is* a horse. It's only natural that a horse can hold more horse manure than a human, however great his capacity. Don't you remember Princess Z, that filly that ran in the fifth at Belmont? We bet on her and lost a bundle, practically our last dollar. And you said: "It's just like Uncle Bud used to say—'Never put your money on a horse named Princess.'"

TC: Uncle Bud was smart. Not like our old cousin Sook, but smart. Anyway, who do we Strongly Like? Tonight, at least.

TC: Nobody. They're all dead. Some recently, some for centuries. Lots of them are in *Père-Lachaise*. Rimbaud isn't there; but it's amazing who is. Gertrude and Alice. Proust. Sarah Bernhardt. Oscar Wilde. I wonder where Agatha Christie is buried—

TC: Sorry to interrupt, but surely there is someone alive we Strongly Like?

TC: Very difficult. A real toughie. Okay. Mrs. Richard Nixon. The Empress of Iran. Mr. William "Billy" Carter. Three victims, three saints. If Billy Graham was Billy Carter, then Billy Graham would be Billy Graham.

TC: That reminds me of a woman I sat next to at dinner the other night. She said: "Los Angeles is the perfect place to live—if you're Mexican."

TC: Heard any other good jokes lately?

TC: That wasn't a joke. That was an accurate social observation. The Mexicans in Los Angeles have their own culture, and a genuine one; the rest have zero. A city of suntanned Uriah Heeps.

However, I *was* told something that made me chuckle. Something D. D. Ryan said to Greta Garbo.

TC: Oh, yes. They live in the same building.

TC: And have for more than twenty years. Too bad they're not good friends, they'd like each other. They both have humor and conviction, but only *en passant* pleasantries have been exchanged, nothing more. A few weeks ago D.D. stepped into the elevator and found herself alone with Garbo. D.D. was costumed in her usual striking manner, and Garbo, as though she'd never truly noticed her before, said: "Why, Mrs. Ryan, you're *beautiful*." And D.D., amused but really touched, said: "Look who's talkin'."

TC: That's all?

TC: *C'est tout.*

TC: It seems sort of pointless to me.

TC: Look, forget it. It's not important. Let's turn on the lights and get out the pens and paper. Start that magazine article. No use lying here gabbing with an oaf like you. May as well try to make a nickel.

TC: You mean that Self-Interview article where you're supposed to interview yourself? Ask your own questions and answer them?

TC: Uh-huh. But why don't you just lie there quiet while I do this? I need a rest from your evil frivolity.

TC: Okay, scumbag.

TC: Well, here goes.

Q: What frightens you?

A: Real toads in imaginary gardens.

Q: No, but in real life—

A: I'm talking about real life.

Q: Let me put it another way. What, of your own experiences, have been the most frightening?

A: Betrayals. Abandonments.

But you want something more specific? Well, my very earliest childhood memory was on the scary side. I was probably three years old, perhaps a little younger, and I was on a visit to the St. Louis Zoo, accompanied by a large black woman my mother had hired to take me there. Suddenly there was pandemonium. Children, women, grown-up men were shouting and hurrying in every direction. Two lions had escaped from their cages! Two bloodthirsty beasts were on the prowl in the park. My nurse panicked. She simply turned and ran, leaving me alone on the path. That's all I remember about it.

When I was nine years old I was bitten by a cottonmouth water moccasin. Together with some cousins, I'd gone exploring in a lonesome forest about six miles from the rural Alabama town where we lived. There was a narrow, shallow crystal river that ran through this forest. There was a huge fallen log that lay across it from bank to bank like a bridge. My cousins, balancing themselves, ran across the log, but I decided to wade the little river. Just as I was about to reach the farther bank, I saw an enormous cottonmouth moccasin swimming, slithering on the water's shadowy surface. My own mouth went dry as cotton; I was paralyzed, numb, as though my whole body had been needled with Novocaine. The snake kept sliding, winding toward me. When it was within inches of me, I spun around, and slipped on a bed of slippery creek pebbles. The cottonmouth bit me on the knee.

Turmoil. My cousins took turns carrying me piggyback until we reached a farmhouse. While the farmer hitched up his mule-drawn wagon, his only vehicle, his wife caught a number of chickens, ripped them apart alive, and applied the hot bleeding birds to my knee. "It draws out the poison," she said, and indeed the flesh of the chickens turned green. All the way into town, my cousins kept killing chickens and applying them to the wound. Once we were home, my family telephoned a hospital in Montgomery, a hundred miles away, and five hours later a doctor arrived with a snake serum. I was one sick boy, and the only good thing about it was I missed two months of school.

Once, on my way to Japan, I stayed overnight in Hawaii with Doris Duke in the extraordinary, somewhat Persian palace she had built on a cliff at Diamond Head. It was scarcely daylight when I woke up and decided to go exploring. The room in which I slept had French doors leading into a garden overlooking the ocean. I'd been strolling in the garden perhaps half a minute when a terrifying herd of Dobermans appeared, seemingly out of nowhere; they surrounded and kept me captive within the snarling circle they made. No one had warned me that each night after Miss Duke and her guests had retired, this crowd of homicidal canines was let loose to deter, and possibly punish, unwelcome intruders.

The dogs did not attempt to touch me; they just stood there, coldly staring at me and quivering in controlled rage. I was afraid to breathe; I felt if I moved my foot one scintilla, the beasts would spring forward to rip me apart. My hands were trembling; my legs, too. My hair was as wet as if I'd just stepped out of the ocean. There is nothing more exhausting than standing perfectly still, yet I managed to do it for over an hour. Rescue arrived in the form of a gardener, who, when he saw what was happening, merely whistled and clapped his hands, and all the demon dogs rushed to greet him with friendly wagging tails.

Those are instances of specific terror. Still, our real fears are the sounds of footsteps walking in the corridors of our minds, and the anxieties, the phantom floatings, they create.

Q: What are some of the things you can do?

A: I can ice-skate. I can ski. I can read upside down. I can ride a skateboard. I can hit a tossed can with a .38 revolver. I have driven a Maserati (at dawn, on a flat, lonely Texas road) at 170 mph. I can make a soufflé Furstenberg (quite a stunt: it's a cheese-and-spinach concoction that involves sinking six poached eggs into the batter before cooking; the trick is to have the egg yolks remain soft and runny when the soufflé is served). I can tap-dance. I can type sixty words a minute.

Q: And what are some of the things you can't do?

A: I can't recite the alphabet, at least not correctly or all the way through (not even under hypnosis; it's an impediment that has fascinated several psychotherapists). I am a mathematical imbecile—I can add, more or less, but I can't subtract, and I failed first-year algebra three times, even with the help of a private tutor. I can read without glasses, but I can't drive without them. I can't speak Italian, even though I lived in Italy a total of nine years. I can't make a prepared speech—it has to be spontaneous, "on the wing."

Q: Do you have a "motto"?

A: Sort of. I jotted it down in a schoolboy diary: *I Aspire.* I don't know why I chose those particular words; they're odd, and I like the ambiguity—do I aspire to heaven or hell? Whatever the case, they have an undeniably noble ring.

Last winter I was wandering in a seacoast cemetery near Mendocino—a New England village in far Northern California, a rough place where the water is too cold to swim and where the whales go piping past. It was a lovely little cemetery, and the dates on the sea-grey-green tombstones were mostly nineteenth century; almost all of them had an inscription of some sort, something that revealed the tenant's philosophy. One read: NO COMMENT.

So I began to think what I would have inscribed on my tombstone—except that I shall never have one, because two very gifted fortunetellers, one Haitian, the other an Indian revolutionary who lives in Moscow, have told me I will be lost at sea, though I don't know whether by accident or by choice (*comme ça*, Hart Crane). Anyway, the first inscription I thought of was: AGAINST MY BETTER JUDGMENT. Then I thought of something far more characteristic. An excuse, a phrase I use about almost any commitment: I TRIED TO GET OUT OF IT, BUT I COULDN'T.

Q: Some time ago you made your debut as a film actor (in *Murder by Death*). And?

A: I'm not an actor; I have no desire to be one. I did it as a lark; I thought it would be amusing, and it was fun, more or less, but it was also hard work: up at six and never out of the studio before seven or eight. For the most part, the critics gave me a bouquet of garlic. But I expected that; everyone did—it was what you might call an obligatory reaction. Actually, I was adequate.

Q: How do you handle the "recognition factor"?

A: It doesn't bother me a bit, and it's very useful when you want to cash a check in some strange locale. Also, it can occasionally have amusing consequences. For instance, one night I was sitting with friends at a table in a crowded Key West bar. At a nearby table, there was a mildly drunk woman with a very drunk husband. Presently, the woman approached me and asked me to sign a paper napkin. All this seemed to anger her husband; he staggered over to the table, and after unzipping his trousers and hauling out his equipment, said: "Since you're autographing things, why don't you autograph this?" The tables surrounding us had grown silent, so a great many people heard my reply, which was: "I don't know if I can autograph it, but perhaps I can *initial* it."

Ordinarily, I don't mind giving autographs. But there *is* one thing that gets my goat: without exception, every grown man who has ever asked me for an autograph in a restaurant or on an airplane has always been careful to say that he wanted it for his wife or his daughter or his girl friend, but never, *never* just for himself.

I have a friend with whom I often take long walks on city streets. Frequently, some fellow stroller will pass us, hesitate, produce a sort of is-it-or-isn't it frown, then stop me and ask, "Are you Truman Capote?" And I'll say, "Yes, I'm Truman Capote." Whereupon my friend will scowl and shake me and shout, "For Christ's sake, George —when are you going to stop this? Some day you're going to get into serious trouble!"

Q: Do you consider conversation an art?

A: A dying one, yes. Most of the renowned conversationalists—Samuel Johnson, Oscar Wilde, Whistler, Jean Cocteau, Lady Astor, Lady Cunard, Alice Roosevelt Longworth—are monologists, not conversationalists. A conversation is a dialogue, not a monologue. That's why there are so few good conversations: due to scarcity, two intelligent talkers seldom meet. Of the list just provided, the only two I've known personally are Cocteau and Mrs. Longworth. (As for her, I take it back—she is not a solo performer; she lets you share the air.)

Among the best conversationalists I've talked with are Gore Vidal (if you're not the victim of his couth, sometimes uncouth, wit), Cecil Beaton (who, not surprisingly, expresses himself almost entirely in visual images—some very beautiful and *some* sublimely wicked). The late Danish genius, the Baroness Blixen, who wrote under the pseudonym Isak Dinesen, was, despite her withered though distinguished appearance, a true seductress, a *conversational* seductress. Ah, how fascinating she was, sitting by the fire in her beautiful house in a Danish seaside village, chain-smoking black cigarettes with silver tips, cooling her lively tongue with draughts of champagne, and luring one from this topic to that—her years as a farmer in Africa (be certain to read, if you haven't already, her autobiographical *Out of Africa*, one of this century's finest books), life under the Nazis in occupied Denmark ("They adored me. We argued, but they didn't care what I said; they didn't care what *any* woman said —it was a completely masculine society. Besides, they had no idea I was hiding Jews in my cellar, along with winter apples and cases of champagne").

Just skimming off the top of my head, other conversationalists I'd rate highly are Christopher Isherwood (no one surpasses him for total but lightly expressed candor) and the felinelike Colette. Marilyn Monroe was very amusing when she felt sufficiently relaxed and had had enough to drink. The same might be said of the lamented screen-scenarist Harry Kurnitz, an exceedingly homely gentleman who conquered men, women, and children of all classes with his verbal flights. Diana Vreeland, the eccentric Abbess of High Fashion and one-time, long-time editor of *Vogue*, is a charmer of a talker, a snake charmer.

When I was eighteen I met the person whose conversation has impressed me the most, perhaps because the person in question is the one who has most impressed me. It happened as follows:

In New York, on East Seventy-ninth Street, there is a very pleasant shelter known as the New York Society Library, and during 1942 I spent many afternoons there researching a book I intended writing but never did. Occasionally, I saw a woman there whose appearance rather mesmerized me—her eyes especially: blue, the pale brilliant cloudless blue of prairie skies. But even

without this singular feature, her face was interesting—
firm-jawed, handsome, a bit androgynous. Pepper-salt
hair parted in the middle. Sixty-five, thereabouts. A les-
bian? Well, yes.

One January day I emerged from the library into the
twilight to find a heavy snowfall in progress. The lady
with the blue eyes, wearing a nicely cut black coat with
a sable collar, was waiting at the curb. A gloved, taxi-
summoning hand was poised in the air, but there were
no taxis. She looked at me and smiled and said: "Do you
think a cup of hot chocolate would help? There's a Long-
champs around the corner."

She ordered hot chocolate; I asked for a "very" dry
martini. Half seriously, she said, "Are you old enough?"

"I've been drinking since I was fourteen. Smoking,
too."

"You don't look more than fourteen now."

"I'll be nineteen next September." Then I told her a
few things: that I was from New Orleans, that I'd published several short stories, that I wanted to be a writer
and was working on a novel. And she wanted to know
what American writers I liked. "Hawthorne, Henry
James, Emily Dickinson . . ." "No, living." Ah, well, hmm,
let's see: how difficult, the rivalry factor being what it is,
for one contemporary author, or would-be author, to confess admiration for another. At last I said, "Not Heming-
way—a really dishonest man, the closet-everything. Not
Thomas Wolfe—all that purple upchuck; of course, he
isn't living. Faulkner, sometimes: *Light in August*. Fitz-
gerald, sometimes: *Diamond as Big as the Ritz, Tender
Is the Night*. I really like Willa Cather. Have you read
My Mortal Enemy?"

With no particular expression, she said, "Actually, I wrote it."

I had seen photographs of Willa Cather—long-ago ones, made perhaps in the early twenties. Softer, homelier, less elegant than my companion. Yet I knew instantly that she *was* Willa Cather, and it was one of the *frissons* of my life. I began to babble about her books like a schoolboy—my favorites: *A Lost Lady, The Professor's House, My Ántonia.* It wasn't that I had anything in common with her as a writer. I would never have chosen for myself her sort of subject matter, or tried to emulate her style. It was just that I considered her a great artist. As good as Flaubert.

We became friends; she read my work and was always a fair and helpful judge. She was full of surprises. For one thing, she and her lifelong friend, Miss Lewis, lived in a spacious, charmingly furnished Park Avenue apartment —somehow, the notion of Miss Cather living in an apartment on Park Avenue seemed incongruous with her Nebraska upbringing, with the simple, rather elegiac nature of her novels. Secondly, her principal interest was not literature, but music. She went to concerts constantly, and almost all her closest friends were musical personalities, particularly Yehudi Menuhin and his sister Hepzibah.

Like all authentic conversationalists, she was an excellent listener, and when it was her turn to talk, she was never garrulous, but crisply pointed. Once she told me I was overly sensitive to criticism. The truth was that she was more sensitive to critical slights than I; any disparaging reference to her work caused a decline in spirits. When I pointed this out to her, she said: "Yes, but aren't we always seeking out our own vices in others and reprimanding them for such possessions? I'm alive. I have clay feet. Very definitely."

q: Do you have any favorite spectator sport?

a: Fireworks. Myriad-colored sprays of evanescent designs glittering the night skies. The very best I've seen were in Japan—these Japanese masters can create fiery creatures in the air: slithering dragons, exploding cats, faces of pagan deities. Italians, Venetians especially, can explode masterworks above the Grand Canal.

q: Do you have many sexual fantasies?

a: When I do have a sexual fantasy, usually I try to transfer it into reality—sometimes successfully. However, I do often find myself drifting into erotic daydreams that remain just that: daydreams.

I remember once having a conversation on this subject with the late E. M. Forster, to my mind the finest English novelist of this century. He said that as a schoolboy sexual thoughts dominated his mind. He said: "I felt as I grew older this fever would lessen, even leave me. But that was not the case; it raged on through my twenties, and I thought: Well, surely by the time I'm forty, I will receive some release from this torment, this constant search for the perfect love object. But it was not to be; all through my forties, lust was always lurking inside my head. And then I was fifty, and then I was sixty, and nothing changed: sexual images continued to spin around my brain like figures on a carrousel. Now here I am in my *seventies*, and I'm still a prisoner of my sexual imagination. I'm stuck with it, just at an age when I can no longer do anything about it."

q: Have you ever considered suicide?

a: Certainly. And so has everyone else, except possibly the village idiot. Soon after the suicide of the esteemed

Japanese writer Yukio Mishima, whom I knew well, a biography about him was published, and to my dismay, the author quotes him as saying: "Oh yes, I think of suicide a great deal. And I know a number of people I'm certain will kill themselves. Truman Capote, for instance." I couldn't imagine what had brought him to this conclusion. My visits with Mishima had always been jolly, very cordial. But Mishima was a sensitive, extremely intuitive man, not someone to be taken lightly. But in this matter, I think his intuition failed him; I would never have the courage to do what he did (he had a friend decapitate him with a sword). Anyway, as I've said somewhere before, most people who take their own lives do so because they really want to kill someone else—a philandering husband, an unfaithful lover, a treacherous friend—but they haven't the guts to do it, so they kill themselves instead. Not me; anyone who had worked me into that kind of a position would find himself looking down the barrel of a shotgun.

Q: Do you believe in God, or at any rate, some higher power?

A: I believe in an afterlife. That is to say, I'm sympathetic to the notion of reincarnation.

Q: In your own afterlife, how would you like to be reincarnated?

A: As a bird—preferably a buzzard. A buzzard doesn't have to bother about his appearance or ability to beguile and please; he doesn't have to put on airs. Nobody's going to like him anyway; he is ugly, unwanted, unwelcome everywhere. There's a lot to be said for the sort of freedom that allows. On the other hand, I wouldn't mind being a sea turtle. They can roam the land, and they know the secrets of the ocean's depths. Also, they're long-lived, and their hooded eyes accumulate much wisdom.

q: If you could be granted one wish, what would it be?

a: To wake up one morning and feel that I was at last a grown-up person, emptied of resentment, vengeful thoughts, and other wasteful, childish emotions. To find myself, in other words, an adult.

tc: Are you still awake?

tc: Somewhat bored, but still awake. How can I sleep when you're not asleep?

tc: And what do you think of what I've written here? So far?

tc: Wellll . . . since you *ask*. I'd say Billy Grahamcrackers isn't the only one familiar with horse manure.

tc: Bitch, bitch, bitch. Moan and bitch. That's all you ever do. Never a kind word.

tc: Oh, I didn't mean there's anything *very* wrong. Just a few things here and there. Trifles. I mean, perhaps you're not as honest as you pretend to me.

tc: I don't pretend to be honest. I *am* honest.

tc: Sorry. I didn't mean to fart. It wasn't a comment, just an accident.

tc: It was a diversionary tactic. You call me dishonest, compare me to Billy Graham, for Christ's sake, and now you're trying to weasel out of it. Speak up. What have I written here that's dishonest?

tc: Nothing. Trifles. Like that business about the movie. Did it for a lark, eh? You did it for the moola—and to satisfy that clown side of you that's so exasperating. Get rid of that guy. He's a jerk.

tc: Oh, I don't know. He's unpredictable, but I've got a soft

spot for him. He's part of me—same as you. And what are
some of these other trifles?

TC: The next thing—well, it's not a trifle. It's how you answered the question: Do you believe in God? And you
skipped right by it. Said something about an afterlife, reincarnation, coming back as a buzzard. I've got news for you,
buddy, you won't have to wait for reincarnation to be treated
like a buzzard; plenty of folks are doing it already. Multi-
tudes. But that's not what's so phony about your answer. It's
the fact that you don't come right out and say that you *do*
believe in God. I've heard you, cool as a cucumber, confess
things that would make a baboon blush blue, and yet you
won't admit that you believe in God. What is it? Are you
afraid of being called a Reborn Christian, a Jesus Freak?

TC: It's not that simple. I did believe in God. And then I
didn't. Remember when we were very little and used to go
way out in the woods with our dog Queenie and old Cousin
Sook? We hunted for wildflowers, wild asparagus. We caught
butterflies and let them loose. We caught perch and threw
them back in the creek. Sometimes we found giant toadstools,
and Sook told us that was where the elves lived, under the
beautiful toadstools. She told us the Lord had arranged for
them to live there just as He had arranged for everything we
saw. The good and the bad. The ants and the mosquitoes and
the rattlesnakes, every leaf, the sun in the sky, the old moon
and the new moon, rainy days. And we believed her.

But then things happened to spoil that faith. First it was
church and itching all over listening to some ignorant redneck preacher shoot his mouth off; then it was all those
boarding schools and going to chapel every damn morning.
And the Bible itself—nobody with any sense could believe
what it asked you to believe. Where were the toadstools?

Where were the moons? And at last life, plain living, took away the memories of whatever faith still lingered. I'm not the worst person that's crossed my path, not by a considerable distance, but I've committed some serious sins, deliberate cruelty among them; and it didn't bother me one whit, I never gave it a thought. Until I had to. When the rain started to fall, it was a hard black rain, and it just kept on falling. So I started to think about God again.

I thought about St. Julian. About Flaubert's story *St. Julien, L'Hospitalier*. It had been so long since I'd read that story, and where I was, in a sanitarium far distant from libraries, I couldn't get a copy. But I remembered (at least I thought this was more or less the way it went) that as a child Julian loved to wander in the forests and loved all animals and living things. He lived on a great estate, and his parents worshipped him; they wanted him to have everything in the world. His father bought him the finest horses, bows and arrows, and taught him to hunt. To kill the very animals he had loved so much. And that was too bad, because Julian discovered that he liked to kill. He was only happy after a day of the bloodiest slaughter. The murdering of beasts and birds became a mania, and after first admiring his skill, his neighbors loathed and feared him for his bloodlust.

Now there's a part of the story that was pretty vague in my head. Anyway, somehow or other Julian killed his mother and father. A hunting accident? Something like that, something terrible. He became a pariah and a penitent. He wandered the world barefoot and in rags, seeking forgiveness. He grew old and ill. One cold night he was waiting by a river for a boatman to row him across. Maybe it was the River Styx? Because Julian was dying. While he waited, a hideous old man appeared. He was a leper, and his eyes were running sores, his mouth rotting and foul. Julian didn't know it, but this repulsive evil-looking old man was God. And God tested him to see if all his sufferings had truly changed Julian's savage heart. He told Julian He was cold, and asked to share his blanket, and Julian did; then the leper wanted Julian to embrace Him, and Julian did; then He made a final request— He asked Julian to kiss His diseased and rotting lips. Julian did. Whereupon Julian and the old leper, who was suddenly transformed into a radiant shining vision, ascended together to heaven. And so it was that Julian became St. Julian.

So there I was in the rain, and the harder it fell the more I thought about Julian. I prayed that I would have the luck to hold a leper in my arms. And that's when I began to believe in God again, and understand that Sook was right: that everything was His design, the old moon and the new moon, the hard rain falling, and if only I would ask Him to help me, He would.

TC: And has He?

TC: Yes. More and more. But I'm not a saint yet. I'm an alcoholic. I'm a drug addict. I'm homosexual. I'm a genius. Of course, I could be all four of these dubious things and still be a saint. But I shonuf ain't no saint yet, nawsuh.

TC: Well, Rome wasn't built in a day. Now let's knock it off and try for some shut-eye.

TC: But first let's say a prayer. Let's say our *old* prayer. The one we used to say when we were real little and slept in the same bed with Sook and Queenie, with the quilts piled on top of us because the house was so big and cold.

TC: Our old prayer? Okay.

TC and TC: Now I lay me down to sleep, I pray the Lord my soul to keep. And if I should die before I wake, I pray the Lord my soul to take. Amen.

TC: Goodnight.

TC: Goodnight.

TC: I love you.

TC: I love you, too.

TC: You'd better. Because when you get right down to it, all we've got is each other. Alone. To the grave. And that's the tragedy, isn't it?

TC: You forget. We have God, too.

TC: Yes. We have God.

TC: Zzzzzzz

TC: Zzzzzzzzz

TC and TC: Zzzzzzzzzzz

TRUMAN CAPOTE was born in New Orleans in 1924. He spent most of his childhood in the South, but was educated at various Eastern schools. He is a member of the American Institute of Arts and Letters.